Queen Mary's Women

This item must be returned or renewed on or before the latest date shown

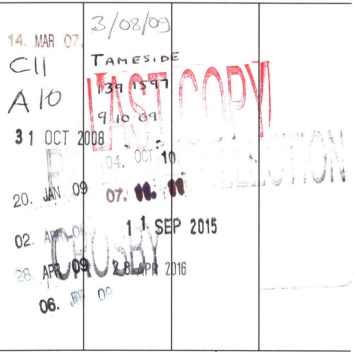

3/08/09

14. MAR 07

C11

TAMESIDE

A 10

LAST COPY

31 OCT 2008

04. OCT 10.

20. JAN 09   07.

1 1 SEP 2015

02. APR 09

28 APR 2016

28. APR 09   CROSBY

06.

Queen Mary's Women

Female relatives, servants, friends and enemies
of Mary, Queen of Scots

Rosalind K. Marshall

John Donald

First published in Great Britain in 2006 by
John Donald, an imprint of Birlinn Ltd

West Newington House
10 Newington Road
Edinburgh
EH9 1QS

www.birlinn.co.uk

ISBN 10: 0 85976 667 5

ISBN 13: 978 0 85976 667 8

British Library Cataloguing-in-Publication Data
A catalogue record for this book is available on request from
the British Library

Typeset by Palimpsest Book Production Limited,
Grangemouth, Stirlingshire
Printed and bound in Britain by
Creative Print and Design, Wales

For Susan Groag Bell

Contents

List of Illustrations   ix
Genealogical Tables   x
Chronology   xiii
Acknowledgments   xiv

Introduction   1

Chapter 1   Mother and Daughter   3

Chapter 2   French Relatives: Antoinette de
                 Bourbon and Catherine de Medici   18

Chapter 3   The Governesses and the Early Household   39

Chapter 4   The Queen of France's Ladies (1)   57

Chapter 5   The Queen of France's Ladies (2)   74

Chapter 6   Three Favourites: The Countesses
                 of Argyll, Mar and Moray   90

Chapter 7   Aunt and Mother-in-Law:
                 The Countess of Lennox   107

Chapter 8   The Countess of Bothwell
                 and Lady Douglas   126

Chapter 9   The Four Maries   141

Chapter 10   The Scottish Retinue   155

Chapter 11   Bess of Hardwick and the English Years   176

Chapter 12   Elizabeth I of England   192

Conclusion   211

Bibliography   215
Index   227

Illustrations

1 *Mary of Guise* attributed to Corneille de Lyon (Scottish National Portrait Gallery)

2 *Antoinette de Bourbon, Duchess of Guise* by Léonard Limosin (Musée Condé, Chantilly © Photo RMN – © Gérard Blot)

3 *Catherine de Medici* by Corneille de Lyon (Château de Versailles © Photo RMN – © Daniel Arnaudet)

4 *Anne d'Este, Duchess of Guise* by an artist of the French School (Musée Condé, Chantilly © Photo RMN – © Rights Reserved)

5 *Guillemette de Sarrebruche, Duchess of Bouillon* by Jean Clouet (Musée Condé, Chantilly © Photo RMN – © Harry Bréjart)

6 *Lady Agnes Keith, Countess of Moray* by Hans Eworth (In a private collection)

7 *Lady Margaret Douglas, Countess of Lennox* by an unknown artist (The Royal Collection © 2006 HM Queen Elizabeth II)

8 *Lady Jane Gordon, Countess of Bothwell* by an unknown artist (Scottish National Portrait Gallery)

9 *Elizabeth Talbot, Countess of Shrewsbury* by an unknown artist (National Portrait Gallery, London)

10 *Elizabeth I of England*, in about 1588, attributed to George Gower (National Portrait Gallery, London)

11 Monument to Elizabeth and Barbara Curle, St Andrew's Church, Antwerp (© IRPA-KIK, Brussels)

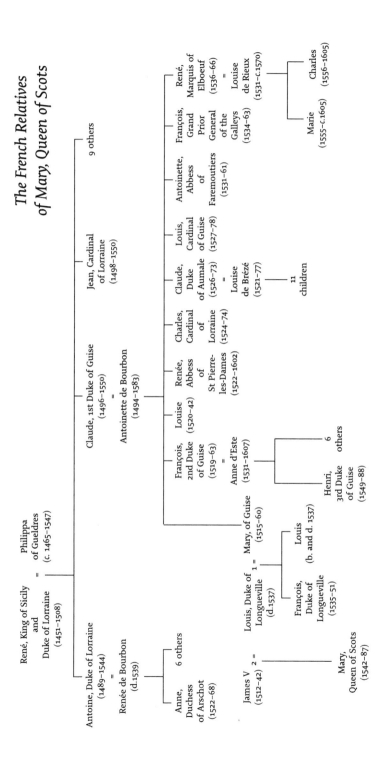

*The French Relatives
of Mary, Queen of Scots*

The French Royal Family

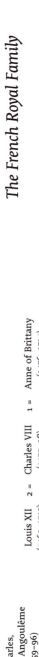
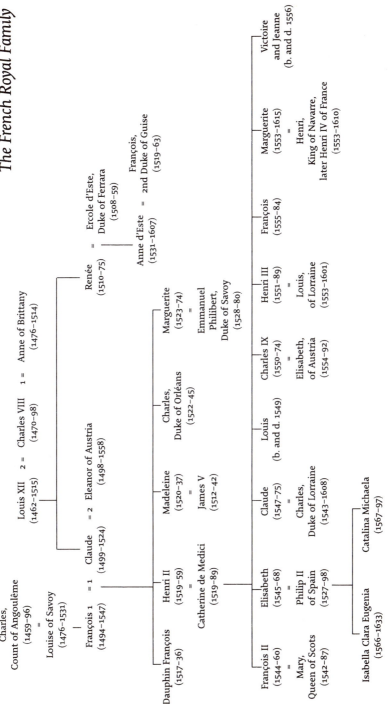

The Succession to the English Throne

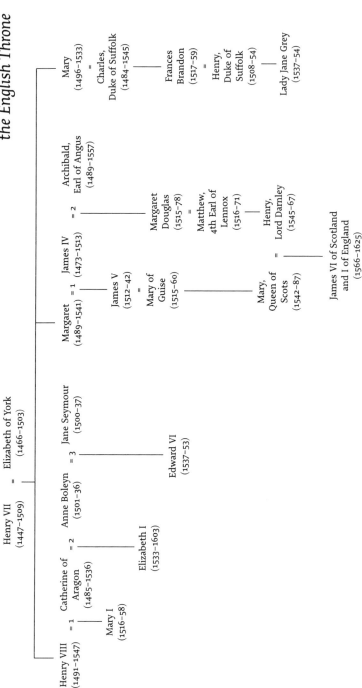

Henry VII (1447–1509) = Elizabeth of York (1466–1503)

Henry VIII (1491–1547)

= 1 Catherine of Aragon (1485–1536)
— Mary I (1516–58)

= 2 Anne Boleyn (1501–36)
— Elizabeth I (1533–1603)

= 3 Jane Seymour (1500–37)
— Edward VI (1537–53)

Margaret (1489–1541)

= 1 James IV (1473–1513)
— James V (1512–42) = Mary of Guise (1515–60)
— Mary, Queen of Scots (1542–87)

= 2 Archibald, Earl of Angus (1489–1557)
— Margaret Douglas (1515–78) = Matthew, 4th Earl of Lennox (1516–71)
— Henry, Lord Darnley (1545–67)

Mary, Queen of Scots = Henry, Lord Darnley
— James VI of Scotland and I of England (1566–1625)

Mary (1496–1533) = Charles, Duke of Suffolk (1484–1545)
— Frances Brandon (1517–59) = Henry, Duke of Suffolk (1508–54)
— Lady Jane Grey (1537–54)

MARY, QUEEN OF SCOTS CHRONOLOGY

1542   Born at Linlithgow Palace, the daughter of James V
        of Scotland and Mary of Guise
        Six days later, becomes Queen of Scots, on the death
        of her father
1544-5 English invade Scotland in the campaigns known as
        The Rough Wooing
1548   Mary sails to France, to be brought up at the French
        Court as the future bride of the Dauphin François
1558   Mary marries the Dauphin
1559   Becomes Queen of France when her husband inherits
        the throne as François II
1560   Death of Mary of Guise Death of François II
1561   Mary returns to Scotland
1565   Marries Henry Stewart, Lord Darnley
1566   Murder of her secretary, David Riccio. Birth of Mary's
        son, the future James VI
1567   Murder of Lord Darnley. Mary marries James, 4th Earl
        of Bothwell Confronts her Protestant Lords at
        Carberry Hill, surrenders and is held prisoner in
        Lochleven Castle
1568   Escapes, only to be defeated at the Battle of Langside
        Flees to England. Held captive
1587   Executed at Fotheringhay Castle

ACKNOWLEDGMENTS

I should like to thank Dr Athol L. Murray for kindly reading the text of this book in its entirety, and Professor Margaret M. McGowan for looking at the chapters on the French years. Their expertise is much appreciated. I am likewise grateful to Dr Dana Bentley-Cranch, Dr Armel Dubois-Nayt, Kristof Duran, Joan Noble, Dr Bert Remijken, Dr Herman Reybrouck, Dr Margaret H.B. Sanderson, Dr Jane B. Stevenson, Dr Alison Rosie of the National Register of Archives (Scotland) and her colleagues, Anne Monseur, administrative assistant at the Stadsarchief Antwerpen, the staff of the various Picture Libraries who supplied the illustrations and the anonymous owner who allowed me to consult his archives and reproduce one of his portraits.

RKM
Edinburgh

Introduction

Much has been written about the relationship between Mary, Queen of Scots and the various men in her life: husbands, alleged lovers, loyal servants and bitter enemies. Far less has been said about the women she knew. Major figures like Elizabeth I of England are usually analysed as political adversaries, while members of Mary's own household are dismissed as minor characters of no importance, a sort of Greek chorus watching in the background as she travelled from early promise to final tragedy. It is reasonable to suppose that even queens are influenced by those with whom they spend their days and so it is worth identifying the women who were closest to Mary, either bound to her by ties of affection or simply taking up her time and her attention. Did they help to make her the woman she became, and how did their dealings with her affect their own lives?

Mary's dramatic story is too well known to require detailed repetition here. Suffice it to say that she was only six days old when her father, James V, died in 1542 and she became Queen of Scots. Her earliest years were overshadowed by the threat of English invasion and, when she was five, her mother, Mary of Guise, agreed to send her to France, to be brought up there as the future bride of King Henri II's son and heir, the Dauphin François. Her marriage took place on 24 April 1558 and she became Queen of France a year later, when her father-in-law was fatally wounded in a jousting accident. Her central position at the French Court was to be brief, however, for on 5 December 1560 her delicate young husband succumbed to an ear infection. Her mother had died less than six months earlier and, despite the warnings of family and friends,

Mary returned to Scotland in August 1561, a Roman Catholic monarch about to rule a newly Protestant realm.

Ecclesiastical tensions apart, it was obvious that she would have to marry again, so that she could bear heirs to the throne. Her choice of Henry, Lord Darnley proved disastrous. They did have one son, the future James VI, but the petulant, jealous and immature Darnley's involvement in the killing of his wife's secretary, David Riccio, ended any feelings of affection Mary had for him. Darnley had by now alienated many of the Scottish nobility and on 9 February 1567 he was murdered at Kirk o' Field. Mary made her greatest mistake when, less than three months later, she married James Hepburn, 4th Earl of Bothwell, after he had allegedly abducted her, but probably with her collusion. She may have seen him as the strong protector she needed, but he was the man most people held responsible for Darnley's assassination and so even her friends and supporters were shocked by her rush to disaster.

Confronted by her Protestant lords at Carberry Hill, Mary surrendered and was held prisoner in Lochleven Castle, where she miscarried twins. Although she escaped the following spring and gathered her forces, she was defeated on 13 May 1568 at the Battle of Langside. Confident that Queen Elizabeth I of England would help her, she fled south, only to be kept captive until her eventual execution at Fotheringhay Castle in Northamptonshire on 8 February 1587.

1

Mother and Daughter

Naturally enough, the first woman to be important to Mary Stuart was her French mother, Mary of Guise, and there were powerful reasons why there was a particularly strong bond between them. Royal children often saw relatively little of their parents. They lived in their own households, while the king and queen led a peripatetic existence, moving constantly from one royal residence to the next in order to use up the food which came to them in rents from their estates and to allow periodic cleansing of the various houses at a time when sanitation was primitive, to say the least. The children's household moved about too, but their journeys did not coincide with those of the Court and so the extent to which princes and princesses formed real bonds with their fathers and mothers depended very much upon the attitudes of the parents themselves. Some had little time for their numerous offspring, others formed real attachments, visited the children when they could and worried about their welfare. Of course their relationships always involved a great deal of formality. Kings and queens were monarchs first and foremost, parents second, and so they always had to be treated with the deepest respect both in person and in any childish letters their sons and daughters were encouraged to send them.

Had circumstances been different, Mary, Queen of Scots might well have lived this sort of life, brought up at Stirling Castle, say, while her parents moved around the country, spending much of their time in Edinburgh, a considerable distance away. As it was, her father's death when she was only six days old left her in a perilously vulnerable position. However, her mother, Mary of

Guise, was determined to do everything in her power to protect her child, not least because past events in her own life had given her a deep emotional need to keep this precious daughter close to her.

Mary of Guise came from a powerful and energetic family famous, indeed notorious, for the ambition of its various members and for their loyalty to the Roman Catholic Church. Her father, Claude, Duke of Guise, was a close friend of François I of France, and her mother, Antoinette de Bourbon, was herself a descendant of French kings. Mary of Guise, their eldest child, was born on 20 November 1515. It seems that she was at first destined for a career in the Church, for she spent a period in the convent of Poor Clares at Pont à Mousson, where her paternal grandmother, Philippa of Gueldres, was living in retirement, and left only after a visit from her uncle. Antoine, Duke of Lorraine was head of the family and, meeting the tall, attractive teenager, he soon decided that she could be more usefully deployed elsewhere. By marrying well, she could bring in valuable allies and so he and his wife took her home to Nancy with them, instructed her in all the necessary social graces, and presented her at Court, where she immediately became a popular figure and a friend of the royal princesses.

If Duke Antoine harboured hopes of marrying Mary to a royal prince, he was disappointed but, on 4 August 1534, she became the bride of Louis, Duke of Longueville, Grand Chamberlain of France, a pleasant young man whom she would have known well. She spent the next few years moving about their estates, devoting a significant amount of time to the welfare of the tenants. Her first child, born on 30 October 1535, was christened François, after the French King, François I. By the spring of 1537 she was pregnant again, but her young husband suddenly died of a fever at Rouen on 9 June. Mary's second child, Louis, whom she named after him, was born eight weeks later, but he died at four months old. By this time, Mary had received a disturbing message from François I. Instead of looking after the Longueville estates for her surviving son, she was to marry James V of Scotland. She was horrified, not least because she knew that she would not be allowed to take little

François with her. As Duke of Longueville and hereditary Grand Chamberlain, he had to remain in France.

Mary and her mother tried every means at their disposal to persuade the King to change his mind, but he was adamant and she had to obey. She was married by proxy at her castle of Châteaudun and, a year and a day after her first husband's death, she set sail for Scotland.[1] Two-year-old François was left behind, in the care of her parents. Her mother wrote frequently, with reassurances about his health, portraits of him, and even, on one occasion, a piece of string to show how tall he had grown. Once he was old enough, he wrote to her himself, and his childish letters still survive, because Mary of Guise preserved them with loving care.[2]

Life as James V's consort was not always easy. Mary's new husband was a difficult, neurotic man whose disturbed childhood had left him with an almost paranoid suspicion of those around him. The tone of his four surviving letters to her, preserved in the National Library of Scotland, suggests, however, that she may have been the dominant partner in their personal relationship. Writing to her he signed himself 'Your humble husband', and on one occasion begged her to be 'not so thundering' when he forgot a small commission he had promised to do for her.[3] One of Mary's principal purposes in coming to Scotland, of course, was to provide him with sons. He had at least eleven illegitimate children already, but he needed a legitimate heir. As the months went by, Mary and her own relatives began to worry that she showed no signs of pregnancy, but she conceived in the late summer of 1539 and on 22 May 1540 she gave birth to the much desired boy, Prince James. Less than a year later, on 24 April 1541, she had another son, Prince Robert. Apart from the fact that she had done her dynastic duty, Mary must have experienced considerable emotional satisfaction in the creation of her second family and subsequent events were all the more horrifying.

Celebrations for the birth of the second prince were brutally cut short when both babies died, within twenty-four hours of each other, the elder in St Andrews, the younger in Stirling.[4] The bereaved parents were plunged into grief, the loss of the infants

[5]

placed a severe strain on their marriage and James began to see his mistresses again. Mary conceived once more in the spring of 1542,[5] but it was not a time of happy optimism. Henry VIII of England had made himself Head on Earth of the Church of England when the Pope refused to grant him a divorce from his first wife, and he wanted James V to follow his example and break with Rome. He also wanted James to end Scotland's traditional alliance with France. James refused to listen to any of this advice, with the result that Henry sent his army north and defeated the Scottish forces at Solway Moss, on 24 November 1542. James was not present at the battle but he seems to have suffered a complete collapse shortly afterwards. Distraught, he retreated to Falkland Palace, where he took to his bed with a high fever, received the unwelcome news that his wife had given birth to a daughter instead of the son they had been hoping for, turned his face to the wall and died.[6]

Widowed for the second time in her life, with three baby sons dead in infancy and her other son far away in France, it was hardly surprising that Mary of Guise was fiercely protective of her only daughter. Under other circumstances, she could have been expected to assume the regency, but because she had newly given birth and had to spend a month officially recovering, she was ruled out and the position was taken by the next eligible person, James Hamilton, Earl of Arran, who now became Regent with the title of Lord Governor. This was a source of considerable worry to Mary of Guise, for he was the heir presumptive to the throne. If anything were to happen to the little Queen, then the crown would be his. Certainly Arran had a reputation for being weak and irresolute, but could he resist the temptation of making away with the baby or kidnapping her and sending her to Henry VIII?

In the end neither of these dreaded events came to pass, but for years Mary of Guise suffered torments of anxiety as to his intentions. She felt that the only way she could secure her daughter's future was to wrest the regency from him, and so she embarked on a lengthy power struggle with him, in the meantime safe-guarding her daughter in every way she could. Historians have sometimes wondered why she did not simply retire to France after the death of James V, but of course she could not have done that because she knew that the Scots would never permit their infant monarch to leave the country, nor could she somehow have whisked her child away and allowed Arran to take the throne.

There were other factors in her decision too. Although she had been in Scotland for only four and a half years at the time of her husband's death, Mary of Guise had already taken to heart the notion that Scotland must be modernised, given an efficient government and transformed into an even more effective, reliable ally for France against the English. It seems probable that she and James V had discussed such ideas, and now she was all the more determined to carry through these policies of improvement to her daughter's kingdom. Interestingly, her own identification with Scotland and her commitment to the country's future can be seen in her attitude to the Scots language. It seems that James V had always written to her in French,[7] but we know that she learned Scots. Her signature on letters is often preceded by a few words in that language and in his *History of the Reformation* John Knox satirises her French accent.[8] Moreover, when Mary, Queen of Scots was old enough to learn to speak, she was taught only Scots, not French. This must have been a deliberate decision by Mary of Guise, but she must have had difficulty in preventing herself from addressing the little girl in her own mother tongue.

One of the few glimpses we have of them together comes in a letter written by the English envoy, Sir Ralph Sadler. He had been sent north by Henry VIII to assess the various loyalties of the principal players in Scotland. After lengthy and confusing conversations with all the leading nobles, Sir Ralph made his way to Linlithgow Palace, where Mary of Guise received him graciously and did everything she could to dispel persistent rumours put about by Arran to the effect that her daughter was a sickly child, unlikely to survive. 'You shall see whether he says true or not,' she declared and, with maternal pride as well as political calculation, led Sadler through to the royal nursery where she ordered the nurse to unwrap the baby's swaddling clothes so that he could observe for himself what she was really like. 'I assure Your Majesty,' he reported to Henry VIII, 'it is as goodly a child as I have seen of her age, and as like to live, with the grace of God.'[9]

In order to avert the imminent English invasion, Arran thought it best to declare that he was a Protestant and to sign the Treaties of Greenwich with England, a course all the more strongly opposed by Mary of Guise because one of the principal terms was that her daughter should marry Henry VIII's son and heir, the future Edward VI, as soon as she was old enough. With considerable difficulty, she persuaded Arran to allow her to move with the little Queen to the greater safety of Stirling Castle, and the baby was crowned in the Chapel Royal there on 8 September 1543.[10] Mary of Guise was not alone in opposing the rapprochement with England, Arran was persuaded to change his mind and by the end of 1543 the Scottish parliament had declared that the Treaties of Greenwich were null and void. Furious, Henry VIII launched the series of invasions of Scotland known as 'The Rough Wooing'.

These campaigns were continued after his death by the Duke of Somerset, ruling England as Lord Protector for the young Edward VI, and there was a very real danger that Mary, Queen of Scots would be captured. When the Scottish army was defeated at the Battle of Pinkie on 10 September 1547, Mary of Guise sent her daughter for about three weeks to the secluded island of Inchmahome, on the Lake of Menteith, in case the English should try to seize her.[11] It was at this point that Henri II of France came up with a possible solution to the problem and suggested that the Queen of Scots should be sent to marry his eldest son, the Dauphin François, thereby trapping irrevocably their shared enemy the English between Scotland and France. Since Mary was only five and the Dauphin two years younger, the wedding could not take place for some years yet but, in the meantime, Henri would require the little Queen to come and live at the French Court. This was a perfectly conventional stipulation, and it would be useful to the Scots because it would remove their child monarch from the imminent danger of capture by the English.

The Regent Arran was persuaded to agree to the arrangement when Henri II made him Duke of Châtelherault, the only duke in

Scotland, and the new marriage treaty was signed near Haddington on 7 July 1548. For all that, the decision to send her daughter to France must have been one of the most painful Mary of Guise ever made. Leaving behind her son the Duke of Longueville had been difficult enough, but now she was going to have to send away the much-loved child who had been her consolation in the difficulties of the past five years and more. However, concern for her daughter's safety had to take priority over all other considerations and Mary of Guise did all she could to make the transition comfortable for the little girl. She could not take her daughter to France herself, much as she might have liked to do so, for the Scots would never have agreed to both of them leaving. However, she arranged for an impressive escort to go in her place, led by her daughter's official guardians, Lord Erskine and Lord Livingston, and including not only one of young Mary's aunts and three of her father's illegitimate sons, but a crowd of aristocratic children of about her own age. These familiar friends would provide reassuring company as she set off for her new life.[12]

On 29 July mother and daughter parted from each other at Dumbarton, where the little Queen boarded one of the royal French galleys sent by Henri II to collect her.[13] There then ensued a trying delay when storms blew up and contrary winds meant that they could not set sail. Unable to endure the prospect of long-drawn-out farewells, Mary of Guise said goodbye to her daughter and rode back to Edinburgh. The fleet finally sailed a week later, on 7 August 1548. 'The old Queen doth lament the young Queen's departure', an English spy reported, no doubt with considerable understatement.[14] The voyage took almost a week, and Mary of Guise must have endured agonies of suspense until word finally arrived that the little Queen had landed safely near Roscoff, in Brittany, and was on her way to St Germain-en-Laye, where she would meet King Henri II and the French royal children.

A young child's memories of her only surviving parent would inevitably have faded with the passage of time, but her Guise relatives made sure that Mary's mother remained very much in her mind and Mary of Guise's many friends at the French Court were eager to send her admiring reports of her daughter. Even so, as the months went by, Mary of Guise became increasingly anxious for a reunion and in 1550 she decided to visit France herself. This was a daring decision in many ways. It was virtually unheard of for any foreign bride, least of all a queen consort, to make a trip back to her country of origin, not least because sea travel was so dangerous. However, Mary had discovered on her way to Scotland that she was a good sailor, and the Guise women were energetic and courageous. 'If only I were younger I would be tempted to risk it myself and come to see you,' her mother had even said, 'but I cannot think of it at my age.'[15] More worrying was what might go on in Scotland during Mary of Guise's absence. What would Châtelherault and the machinating nobles do were she to leave them to their own devices?

The arguments in favour of making the journey were, however, more telling. Apart from the fact that she was desperate to see her own children, the death of her father in the spring of 1550 had made Mary of Guise anxious to visit her mother. Moreover, there was a vital political motive. Henri II was an old friend. There had even been rumours before she left France that he had fallen in love with her and would have liked to put away his wife, Catherine de Medici, to marry her instead.[16] Royal courts were always full of such gossip but whatever Henri's true feelings, Mary enjoyed a good relationship with him, as his surviving letters to her bear witness.[17] She set great store by personal contact and she was convinced that if she could speak to him in person, she would be able to persuade him to support her in her bid to replace Châtelherault as Regent of Scotland.

She decided to solve the problem of the Scottish nobles by taking a large number of them with her. Henri was agreeable to her visit, invited her to be godmother to his newborn son, postponed the christening so that she could attend, and sent six of his galleys to collect her, the mariners and galley slaves specially attired for the voyage in white damask. Unfortunately a quarrel between two of the leading Scottish nobles, the Earl of Huntly and the Earl of Cassillis, meant that Mary had to postpone her departure, with the result that she missed the royal baptism, but she embarked at Leith in mid-September and sailed into Dieppe on 19 September to find a large welcoming party led by her brothers waiting to greet her. She had been away for twelve years, and it would have been an emotional occasion. They escorted her to Rouen, where Henri II was waiting with her children, seven-year-old Mary and François, Duke of Longueville, now almost fifteen.[18] The reunion must have been a touching one, and observers saw the close resemblance between Mary of Guise and her daughter. The Queen Dowager was of the largest size of women, as a contemporary once noted,[19] with dark auburn hair and a creamy skin,[20] and already her daughter was unusually tall and well made, with similar colouring, although from her portraits the younger Mary's eyes were brown whereas her mother's were grey.

The time the two could spend together was, of course, limited, because Mary of Guise engaged in long political discussions, gaining, as she had hoped, the support of the French King in her bid for the regency. Beneath the formality of royal etiquette, however, was great depth of feeling and when in April 1551 a plot to poison Mary, Queen of Scots was discovered, it was reported that 'The old Queen is fallen suddenly sick upon the opening of these news unto her'.[21] Although Mary of Guise's plans for her return voyage to Scotland had been well advanced, she immediately postponed her departure and stayed on for another six months. Her grief at the prospect of parting was cruelly intensified when her son, the Duke of Longueville, escorting her to the coast, fell ill at Amiens and died, despite her careful nursing.[22] No doubt with fervent promises of a return visit, Mary of Guise set sail from Dieppe soon after 18 October.[23]

Mary, Queen of Scots was by now old enough to correspond with her mother herself, and fourteen of the letters she wrote are preserved in the National Library of Scotland. Most are undated, but the first in the series is from 23 June 1554, the year that Mary of Guise finally succeeded in replacing Châtelherault as Regent. It is a polite little letter, written out by a secretary. The Bishop of Galloway had been visiting France and was going to Mary of Guise with the latest report about her daughter, so the younger Mary took the opportunity of declaring that her greatest pleasure was to have frequent news of her mother's prosperity and good health. The letter was written in French, for Henri II, horrified that his future daughter-in-law spoke only Scots, had immediately arranged for her to be taught the language of her new country, and it ends in that language, 'Your very humble and very obedient daughter, Marie'.[24]

Subsequent letters are holograph, entirely written out by Mary, Queen of Scots herself in a very regular, neat, rather tight and angular italic hand, the signature much larger than the rest of the letter, the tone always very respectful. Sometimes there were family occasions to report: a gathering at her uncle the Cardinal of Lorraine's house of Meudon for a cousin's baptism, attended by Henri II and his Queen, or a little supper party in her own household for the Cardinal. She was content to leave it to others to convey all the news of public affairs, but she was always anxious that her mother should know how eager she was to please her. As the months went by, her writing became larger, more relaxed, less tidy and rather more like her handwriting in adult life. The tone is more personal too.

Her messages no longer resembled short exercises in calligraphy but expressed her feelings as well as the conventional courtesies. She referred quite frequently to her servants, making repeated requests that some of them should receive higher salaries. Moreover, it becomes clear that Mary of Guise was instructing her in the art of statecraft, outlining current problems, asking her daughter's approval for the action she had taken, and encouraging young Mary to make suggestions of her own. Naturally enough, when her daughter was still in her early teens, she relied heavily on her Guise uncles to tell her how to answer and in one letter, which probably dates from about 1555, she mentioned that she was enclosing fifty blank sheets of paper which she had signed with varying degrees of formality so that her mother could use them to send out her instructions to Scottish courtiers and officials.

Another letter, assigned by Prince Labanoff, the nineteenth-century editor of her correspondence, to the year 1552, must actually come from later than that, for both the style of the handwriting and the internal evidence of the document place it in the summer of 1556. It was in answer to a letter sent by her mother discussing confidential affairs of state, it seems, and there is reference to the fact that the young Queen's former suggestions about the Abbot of Kilwinning had proved acceptable to the Queen Regent. When Mary of Guise asked her, however, to approve what she had done with regard to a financial matter concerning Lord Erskine, young Mary was embarrassed, and begged her mother never to seek her approval but to treat her as 'your very humble and very obedient daughter and servant'.[25]

By this time the letters of Mary, Queen of Scots were not merely a paragraph or two long. Written on sheets of approximately foolscap size, they run to two pages and more, and one of them covers four pages with energetic, fluent writing, devoid of scorings-out or hesitations. Her mention of the marriage three or four days previously of Diane de France, Duchess of Castro to Constable Montmorency's son, places this letter at the very beginning of May 1557, for the wedding took place on 4 May that year. Mary also complained that while her royal lands remained small, the Scottish nobility were increasing their holdings. She would not have mentioned this, she said, had not Mary of Guise commanded her to give advice on all the Queen Regent's affairs.

What, then, may we infer from this set of letters? Written by Mary, Queen of Scots between the ages of eleven and fourteen, they show her eager to please her mother and heavily reliant on her uncles for advice, struggling to give an opinion on matters about which she knew little. The most intriguing aspect of these exchanges is that Mary of Guise was so diligent in trying to train her up to be an effective and active Queen of Scots. Since young Mary would presumably marry the Dauphin one day and become Queen Consort of France, Mary of Guise might have considered that there was no need for her to know anything about Scottish affairs. The country could go on being ruled by herself or by a succession of regents under the guidance of the French King. Mary of Guise had never seen the situation in this light, however. From the very beginning she had raised her daughter not as a future Queen of France but as the Scottish monarch. Life was uncertain, death had all too often interfered with her own plans and there was always the fear that the French might not go through with the Dauphin's marriage. Even if everything did go smoothly, Mary, Queen of Scots must always remember that she was no mere queen consort but a monarch in her own right, with her own particular heritage.

The correspondence between mother and daughter continued as the months went by, and further letters are preserved in a variety of archive repositories. Apart from discussing financial and political affairs, there is an increasing exchange on more personal matters. In about May 1557, for example, Mary, Queen of Scots was apologising for the delay in sending her mother a watch that struck the time and asking for some sleeves, which were detachable from dresses at that period, as well as some good palfreys, the light saddle horses ridden by women. At the end of that particular letter, she begs Mary of Guise most humbly to come to see her as soon as she could safely do so.[26] The following year, it seemed that this was about to happen. Henri II finally decided that the time had come for his eldest son's marriage to take place. Mary of Guise fully intended to be at Notre Dame in Paris for her daughter's wedding in 1558 and announced her plans. It must have been a desperate disappointment for both of them when she was forced to decide that the political situation made it too dangerous for her to leave Scotland.[27] The marriage took place without her, and her daughter hastened to write reassuringly afterwards to say how happy she was and how well she was treated.[28]

Even with her child's future secured, Mary of Guise had no thought of retiring to France and she remained indomitable in her efforts to make her daughter's realm into a modern, well-governed country, France's unshakeable ally. When her old friend Henri II died after a jousting accident in 1559, Mary of Guise's regret must have been mingled with the satisfaction of knowing that her daughter and her son-in-law were now Queen Consort and King of France. Scottish Protestants were, however, becoming increasingly alarmed by the thought that their country was set to become a mere province of France, and the accession of Elizabeth I to the English throne in 1558 had given them hopes of a powerful ally. Despite all her efforts, Mary of Guise was ultimately unable to hold back the rising tide of the Reformation. She was not a persecutor, she knew very well the abuses that affected the Roman Catholic Church but she believed that most of the Scots who had converted to Protestantism had done so not out of religious conviction but because they had been led astray by leaders who were challenging her authority for purely secular reasons. In July 1559 Mary, Queen of Scots wrote from Paris to the Duke of Châtelherault to thank him for the assistance he was giving her mother in such troubled times but the situation was deteriorating rapidly.[29] John Knox arrived back from continental exile to preach his inflammatory sermons, more and more of the nobility were joining the Lords of the Congregation, as the Protestant leaders were known, and on 21 October they announced that Mary of Guise's regency was suspended.[30]

After lengthy consideration, Elizabeth I of England sent forces to help the Scottish Protestants besieging Leith, which was being held for Mary of Guise by French soldiers who had come to assist her. Mary of Guise's health had by this time broken down under the strain of her long years of struggle, and Mary, Queen of Scots anxiously awaited reports of how she was in the early months of 1560, begging her to take care of herself and urging her to trust in God to help her in her adversities, as he had so often done in the past. She asked Mary of Guise to forgive her for her boldness in making these remarks and assured her that François II had promised that he would send more help to Scotland in response to her repeated requests for further assistance. She would not allow him to forget to do so, she said, nor would his mother, Catherine de Medici, who had wept bitter tears when she had heard of the Queen Dowager's tribulations.[31]

Mary of Guise finally died in Edinburgh Castle on 11 June 1560, probably from chronic heart disease. The news reached France the following week, but it was kept from Mary, Queen of Scots for another ten days. The Venetian ambassador reported that her uncle, the Cardinal of Lorraine, who was himself deeply distressed,[32] finally told her what had happened, whereupon she 'showed and still shows such signs of grief, that during the greater part of yesterday she passed from one agony to another'.[33] Less than six months later, François II died, leaving Mary, Queen of Scots a widow at eighteen, contemplating her return to Scotland. She went back the following year, and the very first time she met John Knox, on 4 September 1561, she opened their debate by accusing him of raising a number of her subjects against her mother and herself. She was painfully aware of all the difficulties that Mary of Guise had faced.[34]

The Venetian ambassador once observed that Mary 'loved her mother incredibly, and much more than daughters usually love their mothers'.[35] She and Mary of Guise had spent less than seven years together, but the emotional bond between them had if anything been strengthened by absence. Without that deep affection, the younger Mary might never have taken any interest in her own kingdom, and indeed might never have returned to it after the death of her first husband. As it was, throughout the tribulations of her personal rule and during her captivity, she constantly emphasised the fact that she was Queen of Scots. Politically, it suited her to do so, of course, but there is no doubt that her mother had given her a strong sense of identity.

Notes

1. Bouillé, *Histoire des Ducs de Guise*, i, 41–60, 220–2; Forneron, *Les Ducs de Guise*, i, 1–9; Fontette, *Les Religieuses*, 129–51; Merigot, *Philippe de Gueldres*; Strickland, *Queens of Scotland*, i, 343–5; *Foreign Correspondence*, 1537–48, 1548–57, *passim* ; *LPFD, Henry VIII*, 11, 150, 292–302, 336–7, 348, 421–2, 449, 453–4; Marshall, *Mary of Guise* (1977), 1–54; Marshall, *Mary of Guise, Queen of Scots* (2001)
2. *Foreign Correspondence*, 1548–57, 13, 20, 23, 31, 51
3. NLS, Balcarres Papers, 29.2.1/6

4. *Diurnal of Occurrents*, 23–4; *Historie, Pitscottie*, i, 382, 394; Holinshed, *Chronicles*, v, 515–7; Marshall, *Mary of Guise* (1977), 78–87
5. *Foreign Correspondence*, 1537–48, i, 228
6. *CSP Spanish, Henry VIII*, vi, part ii, 189–90; *Hamilton Papers*, i, 323, 324, 328, 333, 337
7. NLS, Balcarres Papers, 29.2.1/6
8. Knox, *History of the Reformation*, i, 126
9. *State Papers, Sadler*, 87
10. Donaldson, *Scottish Historical Documents*, 110–11; *Historie, Pitscottie*, ii, 15
11. Hay Fleming, *Mary, Queen of Scots*, 191, n.73
12. *CSP Scot.*, i, 157; Stoddart, *Girlhood*, Appendix; Hay Fleming, *Mary, Queen of Scots*, 196–8
13. *APS*, ii, 481–2
14. *Hamilton Papers*, ii, 618
15. *Foreign Correspondence*, 1548–57, 7
16. Coste, *Eloges*, i, 231
17. NLS, Balcarres Papers, Adv. MS., 29.2.1/39–79
18. Beaugé, *Histoire*, 76–7, 126–43; Lesley, *History*, ii, 315–17, 327, 333–5; *CSP Scot.*, i, 169–71; Marshall, *Mary of Guise* (1977), 177–86
19. *State Papers, Sadler*, i, 84–8
20. See, for example, the portrait of her attributed to Corneille de Lyon, in the Scottish National Portrait Gallery, PG1558
21. *CSP Foreign*, 1547–53, 93
22. NLS, Balcarres Papers, Adv. MS., 29.2.1/90; Pimodan, *Mère des Guises*, 143
23. *Lettres du Cardinal de Lorraine*, 156
24. NLS, Balcarres Papers, Adv. MS., 29.2.1/10–31
25. Printed in *Lettres*, ed. Labanoff, i, 5–8
26. *Ibid.*, i, 45
27. Ruble, *Première jeunesse*, 147
28. *Lettres*, ed. Labanoff, i, 57
29. *Ibid.*, i, 67–8
30. *CSP Scot.*, i, 255; *CSP Foreign* 1559–60, 46–7
31. *Lettres*, ed. Labanoff, i, 70–1
32. *Lettres du Cardinal de Lorraine*, 404
33. *CSP Venetian*, vii, 234
34. Knox, *History*, ii, 13–20
35. *CSP Venetian*, vii, 227

2

French Relatives: Antoinette de Bourbon and Catherine de Medici

M ary, Queen of Scots spent almost a third of her life in France, arriving when she was five and leaving again at eighteen. During that time she lived at the centre of the French royal family, affectionately treated by King Henri II, brought up along with his children, and protected by her vigilant uncles, François, Duke of Guise and his younger brother, Charles, Cardinal of Lorraine. These men dominated her life, but she also came into contact with a number of powerful women who influenced her in different ways. Two were of particular importance: her own grandmother, Antoinette de Bourbon, Duchess of Guise and Henri II's wife, Queen Catherine de Medici.

Each has a sinister reputation in history. An enamel miniature of 1560 by Leonard Limousin shows Antoinette de Bourbon in a chariot, holding the Eucharist as she rides triumphantly over the mangled bodies of dying heretics.[1] The Guise family had become synonymous with the ruthless persecution of Protestants, and Antoinette was very much the matriarch, advising and directing her ambitious, enterprising sons. Meanwhile, Catherine is often portrayed as a wicked Black Widow, 'Madame Serpent', a Machiavellian plotter who allegedly did not hesitate to use poison to further her devious schemes and who gloated over the massacre of French Protestants on St Bartholomew's Day 1572. Nor do her surviving portraits help. The best known, by François Clouet, shows her swathed in black, her heavy features and watchful eyes apparently bearing out her contemporaries' worst opinions of her.[2] So how did young Mary fare in the company of two such formidable females, and was she influenced by their apparently unfortunate personalities?

Religious prejudice has all too often distorted our mental image of people of the past and Protestant historians heartily disliked both of these women who were, in fact, very different in their religious views. Let us turn first to Mary's grandmother, Antoinette de Bourbon, Duchess of Guise. Born on Christmas Day 1494, she was the daughter of François de Bourbon, Count of Vendôme and his wife, Marie de Luxembourg and she numbered among her ancestors Louis IX of France (St Louis).[3] The elder of two daughters, Antoinette grew up to be a sturdy young woman of middle height with aquiline features, chestnut-coloured hair and fine blue eyes. When she was nineteen, she married Claude, Count of Guise, who was two years younger than herself.

Claude's father, René, Duke of Lorraine and King of Sicily, had owned not only the vast territories of Lorraine, an independent duchy lying on the French border with Germany, but substantial properties in France itself. When he died in 1508, he divided his lands between his first two sons. Antoine, his eldest, became Duke of Lorraine while Claude received the French possessions and became a naturalised Frenchman. Settling at the Court of Louis XII, Claude was the close friend of the heir to the throne, the future François I, not least because their mothers were cousins. When Claude and Antoinette first met, it seemed unlikely that they would marry, for it was rumoured that Louis XII wanted Claude as a husband for one of his own daughters. However, it seems that Claude and Antoinette had fallen in love, and he was bold enough to refuse the Princess. His marriage contract was signed on 9 June 1513 and the wedding was celebrated with much splendour in the Church of St Paul, Paris soon afterwards.[4] Claude then pursued a brilliant military career, accompanying François on his Italian campaigns and surviving near-fatal wounds at the Battle of Marignano in 1515. While he fought in the royal army and attended the King at Court, Antoinette settled first at Bar-le-Duc, an impressive fortress lent by her brother-in-law, Antoine, Duke of Lorraine, and then at Joinville, an elegant, turreted Castle above the River

Marne. There, she raised her large family, ran the estates during her husband's frequent absences, extended Joinville Castle and laid out fine new gardens.[5]

Meanwhile Claude, urged on by his own mother, the pious Philippa of Gueldres, fought not only foreign adversaries but enemies of the Roman Catholic Church. Heresy must be rooted out, his mother had told him,[6] and when he drove back the Anabaptists who were threatening to invade Lorraine in 1525, not only was he congratulated by the Pope but the following year his friend the Dauphin, now François I, created him Duke of Guise. Soon he had gained an iconic reputation as a great Roman Catholic hero and protector of the faith, a soldier of God who appeared at the head of his army in a nimbus of light, a flaming sword in his hand. Protestants, of course, took a very different view of him. For them he was far from being a hero. Instead, he was 'The Great Butcher', a savage murderer of the innocent, perpetrating hideous atrocities against the Lutherans in the name of religion.[7]

Antoinette shared her husband's devotion to the Roman Catholic Church. Although her surroundings were luxurious, she lived frugally, dressing with severe simplicity. She attended Mass daily, collected relics, went on pilgrimages, founded religious houses, and felt a strong sense of responsibility for the spiritual welfare of the people who lived on her husband's estates.[8] Joinville Castle had its own chapel, and successive generations of the family had enriched the interior with precious relics and jewelled images. Claude and Antoinette installed nine canons and four choristers to sing the daily services, and Claude, passionately fond of music, employed there a series of composers including the famous Clément Jannequin. The Church, of course, gave excellent career opportunities for intelligent, capable people and Antoinette's brother Louis, her brother-in-law Jean, Bishop of Metz and two of her sons became cardinals while her aunt, her only sister and two of her daughters were abbesses.[9]

By the time Mary, Queen of Scots arrived in France, her grandmother was an energetic fifty-three-year-old and the experienced mother of twelve, eight sons and four daughters, all of whom seem to have been unusually accomplished. The eldest sons were now in their twenties, the youngest just six years older than Mary herself, and of course Antoinette was also bringing up Mary of Guise's only surviving boy, the Duke of Longueville. No cold ascetic, Antoinette shows herself in her letters to her children to have been a warm-hearted, sympathetic woman who was practical, perceptive and imaginative in her dealings with her family and friends. As soon as she received word that Mary, Queen of Scots had landed, Antoinette hurried to Brittany to meet her, taking time only to write a hasty note of reassurance to the child's mother. She sympathised with Mary of Guise over the anxiety she must have felt during little Mary's voyage and promised that she would look after her with the greatest care. We have no description of that first meeting, but, like everyone else, Antoinette was impressed with her granddaughter. 'This little lady is very pretty indeed and as intelligent as can be. She is a clear-skinned brunette and, I think . . . will be a beautiful girl,' she told her son Charles when she wrote to him from Tours.[10]

She was taking Mary to St Germain-en-Laye, where they would meet the royal children.[11] Henri II joined them there, and to the Guise family's great relief he was very taken with his future daughter-in-law. She was large for her age, pretty and her bright, intelligent manner delighted him. Better still, she and her future husband, the regrettably dull and unresponsive Dauphin, already seemed to be the best of friends. Well satisfied, Antoinette stayed for a few days while Mary settled down and then she went home to Joinville. She would be back from time to time, of course, because she was one of Catherine de Medici's ladies-in-waiting, but in her absence her two eldest sons would keep a watchful eye on all that concerned the little Queen.[12]

Her eldest, François, Duke of Aumale, was following in his father's footsteps and was much admired for his military prowess while Charles, her second son, had entered the Church and was already, at twenty-four, a cardinal, a great patron of the arts, and a sympathetic friend to the women his brothers married. He swiftly became a father figure to Mary, Queen of Scots, who seems to have resembled him in nature, according to one observer. Michel de Castelnau, French ambassador to England, would later comment that Mary had 'as big and restless a spirit' as the Cardinal.[13] Neither François nor Charles needed any prompting to make sure that their niece was treated properly. Family feeling apart, she was their great hope for the future. Once her marriage to the Dauphin was safely accomplished, they would be in an unassailable position of power, or so they believed. Their greatest fear was that their rivals would prevent the marriage from taking place, and so they were determined to emphasise Mary's status at every opportunity. She was, after all, no mere princess but a queen in her own right.

When Mary, Queen of Scots was old enough, she corresponded with Antoinette and a few of the letters she sent to 'Madame my grandmother' have survived. The excited note she dispatched on 3 June 1550 gives us a glimpse of the affectionate relationship between the two. Mary had just heard from Mary of Guise that she was coming to France, and she could not resist passing on 'the joyous news' immediately. 'Soon, you and I will see her here, which is for me the greatest [honour] that I could wish for in this world,' she said, and she begged Antoinette to add to her joy by coming to see her as soon as possible. She signed the letter, as she always did, 'Your most humble and obedient daughter, Marie'.[14] As the years went by, she discussed public affairs with Antoinette as well as private concerns. In late August 1557, when she was fourteen, she was sympathising with her grandmother over the capture of St Quentin by the Duke of Savoy. She did not know how they could appease the wrath of God in order to prevent such disasters, she said, expressing the generally held view that catastrophes were God's way of punishing men and women for their sins, and then on a lighter note she thanked her grandmother warmly for the fine collars she had sent.[15]

She was growing up fast. The following year, her Guise relatives triumphantly attended her marriage to the Dauphin and Ronsard's short poem in praise of Antoinette spoke of the pleasure she must be experiencing at seeing her sons so close to the King.[16] None of them could for one moment have imagined that in less than three years both the bridegroom and his father would be dead. When she was widowed, it was to her grandmother that Mary turned for consolation. Antoinette came to stay with her, sharing her chamber and eating with her before accompanying her to one of the royal palaces near Orléans and then carrying her off to Lorraine to visit her relatives. She spent three weeks in the Abbey of Saint Pierre-les-Dames, Rheims where her aunt, Antoinette's third daughter Renée, was abbess. It was while she was travelling from Rheims to Nancy to call on the Duke and Duchess of Lorraine that she received a visit from her half-brother, Lord James Stewart, inviting her to come back to Scotland. Mary decided to go, and that August she and Antoinette saw each other for the last time.[17]

There is no indication of how Antoinette felt about Mary's decision to leave France. Was she one of those relatives who warned against such a rash step, or did she agree that Mary must begin to rule her own kingdom in person? We simply do not know but, whatever her attitude, Mary's affectionate relationship with her continued. Indeed, as late as 25 January 1564, she was assuring Antoinette that she was anxious only to serve her, 'my good mother, who takes the place of all my paternal and maternal relatives'. As usual, she signed herself, 'Your very humble and very obedient daughter'.[18] We do not know what Antoinette thought of Mary's marriages to Lord Darnley and then to James, 4th Earl of Bothwell, but from her English imprisonment Mary was still sending her grandmother loving messages, and in the early months of 1573 Antoinette managed to get a book to her, probably a prayer book.[19] The old lady was in her late seventies by then, but she lived on for another ten years, finally dying at Joinville on 29 January 1583, at the age of eighty-eight. She was buried beside her husband in the Church of St Laurent, beneath a magnificent marble monument which she had commissioned when Claude died in 1550. Carved in Florence, it was decorated with effigies of Claude and herself, kneeling beneath trophies of victory.[20]

Close though Mary was to her Guise relatives, her day-to-day life in France was governed by the royal family. Henri II always enjoyed her company, while his eldest daughter, Elisabeth, was her constant companion. They shared the same bedchamber and they were taught together, both receiving the fine Renaissance education in languages and the classics judged appropriate for royal women. Henri's unmarried sister, Marguerite, later Duchess of Savoy, was well known for her learning and so was his queen, Catherine de Medici. Marguerite took a kindly interest in Mary, helping to nurse her when she fell ill,[21] but Mary's dealings with Catherine were more problematic. We must remember, of course, that when Mary joined the French Court in 1548, Catherine was not the malevolent widow of later historical accounts but a large, graceful twenty-nine-year-old with dark hair, the big dark eyes which were a Medici characteristic and rather heavy features. As Henri II's consort, she always treated him with great deference and she was deeply attached to their young children, but if she often seemed inscrutable and reserved, that was hardly surprising. She was having to share the husband she adored with his longstanding mistress, whom she publicly accepted but privately loathed.

Catherine was Italian by birth, and she had survived a dangerous and difficult childhood. Born on 13 April 1519, she was the daughter of Lorenzo de Medici, Duke of Urbino, grandson of the famous Lorenzo the Magnificent, and his aristocratic French wife Madeleine de la Tour d'Auvergne. The Medicis had originally made their money in banking, but they had since become the most powerful family in Florence, and in spite of his youth, Catherine's father was already a significant figure on the international scene. However, within three weeks of his daughter's birth, both he and his wife were dead, she of puerperal fever and he allegedly of syphilis. In consequence, for the first months of her life, Catherine was cared for first by her paternal grandmother, Alfonsina Orsini, and then by an aunt, Clarissa de Medici, wife of Philip Strozzi.[22]

During Catherine's childhood, Italy was in turmoil as François I of France pursued his political ambitions there and the Holy Roman Emperor, Charles V, tried to stop him. Charles triumphed, not only defeating the French at the Battle of Pavia in 1525 but subsequently sacking Rome. In the aftermath, the popular party in Florence rose and drove out the Medici. The rebels tried to seize

Catherine, but she and her aunt found refuge in first one convent and then another, in fear of their lives. The situation was further complicated when Pope Clement VII became Charles V's ally and sent papal troops to besiege Florence. Catherine was the Pope's distant relative, and when the city capitulated in August 1530, he had her brought to Rome. By now eleven years old, she had already attracted a string of suitors, for not only was she Duchess of Urbino in her own right but through her mother she was the heir to substantial properties in France. Anxious that she should not be married off to one of his enemies, François I decided that she would make an appropriate wife for his second son, Henri.[23]

After complicated negotiations with the Pope, the marriage contract was finally agreed and in August 1533 Catherine set off for Marseilles. The French royal family were waiting there to greet her and, on 28 October, arrayed in brocade and violet velvet trimmed with ermine and scattered with pearls and diamonds, she married the fourteen-year-old French Prince, Pope Clement himself performing the ceremony. The celebratory banquets and entertainments lasted for more than a month and among the many wedding presents she received were a magnificent gold and rock-crystal casket from the Pope and ropes of the biggest and best pearls ever seen, from her new husband.[24]

This should have been the start of a far more secure life for Catherine, but despite the fact that she was half French, the French courtiers despised her because she was not a royal princess and made it difficult for her to feel accepted. Indeed, from the very first they sneered at her as the daughter of a mere merchant.[25] Determined to secure her position, she set out to win the approbation of her father-in-law, impressing François I with her erudition when she began to study Greek and her panache when she joined the little group of female friends who went hunting with him. She was less successful with her husband, however. The same age as herself, Henri was notoriously taciturn and morose. He too had endured a difficult childhood. His mother, Queen Claude, had died when he was five years old[26] and then, when he was six, his father had been captured at Pavia. Charles V treated François I honourably, but would only agree to set him free on condition that his two eldest sons, the Dauphin François and Prince Henri, were sent to Spain as hostages.

François I agreed, assuming that they would be set free as soon as he paid a ransom for them. To his dismay, Charles refused to negotiate their release and the Princes remained in captivity for the next three and a half years.[27] Throughout that time, Henri was aggressive and defiant, hurling insults at the Spanish and trying to escape whenever he thought he saw an opportunity. All his attempts failed, however, and both boys were much changed when they finally returned to France, their former lively cheerfulness gone. Their father found them wary and withdrawn, and Matteo Dandolo, the Venetian ambassador, commented that Henri rarely smiled.[28] François much preferred his merry youngest son Charles, and seems to have found Henri particularly irritating. His marriage to Catherine had done nothing to improve Henri's disposition but when he was about nineteen Diane de Poitiers came into his life. Thirty-eight years old, tall and statuesque, with dark hair and neat, rather prim features, she was the eldest of three daughters of Jean de Poitiers, Sieur de Saint-Vallier. When she was fifteen, she had married Louis de Brézé, Grand Sénéchal of Normandy, forty years older than she was. Reputed to be one of the ugliest men in France, he was also very kind and extremely wealthy, and in the course of their satisfactory marriage, they had two daughters. When he died in the summer of 1531, he was buried in Rouen Cathedral, where the magnificent tomb Diane erected to him can still be seen.

After his death, Diane returned to the French Court as one of the 'petite bande' of women friends of the King. There was some talk that she became his mistress for a time, but this may have been no more than a rumour. At any rate, when the King complained to her one day about his middle son's unsatisfactory behaviour, she came up with a solution. Henri needed to fall in love, she said. In an era when courtly love provided a safe context for diverting flirtations, it would be perfectly acceptable for her to form a platonic friendship with a young married man.[29] Insecure, unhappy and with no liking for his wife, Henri turned with relief to the comfort of this fascinating, experienced woman's company and very soon their relationship was far from platonic.[30] The King was furious when he realised that they were lovers but, despite his efforts to put an end to the liaison, Henri made it clear that nothing was going to separate him from his mistress.

Painfully aware that her husband had no interest in her, Catherine was alarmed and distressed by this latest development, for by now she was deeply in love with Henri. Her difficulties were compounded by the fact that, although she had been married for more than five years, she still showed no sign of becoming pregnant. Desperately she tried every possible pill and potion provided by her Italian physicians and suggested by her friends, but nothing had any effect. The question of her fertility became even more pressing when Henri's elder brother, the Dauphin François, died in 1536 making Henri the heir to their father's throne. Catherine was terrified that he would send her back to Italy. He would not have been the first royal husband to repudiate a barren wife and it was at this point that there was talk of Henri wanting to marry Mary of Guise instead.[31] Eventually, when rumours of their impending divorce were impossible to ignore, Catherine went to the King in tears and said that she would agree to the ending of her marriage if Henri would allow her either to enter a nunnery or stay on and serve whatever wife he chose instead. Staring at his clever daughter-in-law in dismay, François I proved both sympathetic and supportive, and he made it plain that this was not about to happen. Catherine, Henri and Diane then settled down once more to their customary *ménage à trois*, with Diane living in the Queen's household as one of her ladies-in-waiting.

By 1543, everyone had given up hope of Catherine ever having children but in June, after ten years of marriage, she was able to write to Henri's old friend the Constable Montmorency to tell him her miraculous news. She believed that she was pregnant at last.[32] Sure enough, on 19 January 1544, she gave birth to François, the delicate boy who would one day marry Mary, Queen of Scots, and during the following twelve years she had four more sons and five daughters. Her second son Louis died in infancy, and her last children, twin girls, did not survive their birth, but in spite of being small and weak in infancy, the other seven children did grow up to adult life.[33] Diane de Poitiers usually assisted at Catherine's confinements, helping to nurse her as she recovered, and Catherine was even forced to allow her rival to choose the babies' nurses. After her long and painful wait for children she was an understandably anxious mother, and her concern for her little ones made her demand not only constant reports about them but drawings and portraits of them, so that she could judge for herself the state of their health.[34]

When François I died in 1547, Henri succeeded him, but he did not change his domestic arrangements. Instead, he took the opportunity to shower Diane with valuable properties and some of the crown jewels, creating her Duchess of Valentinois. At Queen Catherine's coronation and official entry into Paris, Diane was prominent as one of her ladies-in-waiting, riding along with two squires in white satin carrying the long train of her mantle. Her influence over the King was publicly acknowledged by everyone, and instead of going to the Queen with messages and petitions to be passed on to Henri, courtiers went to Diane. As John, Lord Erskine told Mary of Guise in 1549, the Duchess of Valentinois 'is very great in credit with the King . . .' and any requests should be addressed to her. Each evening Henri was to be found in Diane's company and Catherine must have known that when he came to her apartments at night it was because his mistress had sent him.[35]

These, then, were the adult complexities facing Mary, Queen of Scots, when she came to live with the French royal children in 1548. She was too young, of course, to appreciate the situation fully, but she knew that she must be polite to both of Henri II's ladies, particularly the Queen. Mary of Guise was always scrupulously correct in such matters herself, and however understanding she may have been about Henri's relationship with Diane, she seems to have impressed upon Mary the need to treat the Queen Consort with the utmost courtesy. For her part, Catherine was apparently pleased with the arrangements made for her eldest son's future bride. In September 1548, before she met Mary, Queen of Scots, she was saying that she was very happy that Mary was joining her children,[36] and some weeks later when she had seen Mary for herself, she wrote to Mary of Guise, praising the little girl's beauty and wisdom. She was marvellously happy, she said, to have such a daughter who would, she hoped, be the support of her old age.[37] 'La reinette' (the little Queen) had only to smile to turn all heads in France.[38]

Mary, Queen of Scots did her best to get on well with Catherine. She wrote her a pleasing letter when the French Queen gave birth to her daughter, Marguerite, in 1553,[39] and she begged an unknown correspondent at one point for a little hackney so that she could follow Catherine to the hunt.[40] When she fell ill with a fever in August 1556, Catherine nursed her tenderly day and night until she recovered.[41] Even so, there is the occasional hint of unease. Courts were always centres of rivalry and gossip, and the simmering tension between Catherine and Diane made it all the more tempting for courtiers and attendants to take sides and stir up strife. When Mary was fourteen she was deeply distressed when she suspected that the Dame de Parois, her governess, was making trouble for her with Catherine.[42]

In the course of a letter home to her mother, pouring out her worries, Mary begged Mary of Guise to allow Catherine to choose her new governess, 'since you want me to be agreeable to the Queen'.[43] This rather suggests that there had already been differences between Mary and Catherine, and that her mother had felt it necessary to remind her of how to behave. Biographers of Mary never fail to repeat her alleged comment that Catherine was merely a merchant's daughter, attributing to this incautious remark a subsequent hostility between the two. However, as we have seen, the French courtiers had always despised Catherine, and this particular jibe had been delivered many times before, by other people. Nevertheless, it does seem that the jealousy between Diane de Poitiers and Catherine was disturbing Mary's life.

Diane was determined to show everyone how friendly she was with the young Queen of Scots. Royal mistresses knew very well that they owed their position entirely to the King's favour, which could vanish overnight. Diane had become an expert in playing off the different factions at Court to her own advantage and in the late 1540s this had involved making a rapprochement with the Guise family. So successful was she that on 1 August 1547 her daughter Louise had married Mary of Guise's young brother Claude, Marquis of Mayenne, creating a permanent link between the two families.[44] Diane was therefore in an excellent position to cultivate a good relationship with Mary, Queen of Scots, not necessarily to annoy Catherine de Medici but to strengthen her own alliance with the Guises. In 1550 she therefore assured Mary of Guise that she would look after Mary, Queen of Scots as though she were her own daughter.[45]

By 1555 Mary was writing to tell her mother how incredibly well not only her uncles but 'Madame de Valentinois' cared for her.[46] In May 1557 she remarked in another letter to Mary of Guise, 'You know how indebted I am to Madame de Valentinois for the love she more and more shows me', and she urged her mother to oblige Diane by arranging a marriage between Diane's granddaughter and the Duke of Châtelherault's eldest son.[47] Of course Catherine de Medici was not going to be happy to see Mary form a close friendship with her own hated rival, and this may well have clouded her relationship with Mary. Even so, Catherine was prepared to be generous when Mary eventually married the Dauphin in 1558. She gave her new daughter-in-law valuable presents, including a collar made from the fabulous pearls Henri II had given her as a wedding present.[48] Mary was fifteen now, no longer a child in the royal nurseries but a tall and beautiful young woman, already famous for her charm, and Catherine's role was changing too. She was at last emerging from her position as the submissive, neglected wife. She had been asked to rule France as Regent when Henri left the country on military campaigns, and although Diane de Poitiers at first persuaded him to limit her powers, when Henri saw his wife beginning to demonstrate real political ability, he came to rely on her. As one recent historian has observed, Catherine now had 'more influence and a larger role in government than any other royal wife of the sixteenth century'.[49]

The following April, France and Spain signed the Treaty of Cateau-Cambrésis ending their wars in Italy, and in fulfilment of one of the conditions, Henri II and Catherine's eldest daughter Elisabeth married Philip II of Spain. The proxy wedding took place on 22 June but eight days later Henri II was mortally wounded when a splinter from his opponent's lance pierced his eye during a celebratory tournament. Although at first there were hopes that he would recover, he died ten days later.[50] Catherine was distraught. Both she and Mary were at his deathbed, and Mary voiced great anxiety afterwards about her mother-in-law, fearing that she would collapse with exhaustion.[51] Only the thought of her son, now François II, would save Catherine from an early death, Mary believed. 'He is so obedient he does nothing but what she wishes,' she told her own mother. Is there a hint of jealousy there, or even of dry humour? Not really, for she goes on to remark that the loss of her mother-in-law would be the greatest misfortune which could come to 'this poor country and all of the rest of us'.[52]

With the death of Henri II, Diane de Poitiers vanished from the scene. When she heard that he had been injured, she came to the gates of the Château des Tournelles in Paris where he lay, only to be turned away on Catherine's orders. Diane had to give back the Château of Chenonceaux and all the crown jewels Henri had lavished upon her, and she was then allowed to retire to her first husband's residence at Anet.[53] Long years afterwards, Catherine de Medici told a friend, 'If I was cheerful toward Madame de Valentinois, it was the King that I really was entertaining, and furthermore I always made him understand that I was doing it against the grain, since never did a woman who loved her husband love his mistress'.[54]

Mary's Guise uncles were determined to rule France through her young husband, but Catherine had other ideas, and she would not rest until she had taken back into her own hands the powers they so eagerly grasped. Even so, she and Mary managed to maintain reasonably amicable relations during the early months of Catherine's widowhood. When Catherine had decided to move from the Château des Tournelles to the Louvre on the very day of her husband's death and was about to enter the leading coach in which François II was already seated, she noticed Mary, standing politely to one side, and remembered their altered position. She therefore insisted that Mary take the place of honour next to the new King.[55] Catherine also had to relinquish her apartments in the royal palaces to Mary,[56] but when they moved to Blois that winter they shared accommodation, attending Mass in their private chapel, receiving visitors together and united in constant worry about the health of François II.[57]

François had never been strong, suffering from chronic catarrh, probably sinus trouble and possibly tuberculosis, in addition to which there were persistent rumours that he and Mary could not have children because he had undescended testicles. He was at last growing tall, it was true, but although Mary's uncles encouraged his passion for hunting in the hope that outdoor exercise would improve his health, he was the victim of recurring fevers. On 16 November 1560 he was out hunting in the Orléans area, seemingly in good health, but the next day he collapsed during vespers, complaining of a sharp pain near his left ear. The infection turned into meningitis and, according to one report, in their agitation Catherine and Mary quarrelled repeatedly at his bedside as to who should look after him. Whether or not that is true, they nursed him devotedly until, after days of delirium, he fell into a coma and died. It was the evening of 5 December. While Mary sat by his body, Catherine de Medici convened a meeting of the Privy Council. She would now rule France as Regent for her next son, Charles IX, who was only ten years old.[58]

Mary had to give back the crown jewels in her possession, put on white mourning and remain shut in her own chamber, as the etiquette of mourning demanded. This was no superficial display. Her incessant tears and grief-stricken lamentations evoked much compassion, said Michaelo Suriano, the Venetian ambassador at the French Court, for she had genuinely cared for her somewhat unappealing young husband.[59] The death of François II also led to a deterioration in Catherine and Mary's relationship. Catherine was fiercely maternal. As long as she and Mary had been united in their support of François II everything had gone smoothly, but now she would defend her son Charles IX's interests at all costs, and the Guise family with their thirst for power were a very real threat. She made carefully correct arrangements for the payment of Mary's jointure from the duchy of Touraine and the county of Poitou, but she also made it plain that her daughter-in-law was now merely the childless Queen Dowager, of no real significance, and that was how Catherine was determined she should remain.

The Guises were not about to give up so readily. Within days of the death of François, Mary's uncles were deep in negotiations for her to marry Philip II of Spain's son and heir, Don Carlos. Catherine was very angry when she found out. The Guises were obviously trying to turn Philip II against her, she believed, and she was convinced that this move would endanger the position of her own daughter Elisabeth, Philip's wife. If charismatic Mary with her powerful connections went to Spain as Philip's daughter-in-law, poor Elisabeth would be pushed aside and there was no knowing what might happen.[60] 'My daughter the Queen of Scots' had become a threat to the stability of Catherine's regency and she immediately moved to end the Spanish match. The Guise brothers continued their negotiations, but it was with palpable relief that Catherine in August 1561 was telling Elisabeth that Mary 'embarked eight days ago and if there is a good wind she will be in Scotland'.[61] For her part, Mary no doubt felt that she had left her domineering mother-in-law behind for good. The two women never met again, but as rulers of their individual countries their relationship was certainly not at an end.

It was in France's interests that Mary should govern Scotland, for the alternative was a Protestant government in Edinburgh which would look to England for support. With this in mind, Catherine kept an eagle eye on everything that went on, dispatching a series of envoys to Scotland during times of particular crisis. Her representative tried to mend matters when Mary and Darnley experienced difficulties in their marriage and again when Mary was imprisoned in Lochleven Castle after her marriage to Bothwell. By now Mary had set aside her resentment of what she regarded as her former mother-in-law's interference and was begging Catherine to send a force to help to free her, but the French were not going to involve themselves in any rash expedition of that nature.

During the first years of her English captivity, Mary continued to look to Catherine for assistance. On 31 March 1568, for example, she was writing to thank her for her 'comfortable letter' and begging for help,[62] but Catherine was more interested in the fate of the famous pearls she had given Mary as a wedding present. These had fallen into the hands of James, Earl of Moray who sold them to Elizabeth I, much to the chagrin of both Mary and Catherine.[63] As time went by, Mary complained that Catherine had abandoned her,[64] although in fact the French Queen was not as unresponsive as Mary would have had her friends believe. She pleaded for Mary's life when the Ridolfi Plot against Elizabeth was revealed and it seemed that Mary would be executed, and she tried to negotiate a treaty with Elizabeth aimed at restoring Mary to her Scottish throne. The trouble was that, whether she acted from compassion or from sheer self-interest, as Mary believed, the political and ecclesiastical complexities of the situation made any restoration impossible.[65] In the end, nothing could save Mary from the scaffold and in February 1587 Catherine received word of what she described as the 'cruel death of the poor Queen of Scotland'. Perhaps she still had some lingering fondness for the little girl she had known so well all those years before.

Catherine's own later life was fraught with difficulty. Exercising power on behalf of her successive sons, she played off Roman Catholics against Protestants, oscillating between friendship with Roman Catholic Spain and alliance with Protestant England. Always a pragmatist, she had long since reached the conclusion that the Protestants were far too numerous to be defeated either by force or by legislation, but in spite of her efforts the wars of religion continued. Charles IX died without ~~children~~ sons in 1574 and was succeeded by his brother, Henri III. Henri had always been a great favourite with his mother but, perhaps because of that, Catherine had less influence over him. She was horrified when in 1588 he ordered the assassination of the Roman Catholic leader, Henri, 3rd Duke of Guise, because she realised that vengeance would surely follow. Wracked by anxiety, she died thirteen days later, on 5 January 1589, at the age of sixty-nine. Henri III was murdered six months after that, just as she had foreseen.

Catherine de Medici was a presence in the life of Mary, Queen of Scots for nearly forty years, during which time their feelings for each other were distinctly ambivalent, but were Mary's attitudes and opinions to any extent moulded by her first mother-in-law? The usual assumption that Mary had learned her propensity for plotting from the Machiavellian Catherine is unconvincing. The two were very different in personality. Manipulation and machin-ation seem to have come naturally to Catherine. Mary was far more open, always ready to give expression to her innermost feelings. She was not the initiator of conspiracies nor was she drawn into them from any love of plotting. Her involvement came about during her captivity because she was desperate to regain her freedom.

More relevant is the question of the extent to which she was influenced in her attitude to religion by Catherine and the *poli-tiques*, those French thinkers who believed that heresy must be tolerated if the only alternative was civil strife.[66] Returning to Scotland in 1561, Mary was certainly resolved to tolerate Pro-testantism for the sake of peace. Her Dominican confessor thought Mary not only a good but a very devout Catholic until she made the mistake of marrying Bothwell,[67] and she certainly seems to have regretted agreeing to a Protestant wedding to him.[68] However, she has been criticised for exploiting religion for her own purposes, declaring undying loyalty to the Roman Catholic Church when she needed money or military support but toying with the notion of converting to Protestantism when she thought it could help her cause.[69] Moreover, early in her captivity in England she did listen to Protestant sermons, probably in the hope that this might encourage Queen Elizabeth to release her, excusing herself after-wards by saying that she only did so because she had been refused the offices of a Roman Catholic priest.

Some writers have thought that when she spoke of dying for her beliefs she was merely trying to gain sympathy and attention, but it was hardly surprising that, during those last desperate years, she turned to her religion for comfort and support, worried about the spiritual welfare of her Roman Catholic attendants, expressed a strong desire for the re-conversion of England and ultimately found the strength to go calmly to her death because she was convinced that in so doing she was furthering the cause of her Church.[70] As one of her Roman Catholic biographers has commented, 'her own strong but primitive faith seems to have remained perfectly unaffected by all the assaults made upon it',[71] a verdict rather strikingly echoed by that of a recent French historian on Mary's grandmother, Antoinette de Bourbon. She, he said, 'seems never to have known doubt. She remained firm in her convictions. Viscerally attached to a Catholicism made up of devout practices, sacramental participation and personal prayers, she kept throughout her life an unfailing fidelity to a religion which was more affective than conceptual . . .'[72] In short, the faith of Antoinette de Bourbon in the end probably meant far more to Mary, Queen of Scots than the agnostic pragmatism of Catherine de Medici.

Notes

1. In the Frick Collection, New York; reproduced in Amico, *Bernard Palissy*. I am grateful to Joan Noble, who drew my attention to this enamel.
2. Frieda, *Catherine de Medici*, p. xix; the portrait by Clouet is in the Musée Carnavalet, Paris
3. Anselme, *Histoire Généalogique*, i, 326–7
4. Bouillé, *Histoire des Ducs de Guise*, i, 44–50; Forneron, *Les Ducs de Guise*, i, 9, 16–20; Pimodan, *Mère des Guises*, 51; Williams, *False Lorraine*, 27–8
5. Pimodan, *Mère des Guises*, 30, 96–8
6. *Ibid.*, 27–9; Merigot, *Philippe de Gueldres*
7. Bouillé, *Histoire des Ducs de Guise*, i, 61–72; Forneron, *Les Ducs de Guise*, i, 23–37; Pimodan, *Mère des Guises*, 51; Williams, *False Lorraine*, 27–8

8. Viard, 'La religion d'Antoinette de Bourbon', 2–7
9. Bouillé, *Histoire des Ducs de Guise*, i, 542; Pimodan, *Mère des Guises*, 97–8
10. *Lettres du Cardinal de Lorraine*, 116 and 116 n.4
11. *Foreign Correspondence, 1548–57*, 6–7
12. Ibid., 6–10
13. Guy, *My Heart is my Own*, 236
14. *Lettres*, ed. Labanoff, vii, 277–8
15. Ibid., vii, 279–80
16. *Pierre de Ronsard, Poésies Choisies*, 872
17. Ruble, *Première jeunesse*, 209–10
18. *Lettres*, ed. Labanoff, vii, 291–2
19. Durkan, 'The Library of Mary, Queen of Scots', 91
20. Anselme, *Histoire Généalogique*, i, 327
21. Russell, *Peacemaking in the Renaissance*, 223; *Lettres du Cardinal de Lorraine*, 243
22. *Lettres de Catherine de Médicis*, i, p. ii; Frieda, *Catherine de Medici*, 13; Baumgartner, *Henry II*, 28
23. *Lettres de Catherine de Médicis*, i, 3–22; Frieda, *Catherine de Medici*, 13–31; Garrisson, *Catherine de Médicis*, 17–21; Castelnau, *Catherine de Médicis*; Bentley-Cranch and Marshall, *John Stewart, Duke of Albany*, 296–8, 300
24. *Lettres de Catherine de Médicis*, i, pp. xxv–xxvi; Frieda, *Catherine de Medici*, 43–6; Garrisson, *Catherine de Médicis*, 27–9
25. Forneron, *Les Ducs de Guise*, 290; Knecht, *The Valois*, 194
26. Bertière, *Reines de France*, 168, 173
27. Knecht, *The Valois*, 142–3
28. Frieda, *Catherine de Medici*, 81
29. Williams, *Henri II*, 124–5
30. *Lettres de Catherine de Médicis*, i, pp. xxx–xxxii; Thierry, *Diane de Poitiers*, 10–11; Frieda, *Catherine de Medici*, 52–3; Benger, *Memoirs*, i, 94, 99; Baumgartner, *Henry II*, 10–28
31. See page 10
32. *Lettres de Catherine de Médicis*, i, 6
33. Ruble, *Première jeunesse*, 24–46; Bertière, *Reines de France*, 293
34. For instance *Lettres de Catherine de Médicis*, i, 62, 66
35. *Foreign Correspondence, 1548–57*, 308; *Lettres de Catherine de Médicis*, i, pp. xxxviii, xl; Bardon, *Diane de Poitiers et le Mythe de Diane*; Thierry, *Diane de Poitiers*, 33–46
36. *Lettres de Catherine de Médicis*, i, 26

37. *Ibid.*, i, 556
38. *Ibid.*, i, p. liv
39. *Ibid.*, i, 557
40. Ruble, *Première jeunesse*, 105
41. *Lettres du Cardinal de Lorraine*, 243
42. See Chapter 3
43. *Lettres*, ed. Labanoff, i, 41–2
44. Baumgartner, *Henry II*, 57–9; Guiffrey, *Dianne de Poytiers: Lettres*, 30 n.3; *Lettres du Cardinal de Lorraine*, 114
45. Maidment, *Analecta*, 352
46. *Lettres*, ed. Labanoff, i, 32
47. *Ibid.*, i, 42–3
48. *Lettres de Catherine de Médicis*, i, pp. xlii n., xxv–xxvi
49. Baumgartner, *Henry II*, 99
50. Frieda, *Catherine de Medici*, 1–9
51. *Lettres de Catherine de Médicis*, i, pp. lvi, 122;
52. *Lettres*, ed. Labanoff, i, 71–2
53. Baumgartner, *Henry II*, 252–3
54. *Ibid.*, 98
55. Fraser, *Mary, Queen of Scots*, 88
56. Montclos, *Fontainebleau*, i, 100
57. Ruble, *Première jeunesse*, 189–95
58. *Ibid.*, 205–6; *Lettres de Catherine de Médicis*, i, pp. lxxxiv–lxxxv
59. Ruble, *Première jeunesse*, 207–10
60. Chéruel, *Marie Stuart et Catherine de Médicis*, 19–27; *Lettres de Catherine de Médicis*, i, pp. xci, 183, 190, 576, 585, 592–3
61. *Lettres de Catherine de Médicis*, i, 605
62. *Lettres*, ed. Labanoff, ii, 64–5
63. *Ibid.*, viii, 129, 132–3; Teulet, *Papiers d'Etat*, ii, 201, 214, 217
64. Chéruel, *Marie Stuart et Catherine de Médicis*, 77
65. *Ibid.*, 57–8
66. Allen, *History of Political Thought*; Frieda, *Catherine de Medici*, 138–9
67. *CSP Spanish, Elizabeth*, i, 662, 665
68. Anderson, *Collections*, i, 27; Keith, *History*, ii, 588
69. *Lettres*, ed. Labanoff, ii, 175–8; vii, 340
70. *Ibid.*, iv, 71–2, 173, 209, 276–8, 279, 375; v, 17
71. Fraser, *Mary, Queen of Scots*, 383
72. Viard, 'La religion d'Antoinette de Bourbon', 10–11

3

The Governesses and the Early Household

When Mary, Queen of Scots was small, Mary of Guise, Catherine de Medici and Antoinette de Bourbon loomed large in her life but the day-to-day care of this important child fell to the women appointed to serve her. Royal princes were often given their own households while they were no more than infants, and that had certainly been so with Mary, Queen of Scots' short-lived brother, Prince James.[1] However, there is no evidence that she herself had her own household during her early childhood years in Scotland. Her nurse Jean Sinclair and the women who rocked her cradle feature as members of her mother's household.[2] Again, although Mary was accompanied by a large number of Scottish courtiers when she set out for France in 1548, many of these were in the nature of a temporary royal escort rather than being seen as permanently in attendance on her. So who was to look after her, see to all the necessities of her daily life, order her clothing and take care of her belongings?

Henri II had already given considerable thought to Mary's domestic arrangements before she arrived. He liked Mary of Guise, he was sensitive to her concerns, and he was also aware that he had secured a very prestigious and diplomatically useful bride for his son. On 24 August 1548 he therefore told Monsieur de Humières, who was in charge of his children's household, that Mary, Queen of Scots was to have precedence over his own daughters, because the marriage with the Dauphin was signed and sealed, apart from which 'she is a crowned queen, and I wish her to be honoured and served as such'.[3] At that stage, he had two daughters, Elisabeth who was three and a half and Claude who was not quite one. Marguerite (known as Margot) was not born until 1553 and so, at almost nine years younger than Mary, she was never a close companion.[4] By mid-September Henri had given orders that spacious rooms for his children and 'my daughter, the Queen of Scotland' should be prepared immediately above the royal apartments at St Germain-en-Laye, to which he himself would travel shortly.[5]

A month later, on 17 October, he decreed that as soon as Mary was installed in the house of Carrières at St Germain, all the foreigners with her were to be sent home. This was a very normal arrangement, and all too often royal brides were deeply upset when the retinues they had brought with them were dispersed. From the monarch's point of view, it was a matter of simple common sense. Apart from the fact that the newcomers inevitably squabbled with the existing attendants, they might well turn into a nest of spies for their native country, not to mention being a drain on the bridegroom's resources. Moreover, this measure was very much in keeping with Henri's desire that Mary should settle down as quickly as possible and grow accustomed to her future husband and his relatives.

What was more unusual was Henri's decision that she should not have her own household of servants, but would be served by his children's attendants. This seemed the obvious arrangement to make, from a practical point of view, but retinues were also important indicators of status, and so his decree immediately gave rise to tension with the Guise family. As we have seen, Mary of Guise, Antoinette de Bourbon, the Duke of Guise and the Cardinal of Lorraine were united in their desire to emphasise that Mary, Queen of Scots was already a queen regnant and they did not rest until it was agreed that although she would live with the French royal children she would be served in the main by her own people.[6] Her personal Scottish attendants would not go home to Scotland. Mary of Guise and the Scots would provide 50,000 livres a year for their upkeep. Henri generously added a further 30,000 livres.[7]

A list of Mary's ladies, maids of honour and chamberwomen survives for the period 1 January 1549 to 31 December 1553,[8] and it records the names of sixteen female attendants and fifteen indoor male servants who included two masters of the household, various valets and kitchen servants, a chaplain, a tailor, a dancing master and Claude Millot the schoolmaster. For the most part, they all stayed at St Germain, but from time to time the children moved to the other royal residences at Fontainebleau, Blois, Amboise and Paris, also paying short visits to Diane de Poitiers at Anet, or the Constable Montmorency at Chantilly, or indeed Mary's own relatives at Rheims.[9]

The little group of women who served Mary, Queen of Scots remained virtually unchanged until at least 1556 and probably until 1558 when she finally married the Dauphin. There was a minor crisis in 1553 when Henri II decided that the Dauphin should now have his own separate household. The royal family was growing rapidly and nine-year-old François had been joined in the nurseries by three small brothers, the short-lived Louis, Charles-Maximilien, later Charles IX, and Edouard-Alexandre, the future Henri III.[10] Catherine de Medici immediately insisted that her daughters should enjoy no such independence but would remain under her own supervision until they married. Elisabeth and Claude were to sleep in her *garderobe* (the chamber where her clothes were kept) or in a room as near to her as she could manage, and they would have with them only Madame de Humières and their own chamberwomen. Catherine made the excuse that, in the past, royal princesses had been given separate households only because their mothers had already died.

The Cardinal of Lorraine was alarmed. He believed that Catherine was really doing this as a means of keeping her daughters 'in fear and obedience'. He did not say so, but she may have acted as she did because she was determined that they should not fall under the influence of Diane de Poitiers. Whatever was in her mind, the Cardinal had no desire to see Mary, Queen of Scots relegated to Catherine's *garderobe* along with the princesses. Mary of Guise alone should be allowed to appoint the person in charge of her daughter and she must make this point forcefully. The young Queen herself was conscious of the need to have a retinue in keeping with her high rank, he said, and so he drew up a draft plan and sent it to

Mary of Guise. By the following spring Mary, Queen of Scots did indeed have her own household under the supervision of Henri Cleutin, Sieur d'Oisel.[11] A list of 1555–6 records the members, but as far as the women were concerned it was little different from the 1549–53 roll, with only one or two new faces.

The most important and trusted attendant was the governess. A governess in this context was not a teacher. She was, rather, the principal lady-in-waiting who supervised the care of the child in her charge, purchased her clothing, oversaw her meals and in many respects took on what we might regard as a maternal role. Moreover, 'Madame de Flamyn', Mary's first governess, was no mere employee but the little Queen's aunt. Jane Stewart, Lady Fleming was the illegitimate daughter of King James IV of Scotland and one of his mistresses, Isabel Stewart, Countess of Bothwell. Illegitimate children were acknowledged by monarchs, and Lady Fleming was a respected figure at the Scottish Court. She had probably been in her mid-teens when she married Malcolm, 3rd Lord Fleming in the spring of 1525. He was in his early thirties. They went on to have two sons and six daughters before Malcolm was killed at the Battle of Pinkie in 1547, along with two of his sons-in-law.[12]

When Lady Fleming boarded the royal galley at Dumbarton with her elder son and two of her daughters, she was a widow in her thirties, small, fair-haired and with considerable aplomb. She did not hesitate to complain to Captain Villegaignon when contrary winds delayed their departure, demanding that she be allowed to take the little Queen ashore to rest until they were able to sail, for Mary had already spent several days cooped up in her cabin. Royal aunt or not, Villegaignon brushed aside her request. He had his orders from Henri II and he was not going to let his precious piece of cargo slip ashore, perhaps never to return. Mary and Lady Fleming remained where they were and set sail soon afterwards.[13]

Waiting at Joinville for news of their arrival, Antoinette de Bourbon already had her own ideas about the person most suitable to be her granddaughter's governess. Mahanet des Essartz, Dame de Curel seemed the obvious choice. She had been in Scotland as one of Mary of Guise's ladies in the 1540s,[14] her husband, Charles de la Haye, Sieur de Curel, had also been in Mary of Guise's household, and both were absolutely loyal to her, said Antoinette. Charles was now to become one of the two masters of the household to Mary, Queen of Scots and if his wife were governess that would fit in very well. Antoinette therefore spoke to Henri II on Mahanet's behalf, only to discover that Mary of Guise had someone else in mind. She was determined that Lady Fleming should be governess. Antoinette reluctantly agreed that it was only sensible for Lady Fleming to stay, since she knew all about the little Queen's upbringing and daily routine, and when she went to the coast and finally met Lady Fleming she began to warm to the idea. The Scottish contingent were a poor-looking lot, she thought, but the governess was a notable exception. Antoinette resolved to be as welcoming as possible to her.[15] By 16 January 1549 she was able to announce that Lady Fleming had sole charge of the little Queen and all her suite, and was everything that Mary of Guise could desire.[16]

Antoinette was not the only person to be impressed. Artus de Maillé, Monsieur de Brézé, who had been sent to escort the little Queen to France, declared, with an enthusiasm which he may have come to regret, that Lady Fleming 'has pleased all this company as much as the six most virtuous women in this kingdom could have done', adding, 'For my part, I would not for the world have had her absent, having regard not only to the service of the Queen but to the reputation of the kingdom of Scotland'.[17] Mahanet was consigned to a secondary role as 'Dame d'atours', which corresponds to 'Lady of the bedchamber', the word 'atours' actually signifying women's attire, so this probably implies that she helped to look after Mary's garments. For this she was paid 300 livres a year.[18]

A vivacious extravert, Lady Fleming settled down rapidly at the French Court and when she was worried about one of her sons, who had been captured by the English, she had no hesitation in pouring out her troubles to Henri II himself.[19] Not only was Henri sympathetic. He was greatly taken with Lady Fleming and in 1550, when Catherine de Medici was recovering from the birth of her fifth child, Charles, and Diane de Poitiers was laid low with a broken leg after a riding accident, he began an affair with the governess. Royal courts being as they were, it was impossible to keep anything secret. Someone saw them and told the Duke of Guise, who immediately passed the information to Diane. Making a miraculous recovery from her accident, she set off at once for St Germain, intercepted Henri as he was about to enter Lady Fleming's apartments and poured out a volley of reproaches. He replied weakly that he was merely visiting Lady Fleming for a chat. He did not, however, give up his new mistress and by December both she and Catherine de Medici were pregnant.[20]

Henri himself would have kept his affair quiet, for he always acted with discretion in such matters, but Lady Fleming was not so diplomatic. She shocked the Court by telling everyone proudly that she was carrying the King's child, announcing her news, that inveterate gossip the Abbé Brantôme said nastily, in her uncouth Scottish-accented French. Mary of Guise was in France, of course, when all this happened. Despite her long friendship with Henri II, it seems that her sympathies lay with Catherine de Medici. No doubt she remembered all too well her own experience of James V's infidelities, and as Lady Fleming's employer it was probably she who ordered the governess back to Scotland that April, to give birth there.[21]

History does not relate how Mary, Queen of Scots felt about her aunt's abrupt departure from the scene, but the disappearance of this mother figure probably meant less because Mary of Guise was with her at the time. As for Lady Fleming herself, she gave birth triumphantly to a son whom she named Henry, and her great ambition was to return to France with the baby. However, Mary of Guise blocked all her attempts, saying she knew that Fleming's reappearance would annoy all the major figures there, especially Queen Catherine.[22] In 1560, as soon as Mary of Guise was dead, Lady Fleming tried again, and that autumn she obtained a passport from Elizabeth I allowing her to pass through England on her way to France with 'Lord Harry de Valois' and a suite of twenty-four people and their horses.[23] Mary, Queen of Scots and her husband had always been fond of Lady Fleming, and they seem to have received her kindly. Harry was made Abbot of La Chaise-Dieu and eventually succeeded Mary, Queen of Scots' uncle, François, as Grand Prior General of the Galleys. Lady Fleming died some time before 1564,[24] when Mary wrote to Harry from Scotland as her 'cousin and brother-in-law', saying she was anxious to have news of his studies.[25] He died in 1586, from a wound received in a quarrel with Philippe, Baron de Castellane.[26]

After the ignominious departure of Lady Fleming from the French Court in 1551, everyone was determined that Mary, Queen of Scots' next governess should be someone of exemplary character and Françoise d'Estamville, Dame de Parois (Parroys or Parroye) was chosen. It is difficult to pin down the exact identity of the Dame de Parois, but everything points to her being from Lorraine, and from a family closely connected with the Dukes of Lorraine. The Sieurs de Parois had their lands in Lorraine, the Dame had a son whose surname was Haraucourt and in the 1520s a Haraucourt of Ormes and Parroye was steward of Lorraine and grand baillif of Nancy, so there is obviously a close connection.[27]

Whatever her background, it is clear from the surviving correspondence that the Dame de Parois was a highly energetic and capable person, completely trusted by the Guise family. With grown-up children of her own, she was of a mature age and unlikely to catch the roving eye of Henri II. By February 1553 the Cardinal of Lorraine was telling Mary of Guise that the Dame could not be better, a sentiment echoed by Antoinette de Bourbon soon afterwards and again the following year.[28] The Cardinal added the reassurance that she was bringing up Mary in the old faith, presumably responding to some rumour of Protestantism in the royal household. Unfortunately, the relationship beween the Dame de Parois and the other attendants was none too harmonious. Madame de Curel quarrelled with her that same year and left in a huff, saying that the post of governess should have been hers,[29] and the Dame fought a long battle with another of her colleagues, the Sieur de Péguillon, continually quarrelling with him in front of Mary, Queen of Scots and Henri II's daughters, and allegedly making herself a laughing stock before the entire Court.[30]

It is true that the Dame had a healthy sense of her own importance, but most of her efforts were directed at protecting her charge's interests and her complaints seem reasonable enough. She demanded three baggage mules to transport Mary, Queen of Scots' bed, for instance, when she discovered that the furnishings were being spoiled by having to be carried in village carts,[31] and in 1553 she was lamenting that she had to arrange Mary's hair herself. 'I do it as best I can while waiting for someone better, but I can't do it as well as I would like,' she admitted.[32] Central to everything, of course, was her relationship with the little Queen herself. Mary was about eight when the Dame took over from Lady Fleming, and the impression given by the reports sent to Mary of Guise is that her daughter was a hard-working, obedient little girl, eager to please and anxious above all else to obey her far-off mother's commands. By the time she was ten she was growing very tall, studying hard and the only quarrels she and the Dame had were over her failure to stand erect. Her height probably made her stoop self-consciously when she was with the small Dauphin, but a dignified posture was vital for a monarch and so of course the Dame de Parois did her best to correct that fault. Apart from that, however, 'she has such a good nature that I believe, Madame, that she will never do anything to displease you', the Dame assured Mary of Guise.[33]

When her charge was eleven, the Dame with some difficulty hired a painter to produce a portrait showing how very tall and beautiful Mary was. Not only was her posture now dignified but she was at ease when she had to give orders, something she did only on Mary of Guise's instructions, of course, the Dame added hastily.[34] At nearly twelve, Mary was making progress in Latin and growing in understanding and judgment.[35] No doubt as the result of the constant reminders from the Cardinal of Lorraine and from the Dame, she had also become conscious of her own status. She wanted a gown of cloth-of-gold or silver for the wedding of one of her relatives, the Count of Vaudemont, because that was what the French princesses always wore to such occasions. Keeping her usual sharp eye on expenditure, the Dame insisted that Mary of Guise be consulted before such costly items were purchased.[36]

As Mary entered her teenage years, her eager obedience was replaced by something resembling adolescent rebellion, and she had a serious quarrel with the Dame about the contents of her wardrobe. The general rule was that a governess could expect to be given the surplus garments of her royal mistress, a valuable gift since they were made of expensive material and often had even more expensive trimmings, but the Dame was apparently removing clothes without Mary's knowledge. A furious quarrel erupted, with the Dame accusing Mary of being mean, unlike her generous mother. Mary forbade her to have anything more to do with her wardrobe, and they both now wrote to Mary of Guise, pouring out their complaints about each other.[37] This crisis took place in the last weeks of 1555. Perhaps the Dame was already ill, for at the beginning of April 1556 the Cardinal of Lorraine told Mary of Guise that she had been unwell for the past four months, was now in Paris and had not been in attendance on Mary, Queen of Scots for some time.

It was thought that the Dame would not live until Christmas, and the Cardinal suggested that Mary of Guise should start thinking about a replacement. It was just as well, he added, because the Dame had been making trouble for Mary, Queen of Scots by misrepresenting her not only to Antoinette de Bourbon but to Catherine de Medici herself. Mary had been so deeply upset as a result that she had made herself ill.[38] As she put it in a characteristically dramatic fashion to her mother, 'She has almost caused my death for the fear I have of being out of your favour and the regret I have to hear by these false reports so many misunderstandings and wrongs done to me'.[39] The Dame de Parois then vanishes from the correspondence and does not seem to have been replaced. After all, at nearly fourteen Mary, Queen of Scots was hardly a child any more. No doubt the other members of the retinue were relieved.

When Mahanet, Dame de Curel had departed after her fracas with the Dame in 1553, she had been succeeded as lady of the bedchamber by Guyonne du Breüil, Dame de Péguillon, who was now the most senior woman. Appointed in 1553 at an annual salary of 300 livres, she stayed with Mary for almost ten years.[40] Guyonne, daughter of Lyonnet de Breüil, Seigneur de Palua and his wife Anne de Baudreuil,[41] had in 1527 married into a family with a long history of service not only to the French Crown but to Mary of Guise. Her husband, Jean de Beaucaire, Sieur de Péguillon,[42] was almost certainly the Monsieur de Péguillon who had been Mary of Guise's trusted representative during the difficult negotiations leading up to her marriage to James V.[43] During the 1540s he was involved in the administration of her Longueville jointure lands and then in 1556 Mary of Guise made him first master of her daughter's household.[44] His brother François, Bishop of Metz, a close associate of the Cardinal of Lorraine, later acted as superintendent of the French finances of Mary, Queen of Scots and was governor of her dower lands.[45] Two of Guyonne and Jean's children found employment in Mary's household, while another relative, Bonaventure de Beaucaire, Seigneur de Boulis, was one of her four cup-bearers when she was Queen of France.[46] This sort of dynasty of attendants was characteristic of both sixteenth- and seventeenth-century Courts, with members of the same family serving over several generations.

Such was Péguillon's loyalty to Mary, Queen of Scots that when she went back to Scotland in 1561, he and Guyonne went with her, taking their son Gilbert along as one of her gentleman carvers. He was probably the Péguillon who had been page to her half-brother, the Duke of Longueville, in the 1540s and had then become one of her store-keepers.[47] Once in Scotland, however, they stayed for only a year. Jean's brother the Bishop came from France in the summer of 1562 to discuss the finances of her dower lands with Mary and when he went back they decided to travel with him. The reason is not clear, but it probably had to do with the fact that another of their sons had been captured by the English and was being held prisoner. The following spring there were unfounded rumours that he might be exchanged for Sir Henry Killigrew, an Englishman captured by the French at the siege of Rouen, and it is likely that Jean and Guyonne went back to France to negotiate their son's release.[48]

Safely back in France, the Péguillon family stayed there. Gilbert had by 1571 become one of the masters of the household to Charles IX,[49] and his parents' names were still on the roll of those servants of Mary, Queen of Scots who were receiving salaries or pensions from her jointure lands in 1567 and again in 1573.[50] Ten years after that, however, on 12 December 1583, Mary was referring to 'the late Sieur de Péguillon' and there is no further mention of Guyonne.[51] She might have been the most senior lady in the retinue, but another of the servants was even closer to Mary, Queen of Scots. This was 'Jehanne de Saint-Clere', who sounds French, but was none other than the Queen's nurse, Jean Sinclair.

Jean had originally been wet-nurse to Mary's elder brother, Prince James, and she had probably served in that capacity when Mary was a baby too. Royal ladies did not normally breast-feed their own children, and so a woman whose own infant had died or who had more milk than she needed was employed to undertake this important task. It is a tribute to Jean's reliability that Mary of Guise was willing to employ her again after the tragedy of the Prince's death, nor could it have been easy for Jean herself to go to France in 1548. However, her husband, son and daughter went too, and she must have been a profoundly comforting presence for the little Queen. Jean was paid sixty livres a year, and had the use of a horse, for of course she had to accompany Mary as she moved from one royal residence to the next.

Perhaps predictably, her relationship with the French attendants was not always easy, as an indignant letter she wrote to Mary of Guise from Blois on 12 April 1549 reveals. She had been downgraded from her proper place at mealtimes, she complained, and felt insulted. 'As Your Grace knows,' she said proudly, 'I am come of honest folks' and she was determined to uphold her position.[52] By 1555–6 she was being paid more than the maids of honour, although her name has slipped down the list of attendants and comes after theirs. Her son was now a secretary in the household, receiving 200 livres a year, but her daughter, who had featured on the first list, had gone by 1555.[53]

The most famous attendants of all were, of course, 'The Four Maries', the four small girls who had come to France with Mary in

1548 and stayed on as maids of honour. They will be discussed fully in a later chapter[54] but, for the moment, suffice it to say that when they arrived Henri II was concerned that the little Queen would never forget Scotland if she were constantly in their company. He therefore decreed that the Maries should be sent to the Priory of St Louis at Poissy to be taught under the supervision of the Dominican prioress, Françoise de Vieuxpont. Sometimes this has been seen as a cruel separation, but in fact Poissy was only a few kilometres from St Germain and the convent had enjoyed important royal connections since the fourteenth century when Charles VI's aunt, Marie de Bourbon, was prioress. Members of the royal circle were educated there and the famous writer Christine de Pizan had spent eleven years in the priory.[55] Lessons at Poissy were therefore a privilege, not a penance. We do not know how long the Maries stayed at Poissy,[56] but throughout their childhood they continue to feature on the household lists of Mary, Queen of Scots as maids of honour, and there was no question of trying to separate them permanently from her.[57]

The Four Maries have undoubtedly overshadowed the other female attendants of Mary, Queen of Scots in the public mind, but there were in fact four other maids of honour during her childhood years, two of them Scottish, two of them French.[58] One of the Scots was a daughter of the Duke of Châtelherault, probably Lady Barbara Hamilton, and the other was Anne (Agnes) Fleming, another of Lady Fleming's children. Barbara Hamilton married Anne's eldest brother James, 4th Lord Fleming in the winter of 1553–4, only to be widowed in 1558. Left with a small daughter, she does not seem to have married again.[59] Agnes became the wife of William, 6th Lord Livingston, brother of one of the Four Maries, also in about 1553, and returned to Scotland where she and her husband would be among the staunchest supporters of Mary, Queen of Scots despite their conversion to Protestantism.[60]

The two French maids of honour were Guyonne, Dame de Péguillon's daughter Marie and Mademoiselle Sunboire. Guyonne's daughter may have replaced Barbara Hamilton, and was given an annual salary of fifty livres, rising to 100 livres by 1555–6.[61]

She retained her position until Mary left for Scotland in 1561. Although reputed to be one of Mary's favourite servants,[62] she had to stay behind because she had recently married Sebastian de Luxembourg, 4th Viscount of Martigues, known to his contemporaries as 'The Fearless Knight'.[63] This handsome man had seen service in Scotland, having been with the French at the siege of Leith, and he was one of the first courtiers Mary, Queen of Scots admitted to her presence after the death of François II.[64] Marie and Sebastian's only surviving child, another Marie, born in the spring of 1562, was a god-daughter of Mary, Queen of Scots.[65] Shortly before the birth of her son in 1566, fearing she might die, Mary drew up an intended list of bequests of jewellery. Madame de Martigues was to have had seven items, including a pendant jewel set with a great emerald, a ruby and pearl collar, a coral belt, and a fur with enamelled crystal head and paws garnished with turquoises, while little Marie was to receive a pearl necklace and other pearl and ruby items.[66]

The final maid of honour, 'Mademoiselle Sunboire', was actually Marie de Gaignon, de Saint-Bohaire. Sixteenth-century spelling is often phonetic. She joined Mary's retinue on 1 April 1555. The daughter of Jean de Gaignon, Seigneur de Saint-Bohaire and Marguerite Chasteigner, she was much praised for her beauty and on 25 June 1559 she was married in the Castle of Blois to an important man, Claude Gouffier, Duke of Rouannais and Marquis of Boisy. His wealth and eminence made him a desirable bridegroom, but he must have been considerably older than Marie, for he had married his first wife as long ago as 1526 and was a widower twice over, with a daughter and three sons. Marie was still a member of the household of Mary, Queen of Scots in 1560, but she stayed behind with her husband when the Queen left for Scotland. No doubt she was pregnant, for she and the Duke had six sons in less than six years, and she died, probably in childbirth, on 15 March 1565. Two years later, her husband married his fourth wife, Claude de Beaune, one of the ladies-in-waiting of Catherine de Medici and the widow of the royal doctor Louis Burgensis. When she too died, he took a fifth and final wife, who managed to outlive him.[67]

These maids of honour were all young girls in their teens when they served Mary, Queen of Scots, and in 1554 the Cardinal of Lorraine decided that they ought to be supervised by their own governess. This position was given to a widow named Claude de Pons, Demoiselle du Mesnil. She evidently had an existing connection with the Guise family, for in the 1540s Mary of Guise had promised to give one of her children a position in the Duke of Longueville's household.[68] Whether this ever happened does not emerge from the correspondence, but in 1554 Claude was expressing very humble thanks to Mary of Guise for being appointed governess to the maids. She felt unequal to the task, she said, but she promised to do her best and she must have proved satisfactory, for she was still in her position in 1560.[69]

The remaining female attendants in Mary's early retinue were the more lowly chamberwomen. Three of them, Rallay, Agathe Burgensis and Barde Courdion, were French. Nothing is known about Barde, other than the fact that she was paid forty livres a year, but Agathe, who was still in her post in 1555–6,[70] could have been a relative of Simon and Louis Burgensis, royal doctors, or of Jacqueline Burgensis, who was chamberwoman in the household of Henri II's children.[71] Rallay earned fifty livres a year, and in May 1557 Mary, Queen of Scots was writing to urge Mary of Guise to allow her twice that amount, for she is 'a very wise and honest maid and as good a servant as it is possible to wish for'.[72] She was to be with Mary for many years. The one Scottish chamberwoman, Mary Jane Seton, must surely have been a relative of Lord Seton, but where she fits into his family is not known.[73]

The household lists are, of course, incomplete, for they are not consecutive, recording as they do the staff from 1549 to 1553 and then in the year 1555–6. Occasionally, some other source gives a fleeting glimpse of those members of the royal children's household who also served Mary, Queen of Scots. Two were Italian: Peronnelle de Gondy, daughter of Catherine de Medici's friend the Dame du Perron, and Livia Pica, known as 'La Contine', daughter of the Count della Mirandola. Livia and her sisters Silvia and Fulvia had been brought to France in 1548 to serve the royal children at

St Germain. Mary must have been fond of her, for among her 1566 bequests of jewellery was a diamond in a red and white enamelled setting, 'To La Contine, for remembrance'.[74] There is also mention of Françoise de Maricourt, daughter of Jean, Seigneur de Maricourt, who served Mary until she left to marry[75] and so did Antoinette de la Tour-Landry, Dame de St Mars.[76] Finally, there was Jeanne de Biencourt, Demoiselle de Poutrincourt, daughter of one of Catherine de Medici's masters of the household, Florimond de Biencourt, Sieur de Poutrincourt, who had seen service in the army of Mary's grandfather, Claude, Duke of Guise. He went on to become master of the household to François II, and so it may have been at this later date that his daughter took up her position in Mary's household. Her name does not, however, appear on any of the official lists.[77]

Our knowledge of Mary's early attendants is all too often tantalisingly brief but even when we know little of their personalities, circumstances or even appearance, we can draw certain conclusions from the short lists and the laconic genealogical details. The Queen's first retinue, small in number because it was not an independent household at all, featured sixteen women but certainly two and perhaps even four were successors to people already there and so at any one time Mary would have had no more than from twelve to fourteen female attendants. Significantly, in spite of Henri II's strictures, ten of her sixteen women were Scottish and although (apart from Lady Fleming) the important posts of governess and lady of the bedchamber were occupied by Frenchwomen or natives of Lorraine, it is clear that these ladies owed their first loyalty to the Guise family rather than to the French King.

The inference we can draw from all this is that despite Henri II's desire to send the Scots home, Mary of Guise had her way in making sure that her daughter had the comforting presence of her nurse and her aunt/governess, not to mention the continuing companionship of her small Scottish maids of honour. This nucleus of Scottish attendants helped to ensure that Mary, Queen of Scots grew up confident in her Scottish identity. French had become her first language for reading and writing, but she never stopped speaking Scots, the language of Jean Sinclair, Lady Fleming and the Four Maries and, although she always preferred to write in French, throughout her life she emphasised the fact that she was Scottish.

Notes

1. *Treasurer Accounts*, vii, 312, 319–20, 325, 333, 396, 403–4
2. NAS, Exchequer Records, E34/23
3. Guiffrey, *Dianne de Poytiers: Lettres*, 33–4 n.1
4. Frieda, *Catherine de Medici*, 61
5. Guiffrey, *Dianne de Poytiers: Lettres*, 33–4 n.1
6. Ruble, *Première jeunesse*, 85
7. Stoddart, *Girlhood*, 20; Guiffrey, *Dianne de Poytiers, Lettres*, 35 and 35n., 46n.
8. BN, Paris, f. fr.11207 f.12, printed in Ruble, *Première jeunesse*, 282
9. Itinerary of the royal children printed in Ruble, *Première jeunesse*, 253–62
10. Frieda, *Catherine de Medici*, 61
11. *Foreign Correspondence*, 1548–57, 140–2; Stoddart, *Girlhood*, 109
12 *Scots Peerage*, viii, 541
13. *CSP Scot.*, i, 157
14. Ruble, *Première jeunesse*, 90; Teulet, *Papiers d'Etat*, 121; NLS, Adv. MS., 29.2.5 f. 31
15. *Foreign Correspondence*, 1548–57, 7–9
16. *Ibid.*, 25–6
17. Stoddart, *Girlhood*, 15, 22–3
18. Ruble, *Première jeunesse*, 282
19. Francisque-Michel, *Les Français en Ecosse*, i, 506
20. Ruble, *Première jeunesse*, 85–6; Baumgartner, *Henry II*, 96; Frieda, *Catherine de Medici*, 97–8
21. *Lettres de Catherine de Médicis*, pp. xlviii, xlix, 39 and 39n.; Ruble, *Première jeunesse*, 86; *Foreign Correspondence*, 1548–57,102n.; Castelot, *Diane, Henri, Catherine*, 227–30; Francisque-Michel, *Les Français en Ecosse*, 2 and 2n.
22. *CSP Spanish*, x, 588
23. *CSP Scot.*, i, 459, 468, 474, 481, 486
24. *Scots Peerage*, viii, 540. There seem to be no details of her date or place of death

25. NLS, Adv. MS., 54.1.4
26. Brantôme, *Lives of Gallant Ladies*, 528, n.774
27. Anselme, *Histoire Généalogique*, ii, 62
28. *Lettres*, ed. Labanoff, i, 16; *Foreign Correspondence, 1548–57*, 146, 183, 210
29. *Ibid.*, 198–9
30. *Ibid.*, 272
31. *Ibid.*, 223, 252
32. *Ibid.*, 199
33. *Ibid.*, 198
34. *Ibid.*, 236–7
35. *Ibid.*, 252–4
36. *Ibid.*
37. *Lettres*, ed. Labanoff, i, 29–31
38. *Foreign Correspondence, 1548–57*, 278
39. *Lettres*, ed. Labanoff, i, 41–2. Labanoff attributes this undated letter to May 1557 but it more probably belongs to the spring of 1556.
40. Ruble, *Première jeunesse*, 282
41. Généalogie Famille de Carné, www.http://a.decarne.free.fr/-gencar/dat32, accessed 17 May 2004
42. Anselme, *Histoire Généalogique*, vii, 714; *Foreign Correspondence, 1548–57*, 327 erroneously gives the name of Guyonne's husband as Gilbert, who was her son.
43. Summarised in *Foreign Correspondence, 1537–48*, 217; *LPFD Henry VIII (1548)*, 540, 544
44. *Foreign Correspondence, 1537–48*, p. xxxii; NAS, Exchequer Records, E34/27
45. *Dictionnaire de Biographie Française*, 1047–9; *Lettres*, ed. Labanoff, i, 148–9; iii, 177–8; Lang, 'Household, 1573', 350; *Lettres du Cardinal de Lorraine*, 168
46. Aubespine, *Négociations*, 746
47. *Foreign Correspondence, 1537–48*, 83
48. *CSP Scot.*, i, 688; Luke MacMahon, 'Killigrew, Sir Henry (1525x8–1603)', *Oxford Dictionary of National Biography*, Oxford University Press, 2004: [http://www.oxforddnb.com/view/article/15533, accessed 27 December 2004]
49. *Lettres du Cardinal de Lorraine*, 627
50. Teulet, *Papiers d'Etat*, ii, 121–2; Lang, 'Household, 1573', 349–50
51. *Lettres*, ed. Labanoff, v, 388
52. *Foreign Correspondence 1548–57*, 312. Wood assigns this letter to 1552

or 1553, but considering the content and Jean's declaration that she had worked for Mary of Guise for the last ten years, 1549 would appear to be a more appropriate date.

53. *Lettres*, ed. Labanoff, i, 26; NAS, Exchequer Records, E34/27; *Foreign Correspondence 1548–57*, p. lv

54 See Chapter 9

55. Bell, *The Lost Tapestries*, 136–7

56. *Foreign Correspondence 1548–57*, 225

57. Ruble, *Première jeunesse*, 282; NAS, Exchequer Records, E34/27

58. *Ibid.*, 282

59. Ruble, *Première jeunesse*, 282; NAS, Exchequer Records, E34/27; *Scots Peerage*, vi, 370; viii, 542. According to the *Scots Peerage* vi, 370, one or two sources say that Barbara actually married Gordon before being widowed soon afterwards, and this may be so.

60. *Scots Peerage*, viii, 541

61. Ruble, *Première jeunesse*, 282; NAS, Exchequer Records, E34/27

62. Brantôme, *Dames illustres*, v, p. xxxvi n.2

63. Poull, *La Maison ducale de Lorraine*, 481–3

64. Broglie, *Les Clouet de Chantilly*, no. 187; Brantôme, *Hommes illustres*, iv, 243–7; Ruble, *Première jeunesse*, 208

65. Ruble, *Première jeunesse*, 282; *Inventaires*, p. xxxvii n.2 and n.3; *CSP Scot.*, i, 621, 635

66. *Inventaires*, 93–9, 100–3

67. Anselme, *Histoire Généalogique*, v, 609–10

68. *Foreign Correspondence 1548–57*, 86

69. *Ibid.*, 263

70. NAS, Exchequer Records, E34/27

71. Ruble, *Première jeunesse*, 275

72. *Lettres*, ed. Labanoff, i, 44

73. Ruble, *Première jeunesse*, 282

74. *Foreign Correspondence 1548–57*, 200; *Lettres de Catherine de Médicis*, x, 97, 507, 513; *Inventaires*, p. lvii n.112

75. *Foreign Correspondence 1548–57*, 200; Anselme, *Histoire Généalogique*, iv, 663; *Lettres de Catherine de Médicis*, 515

76. *Foreign Correspondence 1548–57*, 199; Anselme, *Histoire Généalogique*, v, 610

77. *Lettres du Cardinal de Lorraine*, 112n.; *Lettres de Catherine de Médicis*, x, 97

4

The Queen of France's Ladies (1)

During her childhood, Mary, Queen of Scots had been served by her own nucleus of women attendants within the larger context of the French royal household. When Henri II died and Mary's husband succeeded to the throne of France, however, her position changed dramatically. It was true that she had always been Queen of Scots, but now, as the sixteen-year-old consort of the French King, she had to be surrounded by a large and formal gathering of the most important women in the country, and a list of her attendants in 1560 shows this greatly augmented retinue. In all, Mary had 290 servants, forty-four of whom were women.[1]

Courts were very masculine places. The monarch was surrounded by the great officers of state, his military commanders, and the constantly changing hordes of petitioners who came to seek his favour. The wives of all these men usually stayed at home, bringing up the children and looking after the estates. There are varying theories as to which queens first created their own retinues of female attendants. In England, Edward III (1312–77) is credited with encouraging his wife, Philippa of Hainault, to have a large household of more than thirty ladies of honour as a civilising influence on his Court.[2] In France, it is often said that Anne of Brittany (1476–1514), who was successively wife of Charles VIII and Louis XII, was responsible for gathering around her a formal household of twelve ladies-in-waiting and about forty maids of honour.[3] Some believe that Louise of Savoy, who was never queen but the mother of François I, created the earliest proper female household.[4] His first wife, Queen Claude, in 1523 had no fewer than fourteen ladies in her household while his second, Eleanor of Austria, had five ladies and thirty-eight maids in 1538.[5]

Because of deficiencies in the early records it is difficult to find early Scottish evidence. We know that when Margaret Tudor came north to marry James IV in 1503 and they met for the first time, he greeted her and then politely kissed 'all her ladies'.[6] Mary of Guise's predecessor, Princess Madeleine of France, arrived in Scotland accompanied by her governess, Madame de Montreuil, along with eight other ladies,[7] while Mary of Guise herself in 1543 had thirty-six women in her household of 137 servants. One of her other lists, an undated 'Roll and number of persons being in the service of the Queen', which can also be attributed to the 1540s, begins with six ladies-in-waiting, nineteen maids of honour, twelve chamberwomen and one washerwoman, some of whom were French and some Scottish.[8] In England, Mary I after her accession was attended by seven ladies[9] while her sister Elizabeth I employed seven married ladies-in-waiting, six maids of honour and four women of lesser rank, probably chamberwomen.[10]

The duties of those women ranged from the ceremonial to the very personal. They appeared in processions at great state occasions, sumptuously arrayed in finery sometimes provided by the monarch, their very presence emphasising their mistress's prestige and power. They sat grouped around her, served her at banquets and went with her to Mass. At Court festivities, arrayed in specially created silk garments sewn with paste jewellery, they performed with her in masques, speaking the words composed by Court poets and engaging in stately dance. With its lavish resources, the Court of Henri II had a high and even rarefied level of culture in which aristocratic women fully participated, the ballets in which they performed echoing, it was felt, the structure of the universe and the harmony of the spheres.[11]

Behind the scenes, the ladies looked after all the Queen's clothes and her jewellery, her books, her personal dishes and her dressing plate. They helped to nurse her when she fell ill, they accompanied her when she went out riding, and if she wished to stay quietly indoors they would keep her company, reading, sewing or listening to music together, discussing poetry and sitting for their portraits to artists like François Clouet, whose delicate, sensitive drawings preserve their likenesses for us. Mary, Queen of Scots retained her literary and other interests for the rest of her life. She wrote poetry and during her captivity she managed to assemble a surprisingly large library of books. As late as 1582, slightly more than four years before her death, she was enquiring about Camille Morel, the female French poet and scholar. 'I have a good opinion of her,' she said.[17]

Kings and queens were scarcely ever alone, and for homesick foreign female consorts learning to settle in an unfamiliar world, the companionship of other women meant a great deal, particularly if they were allowed to have attendants of their own nationality. Queens in their own right were in a rather different situation, of course, because they had to do a great deal of business with the men of the Court, but even so they were always surrounded by their little flock of ladies, with whom they developed a close relationship. Elizabeth I of England was notoriously capricious and demanding with her female staff, who had to put up with being pinched, slapped, shouted at, publicly humiliated and embarrassed by her.[13] Mary of Guise, Catherine de Medici and indeed Mary, Queen of Scots on the other hand regarded it as their duty to take a kindly interest in the women who served them.

The ladies-in-waiting were members of the high aristocracy, usually married, and in addition to an annual salary they had access to the Queen and were frequently approached by those wishing to gain her favour. They were therefore seen as having considerable influence, and their appointment brought added distinction to their family. Like all other wives in an age when reliable methods of birth control were unknown, they were often pregnant, and they spent varying amounts of time on their own estates. Some turned out only for important state occasions, but others were favourites and were usually summoned back pretty swiftly. The maids of honour, often the daughters of ladies-in-waiting, were generally still in their teens when they entered royal service and as well as their salary, which was smaller than that of the ladies-in-waiting, they received a courtly education. Moreover, the Queen was expected to arrange suitable marriages for them. Chamberwomen came from further down the social hierarchy, as did nurses and washerwomen.

As we have seen, in her childhood Mary, Queen of Scots had a governess and one lady of the bedchamber, but as Queen of France she was attended by no fewer than twenty-seven ladies-in-waiting, along with the slightly increased number of ten maids of honour still in the charge of their governess Claude de Pons, Demoiselle du Mesnil, one wardrobe woman, three washerwomen and two women who served the maids of honour. By way of comparison, in 1555, when Henri II was still alive, Catherine de Medici had eight ladies at 800 livres a year and thirty-one 'other ladies', along with fifteen maids of honour and fourteen chamberwomen.[14]

Although she could not match the numbers surrounding her mother-in-law, Mary, Queen of Scots was accompanied in public by a full and impressive panoply of female attendants, many of whom had previous experience in other royal households. Indeed, a significant number had transferred from Catherine de Medici's retinue on the death of Henri II, for it was their right to serve the reigning queen. Of the first ten ladies on Catherine's previous list, only Diane de Poitiers did not move to Mary's household and Catherine's was now reduced to five ladies at 800 livres, eighteen 'other ladies', sixteen maids of honour and seven chamberwomen. Mary's time as Queen Consort of France was indisputably brief – a mere sixteen months, over by her eighteenth birthday – and with the death of François II most of her ladies reverted to the house-hold of Catherine de Medici who, as Queen Regent, was once more the first lady in the realm. Only two of Mary's twenty-seven ladies-in-waiting would accompany her to Scotland, but it is instructive to identify the women who served her in 1560, for such details of them as are known can give us a real insight into the milieu in which she lived.

There have been those historians over the centuries who have characterised Mary, Queen of Scots as a frivolous, empty-headed young woman surrounded by a cluster of idle, flirtatious attendants and so it is interesting to find that her French ladies-in-waiting included a number of experienced, middle-aged and indeed elderly women, many of whom had already served not only Catherine de Medici but her predecessor Eleanor of Austria. Deferential they no doubt were, but they were also strong personalities, well used to running their own households and looking after their husbands' estates when the occasion required. Quite often, they brought younger members of their family into the household with them and these little clusters of relatives were often linked to each other by marriage.

It is not surprising to find four of Mary, Queen of Scots' close relatives in her household and this is a sign that, within the conventions of Court etiquette, she was able to choose those she wanted to be with her. Proudly heading the list were her sixty-six-year-old grandmother, Antoinette de Bourbon, Duchess of Guise, and three of Mary's aunts by marriage. The first was the tall, stately Anne d'Este. Like Catherine de Medici, Anne was half Italian and half French. Her grandmother had been none other than the notorious Lucretia Borgia and her father was Ercole, Duke of Ferrara, while her mother, Renée de France, was a daughter of Louis XII.[15] Anne was the second of their two daughters and four sons, but in spite of this sizeable family her parents did not enjoy a happy relationship, for Renée had Protestant sympathies while her disapproving husband was a very orthodox Roman Catholic. Eventually he took the children away from her, but commentators believed that, when she was young, Anne secretly supported her mother's religious views.[16]

Renée, although unprepossessing in appearance, was highly intelligent and learned, and the Court of Ferrara had the reputation of being the most intellectual in Europe. Anne's studies were said to have been supervised by the Baronne de Soubise, the most accomplished female scholar of her time,[17] and as well as being well educated she grew to be extremely attractive. Sigismund, King of Poland was among those who wanted to marry her.[18] However, by the time that she was seventeen, Charles, Cardinal of Lorraine was busily negotiating her marriage to his own elder brother François, Duke of Aumale, later 2nd Duke of Guise. The Cardinal's diligent efforts were not, of course, inspired by Anne's beauty. A marriage to the granddaughter of Louis XII would bring the house of Guise even closer to the French royal family.[19]

Anne was married by proxy in Ferrara Cathedral on 29 September 1548 and then escorted by her uncle, Cardinal Ippolito d'Este, to Grenoble, where she was met by her future father-in-law, Claude, Duke of Guise. Antoinette de Bourbon was waiting in Lyons, where the bride was welcomed with ballets and other celebratory entertainments to emphasise the significance of the match. Afterwards, Anne, her uncle and her parents-in-law set off together for St Germain-en-Laye. François, Anne's fiancé, was with the army, but he would join them there, and while Anne was still on her way he sent her gifts of jewellery and embroideries.[20] Despite this polite gesture, he did not at this point show much interest in his bride and indeed had told his sister Mary of Guise that although some people settle down at home when they marry, he had no intention of doing so. He presumably meant that his military career came first. However, he arrived at Court in good spirits and was as impressed as the rest of his family were by the beauty and imposing stature of his bride. She was not yet eighteen, 'and is as tall as you', he told Mary of Guise,[21] while the Duke of Longueville informed his mother enthusiastically that Anne was 'one of the most beautiful and honest princesses one could hope to see'.[22]

Anne's wedding was celebrated at St Germain on 16 December 1548[23] and, at the celebrations afterwards, Mary, Queen of Scots danced with the Dauphin, delighting all who saw them.[24] In the years that followed, Mary came to know her aunt well. Anne was appointed as one of Catherine de Medici's ladies and so she had to be in attendance at Court whenever possible and she had the opportunity of seeing her niece both privately and at important ceremonial events such as the Queen's coronation in the summer of 1549. When not required, she retired to her family's country residences and often stayed with her mother-in-law at Joinville.[25]

Her husband, as well as being an acclaimed military hero, was tall and handsome, and Anne was soon deeply in love with him. During his lengthy absences with the army she was tortured with anxiety about him. His brother, the Cardinal of Lorraine, was understanding and sympathetic. He and Anne had been firm friends ever since he had negotiated her marriage and he did his best to reassure her, passing on messages from her husband and entertaining her at his own houses, notably at Meudon, which he was beautifying with statues he had brought back from Italy. He took a fatherly interest in her growing family,[26] six sons and a daughter named Catherine Marie, after her god-parents, Catherine de Medici and Mary of Guise.[27] Anne corresponded regularly with her sister-in-law Mary of Guise, and joined in the chorus of reassuring praise about Mary, Queen of Scots, declaring in 1552 that the nine-year-old was the prettiest little Queen in the world and could no longer be regarded as a child, for her conversation and ways were so grown-up.[28]

It must have been about the time when Anne joined Mary's household that the Abbé Brantôme, a connoisseur of female beauty, saw the two dance together at some Court function. He was a great admirer of Anne, whom he described as 'the loveliest woman in Christendom'. She was 'the gentlest, the best, the most unassuming and friendly princess that one could have seen'. Because of her great height and her gravity, people were hesitant to approach her, he said, but when they did speak to her they found only gentleness, candour and friendliness. On the occasion when she and Mary danced together, no one could say who was the more beautiful, but he thought Anne more majestic even though she was not a queen like Mary.[29]

On a less happy note, Anne was in attendance on Mary when the Court went to stay in the medieval castle of Amboise, at the beginning of Lent in 1560. Led by Louis, Prince of Condé, a group of Protestants planned to attack the castle, seize François II and free him from the influence of the Guises. The conspiracy failed because the fortress was too well defended, and afterwards Catherine de Medici, allegedly at the instigation of the Cardinal of Lorraine, ordered the chief rebels to be tortured and then hanged in front of the castle windows, so that the entire Court could observe their fate. Her biographers have often wondered whether

Mary, Queen of Scots witnessed this dreadful spectacle. There is no evidence to prove whether she did or not, but Anne d'Este certainly saw and wept and urged mercy. It was reported that she was upset because she feared that the Protestants would take their revenge on her innocent young sons,[30] but it is not impossible that, apart from her innate sensitivity, the memory of her mother's protection of Protestants was also in her mind.

When Mary, Queen of Scots left for Scotland in 1561, Anne was among those who accompanied her to the coast and an inventory of Mary's jewels, made just before she left, lists a fine collar set with seven cabochon rubies, four emeralds and four clusters of little diamonds and rubies which she gave her aunt as a parting gift at Calais.[31] Anne then returned to her family. Two years later, her worst fears were realised when her husband was shot in the back at the siege of Orléans. The wound was not at first thought to be serious, but six days later he realised that he was dying. He asked Anne to forgive him for the pain his absences had caused her and, when she wept and vowed vengeance on his enemies, he replied, 'Dear wife, do not use words which offend God'. However, after his death on 24 February she did not rest until his murderer was found and punished by being torn apart by four horses, apparently at her insistence.[32]

Anne and Mary corresponded regularly, and shortly before the birth of James VI in 1566, Mary wrote to her aunt confiding that she had recently been transformed from the most contented person possible into one who was battered by continual troubles. She did not enter into details, because the secretary of her ambassador to France would explain everything, but she was obviously thinking of the recent murder of her secretary David Riccio and her unhappy marital relationship with Lord Darnley. She also mentioned Anne's annoyance at something she had said in previous letters. Mary was by nature forthright and no doubt she had made a critical comment about Anne's second marriage, to Jacques de Savoie, Duke of Nemours.

Not only were Anne's Guise relatives unpleasantly surprised that she should contemplate taking a second husband, but the handsome Nemours had in 1556 been involved in an unsavoury scandal which the Cardinal of Lorraine described in a letter to his brother the Duke of Guise on 10 January 1557. Hearing that Françoise de Rohan, one of her maids of honour, had been having an affair with the Duke of Nemours, Catherine de Medici set off late at night for the young woman's chamber, taking Diane de Poitiers and Constable Montmorency's wife with her. Finding Françoise lying in bed, they whipped off the bedclothes and their worst suspicions were confirmed. The maid was heavily pregnant. She had been able to conceal her condition beneath her voluminous, hooped dresses, but now she confessed that the baby was due in about seven weeks' time.

Catherine flew into a dreadful rage, declaring that were it not for the scandal and the bad effect on the reputation of the other maids, she would have her imprisoned. As it was, she would send her away to stay with the Queen of Navarre. Distraught, Françoise protested that she was officially betrothed to the Duke, producing fifteen or sixteen letters from him. Two of them expressed his desire to marry her, but there was no real proof. When taxed with the matter, the Duke of Nemours denied everything, but the Cardinal of Lorraine spoke to him in person and formed the impression that he was lying. 'You can place no great reliance on the words of whores and lechers,' he concluded contemptuously.[33]

When the Cardinal realised that Anne d'Este was intending to marry Nemours, he was affronted and told her so. However, the Duke finally won over the Guises by making generous financial provision for Anne and her children,[34] and during her English imprisonment Mary, Queen of Scots wrote to Anne and her husband whenever she could.[35] The couple had two children in addition to Anne's existing family, and in 1582 when the Abbé Brantôme saw her at a society wedding, wearing an Italian-style cloak, he thought that there was still no lady who could outdo her.[36] Her final years were marred, however, by great personal sorrow. She was widowed for a second time and in December 1588 two of her Guise sons were murdered during the religious troubles. She outlived Mary, Queen of Scots by twenty years, dying in

Paris on 17 May 1607 at the age of seventy-six. She was buried with her second husband in the Church of Notre Dame d'Annency.[37]

Separated in age by only twelve years, Mary and Anne had been the best of friends. The other aunts by marriage to become members of Mary's household were Louise de Brézé and Louise de Rieux. Louise de Brézé's initial claim to fame was that she was a daughter of Diane de Poitiers. In 1545, at a time when the Guise family were anxious to cultivate Diane, Antoinette de Bourbon had arranged her marriage with her fifth child Claude, later Duke of Aumale. The match was a great success. Claude and Louise had eleven children, his mother-in-law was delighted to find that he was a loving and attentive husband, and when he was captured at the siege of Metz in 1552, his enormous ransom was paid by the combined efforts of Antoinette, Diane and the Cardinal of Lorraine.[38] Louise had served both François I's queen, Eleanor of Austria and Catherine de Medici and so she was an experienced attendant.[39] Her husband was killed at the siege of La Rochelle in 1573 and Louise died in 1577, the Cardinal of Lorraine telling Anne d'Este that she had made a very Christian death, 'showing herself extremely obliged to her late husband, whose wishes she followed in all things'.[40]

The third aunt, Louise de Rieux, was the daughter of Claude, Sieur de Rieux, Count of Harcourt and his second wife Suzanne de Bourbon-Montpensier. Born in 1531, Louise was twenty-four when she married the nineteen-year-old René, Marquis of Elboeuf, youngest surviving son of Antoinette de Bourbon. She was twenty-nine when she joined Mary's household, and the mother of two young children. Her little daughter Marie de Lorraine was one of Mary's god-daughters, and she also had a four-year-old son, Charles, no doubt called after the Cardinal of Lorraine. Mary, Queen of Scots would remember the little girl in the bequests she drew up in 1566, leaving her a pendant with a great ruby, another with a sapphire, a large collar of sapphires and pearls, a set of ruby jewellery and two rosaries. Louise outlived her husband by four years, dying in 1570.[41]

When these four Guise ladies accompanied Mary, Queen of Scots on state occasions, splendidly attired, they must have provided a vivid visual reminder of the family's power and influence while in private forming a little group of trusted companions with whom Mary could laugh and gossip. There were very few people with whom a queen could have a truly equal relationship, and so these relatives must have been of very special value to her. As for her other ladies, there were three more who, like Antoinette de Bourbon, could be described as mature matriarchs, brought young relatives with them and had links with competing factions at Court. They were Guillemette de Sarrebruche, Countess of Brenne, in her sixties at least and in charge of all the other ladies, Madeleine de Savoie, wife of the Guise brothers' great rival, the Constable Montmorency, and Jacqueline de Longwy, close to the French royal family but dying of tuberculosis.

Guillemette was a friend of Catherine de Medici and also managed to enjoy a cordial relationship with Diane de Poitiers, but it was her connection with Antoinette de Bourbon which had brought her the prominent position in Mary's retinue. Her relationship with Antoinette was fairly distant, for they were only third cousins, but there may have been other family connections through marriage. In sixteenth-century France, as in sixteenth-century Scotland, kinship mattered a great deal and quite remote relationships were remembered and respected. Antoinette certainly described Guillemette as her relative and good friend. She had referred to her in this way in 1555 when she recommended her to Mary of Guise. This was at the time when the Dame de Parois was troublesome and ailing. Antoinette said that the governess should be replaced by Madame de Brenne, who was not only wise and prudent but very wealthy. Indeed, she had let it be known that, were it not to oblige the Guises, she would never consider taking such a post.

Nothing was done about this idea, but it came up again in the spring of 1557 when the Cardinal of Lorraine told Mary of Guise that Henri II and Catherine de Medici wanted the Countess to be Mary, Queen of Scots' principal lady. No doubt prompted by her uncle, the young Queen herself wrote to her mother in support of this request. The Countess was entirely suitable, she said, and Mademoiselle de Bouillon, her granddaughter, would come too and could carry Mary's train when Madame de Brenne was absent. Moreover, an unidentified niece could sleep in the Queen's chamber when the Countess herself was unable to do so.[42] Mary of Guise apparently rejected this scheme, for she seems to have wanted a Scotswoman to be appointed to the position. However, by 1560, Guillemette was installed as 'lady of honour' and was paid 12,000 livres a year, more than any of the other attendants.[43] A portrait drawing shows her in widow's garments, a lady with a large, long nose, a full mouth and a gentle, rather kindly expression.[44] The daughter of Robert de Sarrebruche, Count of Roucy and Brenne and his wife Marie d'Amboise, she was called after her paternal grandmother, Guillemette de Luxembourg. The lands of Sarrebruche (Saarbrücken) lay immediately to the east of Lorraine and Guillemette was a great heiress, inheriting the title of Countess of Brenne when her father died in 1504.

Six years later she married Robert de la Marck, Duke of Bouillon and Marshal of France. Wounded in battle in 1513, he was imprisoned in Flanders, where he spent his time writing a history of what he termed the memorable events since 1503. After his release, he was awarded the Order of St Michael, but he died young, leaving Guillemette with one son, also called Robert, who became the next Duke of Bouillon.[45] Guillemette's friendship with Diane de Poitiers probably came about when Robert married Diane's elder daughter, Françoise, and we have a glimpse of the amicable relationship of the two mothers in a surviving letter of 1554. Writing shortly after the execution in England of the Protestant Lady Jane Grey, Diane addressed Guillemette as 'Madame my good friend', and told her that she had just had news of 'the poor young Queen Jane'. She could not but weep, she said, at the death of this 'so gentle and accomplished princess'.[46]

Accompanying Guillemette in Mary's household were her daughter-in-law Françoise and her granddaughter, Antoinette de la Marck. Robert and Françoise had married before the entire Court, in the chapel of the Louvre, more than twenty years earlier, on 19

January 1538. They eventually had three sons and six daughters and when Robert was captured at the siege of Hesdin in 1553 he was released only after his wife travelled to Brussels to negotiate his ransom.[47] Sadly, he was seriously ill by then and he died several days after his return to France. Françoise had originally been in the household of Eleanor of Austria, occupied a prominent place at the coronation of Catherine de Medici and then was for many years superintendent of her household.[48] A drawing of her by Clouet probably dating from about 1543–50 shows a calm lady with a firm expression and a strong resemblance to her mother, Diane de Poitiers, around the nose and mouth.[49] Françoise no doubt ruled the various attendants to some effect. Clément Marot, having praised her feminine gentleness in one of his short poems, pointed out that 'always with the rose grows the thorn'.[50]

Antoinette, her eldest daughter, the same age as Mary, Queen of Scots,[51] was the 'Mademoiselle de Bouillon' who could have helped by carrying her train in 1557. That same year, Mary had wanted to arrange a marriage between Antoinette and the Duke of Châtelherault's son and heir, James, Earl of Arran, for that would have ensured that she would remain close to Mary, to whom she was devoted. She would marry anyone, she had said, as long as she could stay with the young Queen. Mary described her as a very wise and virtuous maid, and said that the Cardinal of Lorraine was very fond of her too.[52] Nothing came of the match, for Arran was increasingly under suspicion because of his support for Protestantism, and in any case Diane de Poitiers had other ideas for her granddaughter.

Diane was at this time anxious for a rapprochement with her old enemy, Constable Montmorency, and on 22 December 1558 a marriage contract was signed between Antoinette and the Constable's second son, Henri, Seigneur de Damville. The wedding took place at Chantilly on 20 January 1559.[53] Damville was one of those who accompanied Mary, Queen of Scots when she sailed back to Scotland in August 1561, staying there for a few weeks until 8 October.[54] Meanwhile, Guillemette, Françoise and Antoinette rejoined Catherine de Medici's household.[55] Guillemette died on

20 September 1571 and was buried in the Abbey of Saint Yved of Brenne.[56] Françoise died three years later and was buried beside her.[57] Antoinette had two sons and two daughters, and survived until 1591.[58]

Antoinette had enjoyed not only the company of her mother and her grandmother when she was on duty at Court, but she also had her mother-in-law Madeleine de Savoie, Duchess of Montmorency and her sister-in-law Diane de France with her. This may seem surprising, given the hostility between the Guises and the Montmorencys, but personal feelings had to be set aside when matters of status were at stake, and the distinguished wife of the Constable could not be ignored when Mary's household was being set up. Madeleine had been born in 1510 and so she was fifty when she was one of Mary's ladies-in-waiting. A great heiress, she had royal connections, for she was a cousin of François I, albeit through an illegitimate line. Her father was René, Bastard of Savoy, Count of Villars, Grand Master of France and Governor of Provence while her mother was Anne Lascaris, Countess of Tende. Her marriage contract with Constable Montmorency was signed on 10 January 1526, when she was fifteen, and the fortune she brought him formed the basis of his political greatness.[59]

Madeleine was twenty years younger than the Constable and when she became his wife she deliberately adopted what has been described as an 'obsequiously deferential' manner towards him. He enjoyed that and, before long, began listening to her advice on all manner of things.[60] They had five sons and seven daughters, three of whom became nuns. One of them, Louise, was in the Abbey of Saint Pierre-les-Dames in Rheims while the other two became consecutively Abbesses of La Trinité in Caen. Madeleine ran her household with prudence and economy, always wore modest, old-fashioned clothes, and spent a good deal of time on charitable activities. She too had been a lady-in-waiting to both Eleanor of Austria and Catherine de Medici, and when Mary, Queen of Scots went back to Scotland, she returned to Catherine's household. Later, she was superintendent of the household of Catherine's daughter-in-law, Elizabeth of Austria.[61]

There is no hint as to how Mary, Queen of Scots got on with Madeleine, but when Mary was back in Scotland she wrote from Edinburgh on 10 November 1561 to thank the Constable for a letter he had sent her. Her reply can be read as a straightforward thank you, but it may equally well be an example of her famous irony. 'I was marvellously pleased to hear of your good recollections of me and the good will you bear towards me,' she said, 'because I knew nothing of it until this moment.' At the end of the letter, there is a postscript in her own writing: 'My friend, with your permission I would kiss the hands of Madame Constable [Madeleine] begging her to keep me in the good grace of both of you'.[62] This sounds rather as if she had maintained amiable enough relations with Madeleine while having as little as possible to do with the Constable himself.

Certainly in January 1564, a tantalising entry in Mary's accounts refers to six ells of canvas being used 'to pack up that which was sent into France to Madame de Montmorency',[63] but there is no hint as to what the contents might have been. Presumably it was a gift, or a small commission of some kind, but whatever it was it does indicate continuing contact between the two. The Constable died on 12 November 1567 of wounds received at the Battle of St Denis. As his end approached, someone exhorted him to meet death with patience, to which he replied brusquely that a man who had lived for seventy-five years knew perfectly well how to behave in the quarter of an hour it took him to die. Madeleine commissioned a magnificent tomb for him and she was buried with him in the Church of St Martin de Montmorency when she herself died in 1586.[64]

Notes

1. Aubespine, *Négociations*, 744–50
2. Somerset, *Ladies-in-Waiting*, 5
3. Solnon, *La Cour de France*, 22
4. Clément Marot, *Oeuvres Satiriques*, 326 n.2
5. Jollet, *Clouet*, 127

6. Strickland, *Queens of Scotland*, i, 45
7. *Ibid.*, i, 278, 304
8. NAS, Exchequer Records, E34/23
9. Loades, *Mary Tudor*, 192
10. Hibbert, *The Virgin Queen*, 105–6
11. McGowan, *Ideal Forms*, 176–81, 232–4, 247
12. *Lettres*, ed. Labanoff, v, 23
13. *Ibid.*, v, 252, 282–3
14. *Lettres de Catherine de Médicis*, x, 504, 513–14, 606
15. Poull, *La Maison ducale de Lorraine*, 421; Hollingsworth, *Cardinal's Hat*, 18
16. Benger, *Memoirs*, i, 142–3
17. *Ibid.*, i, 141; Stoddart, *Girlhood*, 24. It seems unlikely that Michel de l'Hôpital was involved in Anne's education as Stoddart claims, since he left Italy when she was only six.
18. Hollingsworth, *Cardinal's Hat*, 19
19. *Foreign Correspondence*, 1548–57, p. viii
20. *Lettres du Cardinal de Lorraine*, 104–5, 110–21
21. *Foreign Correspondence*, 1548–57, 19
22. *Ibid.*, 20
23. Most sources give the date of the wedding as 4 December, but in his letter of 12 December 1548 to Anne's brother Hercule, printed in *Lettres du Cardinal de Lorraine*, 121, the Cardinal states that it will take place 'next Sunday', i.e. 16 December.
24. Anselme, *Histoire Généalogique*, iii, 456; Stoddart, *Girlhood*, 25; Frieda, *Catherine de Medici*, 95
25. *Lettres du Cardinal de Lorraine*, 133–4, 136, 184, 189
26. *Ibid.*, 164–5, 245, 263, 266, 270, 329, 334–5, 480, 505–6
27. *Ibid.*, 154
28. *Foreign Correspondence*, 1548–57, 92, 110
29. Brantôme, *Dames Illustres*, ii, 242–3; Brantôme, *Lives of Gallant Ladies*, 284–5
30. Fraser, *Mary, Queen of Scots*, 93–4; Frieda, *Catherine de Medici*, 136
31. *Inventaires*, 10
32. Brantôme, *Lives of Gallant Ladies*, 468
33. *Lettres du Cardinal de Lorraine*, 251
34. *Ibid.*, 251
35. *Lettres*, ed. Labanoff, iv, 188, 261; v, 43–4; v, 273–4
36. Brantôme, *Lives of Gallant Ladies*, 371–2
37. Anselme, *Histoire Généalogique*, iii, 456

38. Cloulas, *Diane de Poitiers*, 141; Poull, *La Maison ducale de Lorraine*, 433; *Lettres du Cardinal de Lorraine*, 32, 141, 158, 188 n.3; *Lettres de Catherine de Médicis*, ix, 505

39. *Lettres de Catherine de Médicis*, ix, 505; Benger, *Memoirs*, i, 175

40. *Lettres du Cardinal de Lorraine*, 662

41. Poull, *La Maison ducale de Lorraine*, 437; *Inventaires*, p. xxxv n.4, 93, 94, 97; *Lettres du Cardinal de Lorraine*, 189, 243

42. *Foreign Correspondence 1548–57*, 270 and 270n., 280; Ruble, *Première jeunesse*, 89; *Lettres*, ed. Labanoff, i, 42–3

43. Aubespine, *Négociations*, 745

44. Adhémar and Moulin, *Cabinet des Estampes*, no. 326

45. Anselme, *Histoire Généalogique*, vii, 125, 168

46. Cloulas, *Diane de Poitiers*, 220

47. Baumgartner, *Henry II*, 184; *Lettres du Cardinal de Lorraine*, 195–6

48. Anselme, *Histoire Généalogique*, vii, 168; Benger, *Memoirs*, i, 175; *Clément Marot, Oeuvres Diverses*, 243; Solnon, *Cour de France*, 30

49. Broglie, *Les Clouet de Chantilly*, no. 233

50. *Clément Marot, Oeuvres Diverses*, 243

51. Anselme, *Histoire Généalogique*, 605

52. *Lettres*, ed. Labanoff, i, 42–3

53. Cloulas, *Diane de Poitiers*, 280

54. *Lettres*, ed. Labanoff, i, 111

55. *Lettres de Catherine de Médicis*, ix, 505, 509

56. *Ibid.*, ix, 505; Anselme, *Histoire Généalogique*, vii, 168

57. *Ibid.*, vii, 168

58. *Ibid.*, iii, 605–6

59. *Ibid.*, iii, 604

60. Benger, *Memoirs*, i, 172

61. Anselme, *Histoire Généalogique*, iii, 604–5; Cloulas, *Diane de Poitiers*, 76

62. *Lettres*, ed. Labanoff, i, 118–19

63. *Inventaires*, 144

64. Anselme, *Histoire Généalogique*, iii, 604

5

The Queen of France's Ladies (2)

Diane de France was married to Madeleine de Savoie's eldest
son, but she was also an interesting person in her own right
for she was an illegitimate daughter of Henri II, born before he
inherited the throne. Her mother, Filippa Duci, was a young
Piedmontese woman whom the nineteen-year-old Prince had met
during his 1537 military expedition to Italy under the supervision
of the middle-aged Constable Montmorency. According to one
highly coloured account, Henri saw Filippa being carried from a
burning house, instantly fell in love with her and Diane was the
result. A more mundane version of events tells how Filippa's
brother, one of Henri's squires, introduced her to the Prince and
they spent the night together before Henri rode off to join his
troops.

Some weeks later, Montmorency heard that Filippa was
expecting a child and he told Henri who, overcome with paternal
pride, demanded progress reports on the pregnancy. Catherine de
Medici was highly alarmed when the news reached her, for this
was at the time when she was still childless herself and worried
about being repudiated. Henri was at Chantilly, Montmorency's
house, when he heard that his daughter had been born, and he
gave orders for her to be brought to France, while Filippa was
persuaded to retire to a Piedmontese convent. Henri called his
baby daughter after Diane de Poitiers, who became her godmother
and brought her up during her early childhood.[1]

Little Diane was declared legitimate and granted the rank of
princess. Unlike Henri II's other daughters, she apparently bore
a close resemblance to her father, who treated her with great

affection. She grew up to be tall and graceful as well as sweet-natured and kind, and no hint of scandal ever touched her.[2] When she was only nine, Henri decided that she should marry Horace Farnese, Duke of Castro, the grandson of Pope Paul III, and Horace came to live with the royal children too. The marriage contract was signed on 30 June 1547 in the presence of the young couple, Diane wearing Italian costume as a compliment to her future husband. The papal legate was present, and so too were Anne d'Este's husband, and Cardinal Ippolito d'Este. It was some years before the young couple were actually married, and unfortunately, Horace was killed fighting gallantly at the siege of Hesdin in 1553, a few months after his wedding.[3]

Diane had been in Catherine de Medici's retinue ever since she was ten, and after she was widowed at sixteen she remained there.[4] Three years later, Henri II decided to please his old friend the Constable by offering him Diane as a wife for his eldest son, François, and provided her with a handsome dowry. The Constable was delighted, of course, but there was an unforeseen complication. François was a prisoner of Charles V in the Netherlands. His release was arranged, but on his return, he revealed that he had already promised to marry another of Catherine de Medici's maids of honour, Jeanne de Hallwin, Dame de Piennes, daughter of Antoine de Hallwin. The Constable promptly applied his usual solution for superfluous women and had Jeanne shut up in a convent. It was thought that François would have to go to Rome to seek a dispensation to marry, but after pressure from his father he swore that he had never made any promise to Jeanne in the first place and so his wedding to Diane was celebrated at La Ferté-Milnon on 4 May 1557.[5] This union, which began so unauspiciously, had a happy ending for all concerned. Diane and François were delighted with each other although they had no children, and the discarded Jeanne was eventually released from her convent to become the wife of Florimond Robertet the younger, son of the famous French statesman of the same name.[6] Diane became one of the ladies-in-waiting of Mary, Queen of Scots in 1560 and was back with Catherine by 1576. She was widowed in 1579. She did not marry again but spent her latter years in the Hôtel d'Angoulême, the fine house she built for herself in Paris. She died there on 11 January 1619.[7]

The third little family group in Mary's household perhaps illustrates best of all the web of interconnections among the ladies-in-waiting. Jacqueline or Jacquette de Longwy, Duchess of Montpensier had been married since 1538 to Antoinette de Bourbon's cousin, Louis de Bourbon, Duke of Montpensier. With her in the Queen's retinue were her niece Anne Chabot and Louise de Hallwin, who was married to her nephew, Charles Chabot. Jacqueline was accounted a great beauty, and a portrait drawing shows her with a broad forehead, wide-set eyes and a mild expression which belied her energetic and determined character. She had always been at the centre of Court circles, for her mother Jeanne d'Angoulême was an illegitimate sister of François I, making Jacqueline Henri II's cousin.[8] She, Henri's sister Princess Marguerite and Catherine de Medici were all close friends. Described by one contemporary as 'a princess of great spirit, and of a prudence above that of her sex', Jacqueline had one son and five daughters. According to Brantôme, she did everything while her husband did practically nothing. It was Jacqueline who was credited with getting back for his family the dukedom of Châtelherault, given by Henri II to James Hamilton, the Regent Arran. The Hamiltons used the title for several hundred years afterwards, but they did not have possession of the lands of the duchy.[9]

Brantôme declared that Montpensier was the poorest prince in France at the start of his career but, thanks to his wife's efforts, by the time he died he was the second richest.[10] There is probably a good deal of exaggeration in this, for although the Duke may have done little in the way of increasing his family's landholdings, as Lieutenant General of the royal armies he had a long and distinguished military career. However, it remains true that while he was absent with the army, his wife concentrated on increasing her power at Court. Much in favour during the reign of her cousin, Henri II, Jacqueline was apparently greatly relied upon by François II after he became king.[11] However, she was in the last stages of tuberculosis by the time she joined Mary's household, and she died in Paris on 28 August 1561, just weeks after Mary left France. Catherine de Medici was much affected by her death and wrote to the Duke of Savoy, asking him to break the news to his wife, Princess Marguerite. Jacqueline was buried in the chapel of her husband's castle of Champigny.[12]

Anne Chabot, Demoiselle de Brion was the daughter of Jacqueline's sister Françoise and her husband Philippe de Chabot, Admiral of France and governor of Burgundy. In 1538 he had been accused of financial malpractice and had been fined, removed from all his offices and briefly imprisoned. However, he was subsequently released and cleared of all charges, so the marriage prospects of his four daughters were not affected.[13] Indeed, the financial scandal lay well in the past when in 1559 Anne married Charles Hallwin, Duke of Hallwin, later governor of Metz, in Lorraine.[14] She was therefore a new bride when she became one of Mary's ladies, but her subsequent years are a sobering reminder of the realities of life in sixteenth-century France.

She and Charles had five sons and five daughters. Their eldest son, Charles, was murdered in Blois at the age of twenty-four by the servant of a man he had killed in a duel. Their second son, Florimond, was killed in a quarrel in 1592. Robert, their third son, perished at the Battle of Coutras in 1587, while Leonor and Charles, the fourth and fifth sons, died at the siege of Boullères in 1595. Their daughter Louise's husband François, Seigneur de Mesvilliers, was killed at the Battle of Senlis in 1589. Anne's own date of death is not known, but she lived through all these tragedies and was still alive on 24 April 1614.[15]

Anne's sister-in-law Louise de Hallwin, Dame de Cypière was another of Mary's ladies-in-waiting. Her father, Antoine de Hallwin, Seigneur de Buggenhout and Maignelay, had held the colourful office of Grand Wolf-Hunter of France and had been a close ally of the 1st Duke of Guise. Louise began her career in the household of Catherine de Medici, and then she transferred to Mary, Queen of Scots in 1560. By this time she was married to Philibert de Marsilly, Seigneur de Cypière, a distinguished soldier who had fought in Italy. Acting as lady-in-waiting along with Diane de France could have been a source of embarrassment to Louise, for it was her sister Jeanne whom the Constable Montmorency's son had abandoned in favour of Diane. However, that lay in the past, Jeanne was now married to Florimond Robertet the younger, and the famously sweet-natured Diane probably smoothed over any difficulties.[16]

Also in the retinue with Diane and Louise was Florimond Robertet the younger's own sister, Françoise, accompanied by two of her daughters, who were maids of honour to Mary. Françoise's father was the famous statesman and patron of the arts, Florimond Robertet the elder, who had officially occupied the post of Treasurer of France but in fact had acted as first minister to three successive kings, Charles VIII, Louis XII and François I. Françoise, his youngest daughter, must still have been very young when he died in 1527,[17] for it was not until twelve years later that she married Jean Babou, Sieur de la Bourdaisière, master of the wardrobe to Henri II and then to François II. Her family were in this way very close to the monarchy, and indeed when Mary, Queen of Scots gave back to Catherine de Medici the crown jewels in her possession when she was widowed, it was Françoise's husband and brother who were given the task of making an inventory of them.[18]

In her portrait Françoise is a wary-looking, dark-haired person with a large nose and a cleft chin,[19] but perhaps it does not do her justice as Brantôme thought her very lovely. She was a great one to look after herself, he added, saying that she was mortally afraid of night damp and moonlight, which she feared would spoil her beauty. She would, however, have nothing to do with the creams most ladies applied to their complexions and her somewhat bizarre theory seemed to be borne out when she reportedly retained her good looks into old age, not one of her daughters equalling her attractive appearance.[20] She and Jean had four sons and no fewer than seven daughters, including the two who were maids of honour to Mary, Queen of Scots. After her husband's death on 11 October 1569, Françoise married Jean, Marshal d'Aumont, a widower. Her date of death is unknown.[21]

Françoise was not the only lady-in-waiting to come from what might be termed a public-service background rather than the old aristocracy. Marguerite Bertrand was the daughter of Jean Bertrand, First President of the Parlement of Paris and Keeper of the Seals of France, while her husband, Germain-Gaston de Foix, Marquis of Trans, was sent to England as French ambassador to Elizabeth I, who became godmother to their eldest daughter. Sadly, their three sons would all be killed at the siege of Montcrabeau in 1586. Marguerite was still alive in 1591.[22] Another of the ladies-in-waiting, Antoinette de Cerisay, was the wife of the Chancellor of France, François Olivier. In 1549, only a year after his marriage, he was paralysed by a serious illness and had to resign. For ten years he lived quietly with Antoinette and their three sons and two daughters but when François II came to the throne in 1559, he was brought out of retirement. The burden of office was too great, however, and the Chancellor died at Amboise on 30 March 1560.[23]

Several other ladies-in-waiting came from families with a long tradition of service in the French royal household. The very name of Estienette de la Chambre seems to suggest that her ancestors served in this way and indeed the De la Chambre family included a first chamberlain and master of the household to Louis XI[24] and a maid of honour to Catherine de Medici.[25] Likewise, the De Marconnay family supplied various servants in the second half of the sixteenth century. One was Grand Wolf-Hunter, his two sons were squires of the stables to Catherine de Medici, a Jean de Marconnay was a royal cup-bearer and Hilaire de Marconnay, Dame de Berlandière was one of the ladies-in-waiting of Mary, Queen of Scots and a close friend of Constable Montmorency's wife.[26] Marie-Catherine de Pierrevive, the Piedmontese Dame du Perron, another of Mary's ladies, was a valued servant of Catherine de Medici. She was married to Antoine, Seigneur du Perron, who had various marriage connections with the Medicis and who was appointed master of the household to the royal children,[27] while Anne le Maye, Demoiselle de Dannemarie, looked after young Prince Edouard-Alexandre, before she served Mary.[28] Anne de Daillon may have been related to Diane de Poitiers but, more to the point, her mother Anne de Batarnay was on cordial terms with Mary of Guise[29] while her brother, Guy, later Count of Lude, served Henri II's sons and was brought up with them.[30]

As to the remaining four ladies-in-waiting in Mary's household, Anne de Langest, Demoiselle de Comenges remains a shadowy figure. She may have had a Lorraine connection, for she was possibly a sister of the Roger de Comminges, Sieur de Saubole, governor of Metz in the second half of the sixteenth century.[31] Anne Hurault, Dame de Carnavalet was the wife of François de Kernevenog, usually known as Carnavalet, one of the commanders of the royal army and an ally of the Guises,[32] while Marguerite de Lustrac was married to the Marshal of Saint-André, another close friend of the Guise brothers. Solemn-looking, dark-eyed and squarish-faced, she lived with him in the most magnificent style. Their house at Vallery was said to be one of the finest in France, with furniture which surpassed that of the King himself. After her husband's death at the Battle of Dreux in 1562, her career took a sinister turn when she was suspected of poisoning her only daughter and heiress, Catherine. Certainly Catherine died young but there could have been nothing in these rumours, for Marguerite remained friendly with Catherine de Medici and eventually remarried, becoming the wife of Geoffrey, Baron de Caumont, a man said to be the opposite of her first husband in every way, whatever that implied.[33]

Finally, there were Guyonne de Breüil, already in the household, her daughter Marie, Marie de Gaignon and Isabelle Camp, Demoiselle de Cobron, which sounds like a phonetic spelling of the Scottish name, Cockburn. Catherine de Medici had a maid of honour called Bonaventure de Cobron, Demoiselle de Saint-Léger, which seems to place it firmly in a French context but these two women, possibly sisters, may have been of Scottish descent.[34] Isabelle is particularly interesting because she left France with Mary, Queen of Scots in 1561 and was to be found the following year taking her meals at Holyroodhouse alongside the Dame de Péguillon, Madame de Briante and the Four Maries, with her own two servants close by.[35]

Turning now to the maids of honour of Mary, Queen of Scots in 1560, Claude de Pons, Demoiselle du Mesnil, their governess, had only ten to look after, a relatively small number. As we have seen, Eleanor of Austria, Catherine de Medici and Mary of Guise all had at least twice as many maids as ladies, Eleanor actually having seven times more. The reason for this is not clear. It may have been that, because Mary had been Queen of France for such a short time, she had not yet had the opportunity of taking into her household all the eager daughters of ambitious noblemen. It might, of course, have been that it was considered appropriate for mature and matronly queens to assemble groups of young women who could be trained in the ways of the Court and married off to suitable husbands, but when the queen herself was only seventeen she was hardly experienced enough to undertake this role. Whatever the explanation, four of the maids were Scottish – the famous Four Maries, to be discussed later – and the other six were French.[36]

First of the French maids of honour was Suzanne Constant, Demoiselle de Fonterpuy. It seems likely that she was the daughter of a couple who were in the household of Mary of Guise, for about 1538 Anne de Barbancoys, Demoiselle de Fontpertuys and her husband Monsieur de Fontpertuys were dispatched by Mary of Guise from Scotland to France on some errand for her. Contrary winds drove them back to Leith, and Anne declared miserably that no one had ever been as seasick as she had been, adding reproachfully that the Queen would have done a good deed had she sent them by land instead.[37] Whatever her parentage, Suzanne was a favourite of Mary, Queen of Scots and one of the very few French attendants who left France with her in 1561.[38] The following summer, she returned to France in company with the Péguillon family. The English ambassador to Scotland, Thomas Randolph, reported their departure from Edinburgh with some relish, for he disliked the Péguillons. However, he added of Suzanne, 'There is notwithstanding a young French gentlewoman of her grace's chamber, whom she loves marvellous well, whose father is lately dead and she unwillingly forced to return. I think her more worthy of honour than the whole company, and assure you she deserves well'.[39]

Another of the maids seems to have had a Scottish connection, but her identity has proved to be singularly elusive. From 1552 to 1560 Catherine de Medici had a maid of honour named Hippolyte d'Ecosse, Demoiselle de Richebourg, and in 1560 Hippolyte moved to the retinue of Mary, Queen of Scots.[40] Now Jean de Montmorency, Chevalier de Bours had a daughter named Hippolyte de Montmorency, who married Pierre, Marquis of Richebourg, but she was not born until 1560 so she cannot have been Mary's maid of honour. Presumably Hippolyte d'Ecosse belongs to an earlier part of the Richebourg family tree, but it has been impossible to identify her and nothing else is known about her.

The parents of the other French maids are not hard to find. Marie Babou, Demoiselle de la Bourdaisière and her younger sister Françoise were the daughters of Mary's lady-in-waiting Françoise Robertet, Dame de la Bourdaisière. Marie would have been two or three years older than Mary, Queen of Scots, and on 18 September 1559 she married sixteen-year-old Claude de Beauvilliers, Count of Saint-Aignan. Since the wedding took place at Fontainebleau in the presence of the Court, Mary would have been there. The Count was reported to be deeply in love with his bride, who was particularly famed for her lovely hair. They went on to have three sons and six daughters, one a nun and two of the others abbesses. Marie died in 1582, a year before both her husband and her eldest son were killed at the siege of Antwerp.[41] Her younger sister Françoise had an altogether more startling history, if Brantôme is to be believed. Recently married to Antoine d'Estrées, Marquis of Coeuvres when she entered Mary's household, she led an unexceptional if somewhat flirtatious life until 9 June 1593 when, at the age of about fifty-one, she was apparently hanged for adultery with her lover Yves d'Alègre by the people of Issoire.[42]

The final two maids were also about the same age as Mary, Queen of Scots. One was the Demoiselle Olivier, daughter of Chancellor Olivier and Antoinette de Cerisay. Unfortunately the 1560 list does not give her first name, but we know that the

Chancellor and his wife had two daughters. Jeanne, the elder, was a maid of honour to Catherine de Medici from 1551 until 1560 and it was probably she who then transferred to Mary's household. She later became the first wife of Antoine de Monchy, Seigneur de Senarpont and Voisines while Madeleine, her younger sister, married Louis de Sainte-Maure, Marquis of Nesle in 1558 and then, when he died, Jean de Balsac, Seigneur de Montagne.[43] The other maid of honour, Anne Cabrianne, Demoiselle de la Guyonnière, features again in 1570 as 'Anna Cabriana', lady-in-waiting to Catherine de Medici, so she was probably one of the French Queen's Italian servants. She married Philibert de Lignerolles, and was still in Catherine's household in 1572.[44]

What conclusions may we then draw about the women attendants of Mary, Queen of Scots when she was Queen of France? Looking at the twenty-seven ladies-in-waiting together, the most noticeable fact is that twenty-five of them were French, Anne d'Este was Italian and Marie-Catherine de Pierrevive was Piedmontese. None was Scottish. Had Mary, Queen of Scots been Queen Consort of France for longer, this might have changed, in that her Scottish maids of honour would probably have been promoted to ladies-in-waiting in due course as they married or entered their twenties. Interestingly, the twenty-seven ladies cover a wide age span. We do not know the dates of birth of all of them, but it is usually possible to arrive at an approximation of their ages if their marriage dates are known. Most aristocratic young women in the sixteenth century married for the first time between the ages of fourteen and twenty. Using this as a rough guide, we can say that, leaving aside the five whose ages are entirely unknown, half were under the age of forty and half were above it. The youngest was Antoinette de la Marck, who was only eighteen. Her grandmother Guillemette de Sarrebruche, Antoinette de Bourbon and Marie-Catherine de Pierrevive were the oldest, all over sixty with Guillemette perhaps in her seventies.

The imprecise use of the terms 'Dame' and 'Demoiselle' sometimes makes the marital status of sixteenth-century women unclear, but it is possible to say that eighteen of Mary's ladies-in-waiting were married, almost all of them with children, and four were widows. There is no mention of Isabelle, Demoiselle de Cobron having a husband, nor do we know the marital status of four of the others. The occupations of the husbands are significant, of course, and not merely because their status usually determined whether or not their wives were taken into royal service. It is hardly surprising that at least sixteen of the twenty-seven husbands had important military careers, since that was the traditional means of serving the king for members of the peerage, and the long struggle with the Holy Roman Emperor Charles V, the incursions of the French army into Italy and then the lengthy religious wars gave ample opportunity for people like Constable Montmorency and the 2nd Duke of Guise to distinguish themselves.

It would be safe to reckon that the majority of the ladies-in-waiting had close relatives who were at one time or another with the royal army, and the feelings of anxiety they experienced are made abundantly clear in the Cardinal of Lorraine's correspondence with, for instance, his sister-in-law Anne d'Este and with the Marshal of Saint-André's wife. Brought up in this environment, Mary, Queen of Scots was surrounded by women who were constantly waiting for and hearing news of French military successes and disasters. She listened to tales of heroic feats in battle and heard her aunt Anne d'Este described by the poet Ronsard as a Venus worthy of being the wife of 'Our Mars', the Duke of Guise.[45] When she was back in Scotland, Mary would ride boldly at the head of her own army, declaring that she wished she could do all the things a soldier did. After her defeat at the Battle of Langside in 1568 and her flight into England, it was noticed that she delighted in hearing tales of bravery, 'commending by name all approved hardy men of her country, although they be her enemies, and she concealeth no cowardice, even in her friends . . . For victory's sake, pain and peril seem pleasant to her, and in respect of victory, wealth and all other things seem to her contemptible and vile'.[46]

Of those eleven ladies-in-waiting whose husbands were not involved in warfare, three were married to ambassadors, Antoinette de Cerisay's was Chancellor of France and three were the wives of men with important positions in the French royal household, while the Dame de Péguillon's husband had served Mary of Guise. The occupations of the remaining three have not been ascertained. As to the women's own careers, thirteen are known to have been in the household of Catherine de Medici before transferring to Mary in 1560, at least three having previously served Eleanor of Austria. More than half of Mary's ladies-in-waiting were taken into Catherine's household after her departure for Scotland. No fewer than seventeen of the twenty-seven had female relatives in Mary's own household, and as the information is incomplete there could well have been more. Again, at least six had female relatives who served in the households of other French queens past, present and future, and the figure for those with male relatives serving the French kings would be much higher. We can therefore conclude that Mary was surrounded by a tight little group of women who were well known to each other and to her. Moreover, no fewer than fifteen of her ladies had existing links with the Guise family, indicating that she was exercising typical royal patronage to benefit her own relatives but also reflecting the prevailing situation in which her uncles were, apart from Catherine de Medici, the most influential figures at her husband's Court.

Given the Guise brothers' dominating position, it is not surprising that there is little evidence of Protestant sympathies among Mary's ladies during the time that they were in her household. Anne d'Este was the daughter of a notably Protestant mother and she is thought to have demonstrated concern at the hangings of the Protestants at Amboise.[47] Be that as it may, her situation as the adoring wife of that great Catholic warrior François, 2nd Duke of Guise, and the obedient daughter-in-law of the devout Antoinette de Bourbon meant that she must have suppressed any Protestant inclinations in herself. Indeed, two of her sons entered the Roman Catholic Church, one of them becoming a cardinal.[48] Françoise de Brézé's husband Robert de la Marck, Duke of Bouillon is said to have become a Protestant, but he apparently never opposed the King and died a premature death. There is no indication as to whether his wife shared in his conversion.[49] Finally Antoinette de Cerisay's husband, the Chancellor Olivier, is believed to have favoured Protestantism secretly, but that did not affect his own career, the position of his wife as a lady-in-waiting or the appointment of one of their daughters as a maid of honour in Mary's household.[50]

The maids of honour were, of course, a smaller group than the ladies-in-waiting and so any analysis is less statistically significant. What is surprising is that two of the maids, Marie Babou and her sister Françoise, were already married when they joined the retinue. Possibly they were still too young to be ladies-in-waiting and were therefore assigned to the more junior group for the time being. The exact dates of birth of the maids are frequently unknown, but it seems certain that they were all about the same age as Mary, Queen of Scots herself. Young they might be, but some of them were experienced attendants. Hippolyte d'Ecosse, Jeanne Olivier, if she was the 'Demoiselle Olivier', and possibly Anne Cabrianne had already served Catherine de Medici as maids and of course the Four Maries had been in the household since 1548. As for the other three, the Babou sisters and Suzanne Constant, Demoiselle de Fonterpuy were well accustomed to life at Court and both Suzanne and their governess Claude de Pons owed their positions to Mary of Guise.

Four of the maids (three Scottish and one French) came from the old aristocracy, one was the daughter of an important officer of state and the other five came from families who already served the monarchy. Seven of the maids eventually married, five of them twice, Mary Seton remained single and the marital status of the Demoiselles de Fonterpuy and Richebourg is unknown. The maids of honour complete the named women in the household of Mary, Queen of Scots in 1560, but a laconic note records that there were also six chamberwomen. One was a wardrobe woman, three were washerwomen and two served the maids of honour.[51]

Mary, Queen of Scots had grown up at the centre of a sophisticated Court, but any suspicions that she and her women revelled in decadence can be set aside. It is true that Catherine de Medici was criticised for the licentious behaviour of her women, but not at the time when Mary was living with the royal children. It was during her years as Queen Regent of France that Catherine was accused of employing the sexual charms of her various maids to ensnare courtiers in her political machinations. During Mary's childhood, Catherine controlled her ladies strictly. No one was supposed even to speak to her maids of honour unless either the Queen herself or their governess was present. Indeed, Catherine was widely regarded as having restored propriety after the reckless abandon of the Court of her father-in-law, François I.

Any misbehaviour on the part of her women attendants was dealt with severely, as Jeanne de Hallwin and Françoise de Rohan had found to their cost, while the horror evoked by Lady Fleming's affair with Henri II was intensified by the fact that this lady was governess to Mary, Queen of Scots and no hint of scandal must touch the future wife of the Dauphin. Flirtations and love affairs there undoubtedly were, but these were supposed to be conducted with discretion and, as we have seen, Mary's ladies-in-waiting were women with young families and estates to run for their husbands, while the unwed maids were expected to conduct themselves modestly, so that they could be married off to suitable husbands when the time came.

Notes

1. Cloulas, *Diane de Poitiers*, 99–111
2. Williams, *Henri II*, 299
3. Cloulas, *Diane de Poitiers*, 175–6; Williams, *Henri II*, 285
4. *Lettres de Catherine de Médicis*, ix, 505
5. *Lettres du Cardinal de Lorraine*, 263; Bentley-Cranch, 'The Château of Beauregard', 72–3; Anselme, *Histoire Généalogique*, iii, 604; Williams, *Henri II*, 301
6. Bentley-Cranch, 'The Château of Beauregard', 73
7. *Lettres de Catherine de* Médicis, ix, 505; Anselme, *Histoire Généalogique*, iii, 604
8. Bentley-Cranch, 'Marot's *Etrennes*', 69; Bibliothèque Nationale de France, Cabinet des Estampes, no. 290

Queen Mary's Women

9. Anselme, *Histoire Généalogique*, i, 355-6; Brantôme, *Dames illustres*, iii, 276-7
10. Brantôme, *Dames illustres*, iii, 277
11. *Lettres de Catherine de Médicis*, ix, 505; Brantôme, *Dames illustres*, iii, 276
12. *Lettres de Catherine de Médicis*, x, 45; Anselme, *Histoire Généalogique*, i, 355-6
13. Bentley-Cranch, 'Marot's *Etrennes*', 70-1
14. Anselme, *Histoire Généalogique*, iv, 572
15. *Ibid.*, iv, 913
16. See p. 75
17. Mayer and Bentley-Cranch, *Florimond Robertet*, 16
18. *Inventaires*, 202-3
19. Adhémar and Moulin, *Cabinet des Estampes*, no. 304
20. Brantôme, *Lives of Gallant Ladies*, 368-9
21. Anselme, *Histoire Généalogique*, viii, 180
22. *Ibid.*, iii, 388; *Lettres de Catherine de Médicis*, x, 4n.
23. Anselme, *Histoire Généalogique*, vi, 482
24. *Ibid.*, iii, 384
25. *Lettres de Catherine de Médicis*, ix, 508
26. *Ibid.*, 80 and 80n., 89, 100
27. Cloulas, *Diane de Poitiers*, 157; Guiffrey, *Dianne de Poytiers: Lettres*, 15 n.1; Ruble, *Première jeunesse*, 54, 71, 279; *Lettres de Catherine de Médicis*, ix, 508; x, 78-9
28. Anselme, *Histoire Généalogique*, iv, 399
29. *Ibid.*, viii, 191; *Lettres du Cardinal de Lorraine*, 114, 283n., 423; Sutherland, *French Secretaries*, 121
30. Anselme, *Histoire Généalogique*, viii, 191
31. Larcade, 'Le Duc d'Epernon et les Guises', 549n.
32. Sutherland, *French Secretaries*, 162
33. Anselme, *Histoire Généalogique*, vii, 203, 283; *Lettres de Catherine de Médicis*, ix, 506; x, 493; Musée Condé, Chantilly, no. 248; *Lettres du Cardinal de Lorraine*, 102, 303, 506 n.2; *Foreign Correspondence 1548-57*, 62; Sutherland, *French Secretaries of State*, 319-20; Brantôme, *Dames illustres*, iii, 306; Brantôme, *Lives of Gallant Ladies*, 314
34. *Lettres de Catherine de Médicis*, x, 22n., 514; *Lettres du Cardinal de Lorraine*, 293 n.2
35. NAS, Exchequer Records, E33/6/2
36. Aubespine, *Négociations*, 745
37. *Foreign Correspondence*, 1537-48, 76

[88]

38. NAS, Exchequer Records, E33/6/2
39. *CSP Scot.*, i, 645
40. *Lettres de Catherine de Médicis*, ix, 515; Aubespine, *Négociations*, 745
41. Brantôme, *Lives of Gallant Ladies*, 529 n.792; Anselme, *Histoire Généalogique*, iv, 716-7
42. Anselme, *Histoire Généalogique*, viii, 182; Brantôme, *Lives of Gallant Ladies*, 504 n.294
43. *Lettres de Catherine de Médicis*, ix, 515; Anselme, *Histoire Généalogique*, v, 13
44. *Lettres de Catherine de Médicis*, ix, 510; *Lettres du Cardinal de Lorraine*, 610 n.3
45. Pierre de Ronsard, *Poésies Choisies*, 872
46. *CSP Scot.*, ii, 428
47. Frieda, *Catherine de Medici*, 136
48. Benger, *Memoirs*, i, 139-42; Anselme, *Histoire Généalogique*, iii, 456
49. Brantôme, *Dames illustres*, iv, 357
50. Anselme, *Histoire Généalogique*, vi, 482
51. Aubespine, *Négociations*, 746

6

Three Favourites: The Countesses of Argyll, Mar and Moray

'Adieu, France! Adieu, France! Adieu, then, my dear France . . . I think I shall never see you again!' Mary, Queen of Scots is said to have exclaimed as she sailed for Scotland in her great white galley, no doubt recalling with anguish all the people she was leaving behind: her French family, her dead husband's relatives, her galaxy of ladies, her friends and her acquaintances. Who were to take their place in her life? She was going back to her native land, it was true, but she had been away for almost thirteen years and her much-loved mother was dead. So who would be her friends and advisers in this familiar yet unfamiliar environment? According to one observer, during Mary's marriage to Lord Darnley she had three favourite ladies and she confided in them to such an extent that her insecure husband felt jealous.[1] The three were Jean Stewart, Countess of Argyll, Annabella Murray, Countess of Mar and Agnes Keith, Countess of Moray.

We are used to thinking of Mary as an only child which, strictly speaking, she was of course, but because of her father's many affairs she had an array of half-brothers, and Lady Jean Stewart was her half-sister. Jean was born in about 1533 when James V was still a bachelor, the result of his relationship with Elizabeth Beaton, daughter of Sir John Beaton of Creich.[2] The King took responsibility for her, just as he did for his sons.[3] Her nurse, Christian Baxter, features in the accounts of the Lord Treasurer of Scotland from 1538 to 1541[4] and in March 1539 the royal tailor, Thomas Arthur, was making for her a dressing-gown with lapels of sable and a cotton stuff lining. The following month, Mary of Guise's own tailor in Stirling supplied a white taffeta gown for the little girl and a kirtle lined with green to wear underneath it, while that summer Thomas Arthur produced a white satin doublet which she would wear with a long skirt. By July 1540, Jean was old enough to be learning embroidery. Seven hanks of several colours of Paris silk and an ell of fine thin cloth were sent to her 'to be her samplers', and by about 1543, when she was around ten, she features on Mary of Guise's 'Roll and number of persons in the service of the Queen'.[5]

After Mary, Queen of Scots went to France, she and her half-sister did not see each other for the next twelve years and more. In 1538, when her father was still alive, it had been agreed that Jean should become the wife of Archibald Campbell, later 5th Earl of Argyll. She was about five at the time and he only a year old. Obviously their wedding lay some years ahead but for whatever reason he was by 1549 betrothed to someone else, Margaret, daughter of George, 4th Earl of Huntly. Nothing came of that plan, however, and in 1553 Mary of Guise revived the notion of the Campbell match for Jean. Mary was cultivating the 4th Earl of Argyll for political reasons and she saw to it that a new marriage contract was drawn up. The wedding took place in April 1554, and so by the time that Mary, Queen of Scots came back, Jean should have been a mature and settled wife of seven years.[6]

Unfortunately, her marriage was not proving to be a success, for she and Archibald were very different personalities. Attractive and flirtatious, stubborn, spoiled and very conscious of the fact that she was the daughter of a king, Jean was used to life at the royal Court whereas he, moody and resentful, preferred to be on his own estates. To make matters worse, they did not have any children together and, as the months went by, Argyll was more and more conscious of the fact that he needed an heir. This increased his surliness, for he was convinced that the problem lay with Jean. After all, he had various illegitimate sons. As was the custom of the time, his wife was expected to accept his extramarital affairs without complaint, but when she began taking lovers, he ordered his clansmen to seize her and hold her prisoner. This happened on more than one occasion. During the summer before Mary,

Queen of Scots returned to Scotland, for instance, Jean was imprisoned for a fortnight, and it is generally presumed that this was because Argyll had accused her of adultery. His friend John Knox the famous preacher mediated and managed to bring about a reconciliation, but it was obvious that Jean and her husband were incompatible.[7]

Mary, Queen of Scots liked them both, and Jean was often in her company, although she does not appear on the surviving lists of ladies-in-waiting and maids of honour, and we have only an occasional glimpse of her. Her marital troubles continued, and in the spring of 1563, Mary decided to intervene. Her own dealings with John Knox were notoriously difficult but he had helped before and so she summoned him to Lochleven Castle, which she was visiting. She discussed public affairs with him and then, the following morning, met him again and urged him to persuade the Earl of Argyll to show greater kindness to his wife. Knox must not let Argyll know that she had intervened, she said, promising that if Jean 'behave not herself so as she ought to do, she shall find no favours of me'.

Knox duly wrote a firm letter to Argyll telling him that he must perform his marital duties. The Earl was not best pleased, and his relationship with Jean continued to deteriorate.[8] She seems to have been spending all her time at Court and she is perhaps best remembered for the fact that she was the only other woman present when Lord Ruthven and his fellow conspirators burst into the Queen's small supper chamber on the evening of 9 March 1566, and murdered David Riccio. When the table was knocked over in the confusion, it was Jean who snatched up the candelabrum as it fell.[9] A few months later, Mary made her list of jewellery bequests and Jean figured prominently. 'My sister' was the intended recipient of a fur with a gold head and paws, rubies and diamonds round its neck and pearl pendants in its ears, a cabochon ruby in a blue and red setting, a magnificent set of ruby and pearl jewellery, another set in which each item was composed of gold beads filled with perfume and various sapphire, amethyst, ruby and pearl earrings.[10]

When Prince James was christened that autumn, it was Jean who held him at the font, acting as proxy for Elizabeth I, who had agreed to be his godmother. As a result, she found herself in trouble with the Protestant authorities for she had converted to Protestantism, probably at about the time of her marriage to her staunchly Protestant husband. The General Assembly of the Church of Scotland thought that she had no business participating in a Roman Catholic baptism, and they censured her.[11] As long as Mary, Queen of Scots was there to protect her, her position was secure, but when Mary was held prisoner at Lochleven, Jean retired to Argyllshire. However, she simply could not tolerate her husband's company and she left again in August 1567, refusing all his orders to return. Argyll was unable to divorce her for her adultery because they had been officially reconciled, but he immediately demanded that she sue him for divorce on the grounds of his own continuing adultery. He would not contest the action, he said. Jean refused.[12] Her half-brother, the Earl of Moray, a close friend of Argyll, was very much opposed to a divorce, and he seems to have supported her, not only emotionally but financially. On 15 November, by his special command, she was paid £133:6:8.[13]

Argyll was not to be deflected, however, for he was in poor health and more desperate than ever to have an heir. He approached the General Assembly about a legal separation, sent Jean letters formally demanding that she return to him and in the summer of 1570 initiated discussions with her relatives in the hope of reaching some sort of financial settlement, but all to no purpose.[14] That summer Jean was reported as being 'very angry and in great poverty'[15] and in a letter of 2 July to the Earl of Atholl, who was acting for her, she referred in somewhat obscure terms to the behaviour of 'that ungrateful man', presumably her husband, adding in exasperation 'and in the mean time I must take the best of it till God send better'.[16] Argyll obtained a decree of adherence from Edinburgh Commissary Court in the early weeks of 1571 ordering Jean to return to him, but she refused to do so and was officially outlawed.

She was staying in Edinburgh at this time, and the ministers of the town's churches publicly rebuked her and told her that she must return to her husband. Once again she refused, and early in 1573 she found shelter in Edinburgh Castle, which was being held for Queen Mary. The Presbyterian Church excommunicated her on 26 April that year. Argyll was by now Chancellor of Scotland and, after seeking the support of parliament, he at last managed to get a divorce from the Commissary Court on the grounds of their separation. By its terms, Jean was deprived of her dowry and her jointure. To add to her troubles, Edinburgh Castle fell and she was taken prisoner. Terrified that she would be handed over to Argyll, she wrote to Elizabeth I, claiming that she was afraid that, if that happened, he would kill her. Elizabeth responded by telling the Regent Morton tartly that she had no desire to meddle in marriage disputes about which she knew nothing. In fact, Argyll probably had no more desire to see her than she had to encounter him, and she was able to move to Fife, where she was said to be 'comfortable'.[17]

Argyll married again as soon as he was free, taking as his second wife Lady Jean Cunningham, the daughter of his friend Alexander, 4th Earl of Glencairn. However, he died less than six weeks after his wedding, and almost nine months later his posthumous son died at birth. His brother Colin therefore inherited the earldom. As for his discarded first Countess, she pursued what she saw as her marital rights with tenacity. She went to the Court of Session in an attempt to have her divorce arrangements overturned and eventually she was able to reach a private financial settlement with her former husband's widow and Colin, the 6th Earl.[18] There is no known evidence to show whether Jean and Mary, Queen of Scots were ever again in touch with each other, but Jean remained active on her own behalf and on 18 October 1580 received letters of legitimation under the Great Seal. She died in 1588, the year after Mary's execution, and was buried in the royal vault at Holyrood.[19]

Mary's relationship with this wilful and determined half-sister is an interesting one. The Queen viewed her marital difficulties with some disapproval, but she behaved towards her with firmness and sympathy, dealt in an even-handed manner with both parties and was even willing to enlist the help of her own enemy, John Knox, in an attempt to mend the Earl and Countess's marriage. The fact that Jean and her husband were both Protestant does not seem to have upset her in the least and her close friendship with Jean was shattered only when Mary herself had to flee from Scotland. Incidentally, Mary is sometimes said to have had another sister, also illegitimate, named Margaret, who was at one point described as a possible wife for the Master of Home. However, there is no other mention of her anywhere, Jean had once been spoken of in connection with the Master, and it has been suggested that 'Margaret' was simply written in error for 'Jean'.[20]

The second lady who evoked Lord Darnley's jealousy because of her closeness to the Queen was Annabella Murray, wife of John, 6th Lord Erskine. The daughter of William Murray of Tullibardine, she married in 1557. Her husband belonged to a family which had long been close to the Scottish monarchy, and during Mary of Guise's last illness he had compassionately allowed her to enter Edinburgh Castle, despite his declared neutrality during the religious troubles of the time. He became a Protestant shortly after her death, but when Mary, Queen of Scots returned in 1561 she was well disposed to him and in 1565 created him Earl of Mar on the day of her wedding to Lord Darnley.[21] There is little documentary evidence of Annabella's relationship with Mary, but her closeness to the Queen is underlined by the fact that she featured very prominently in Mary's 1566 jewellery bequests just before the birth of Prince James. She was the intended recipient of a particularly important item, a red and white enamelled belt with links made in the shape of roses and a large pendant rose at the end set with a miniature portrait of Henri II of France. It must have been one of Henri's gifts to Mary. Annabella was also to have diamond and ruby bracelets, pearl earrings, a pearl and amethyst belt and a white fur with a gold head set with rubies, diamonds, sapphires and pearls while her daughter Mary, almost certainly called after the Queen, was to have a set of peridot jewellery.[22]

Early the following year, Mary gave her infant son, Prince James, into the care of Lord Mar and his wife. The Erskine family were the traditional keepers of the heirs to the Scottish throne, and Mar was able to retain his position after the Queen's forced abdication. He was, after all, the Regent Moray's uncle. Mar himself became Regent in 1571, when the Regent Lennox was assassinated, but he died on 28 October 1572, leaving Annabella as executrix and guardian of their two children, John and Mary.[23] John was being brought up with Prince James and the two became close friends, but Queen Mary's warmth towards Lady Mar had faded. The Prince regarded Annabella as his surrogate mother and it was hardly surprising if Mary felt jealousy and resentment towards her. In 1578, when she was desperate to get her son out of Scotland so that he could marry Philip II of Spain's daughter, Mary told James Beaton, Archbishop of Glasgow, that the widowed Annabella could easily be bribed to go along with the plan if she were offered some good appointment, for she was no longer in a position of power. 'I know the disposition of this woman,' she wrote, in tones which suggest dislike.[24] That is Mary's last recorded mention of Lady Mar, who continued to enjoy the favour of James VI until her death in February 1603.[25]

Even more significant than the Countess of Mar was the third favourite lady, Agnes Keith, wife of the Queen's half-brother, Lord James Stewart. Theirs was a love match. He was the son of James V and his favourite mistress Margaret Erskine, wife of Sir Robert Douglas of Lochleven, while she was a daughter of the very wealthy William, 4th Earl Marischal and his wife Margaret Keith.[26] Indeed, Agnes was the eldest of their nine daughters, and she had three brothers as well. Many years later, arranging to send the gift of a plaid to the English ambassador, Agnes commented that this was 'in remembrance that I am forced to be a highland woman, howbeit I was brought up in the low country'.[27] This suggests that she may have passed her childhood in Edinburgh, where her father spent much of his time since he played a prominent part in public affairs. He had been a leading Protestant for many years, one of George Wishart the preacher's most influential supporters during Agnes's early childhood. His letters to Agnes are pious in tone, ending with the request that she should remember him in her prayers and signing himself 'Your loving earthly father'.[28]

Lord James had originally been intended as the husband of someone else altogether. His strong-minded mother, Lady Douglas, was a widow with six children when, in 1549, she became the guardian of a three-year-old orphan, Christina Stewart, Countess of Buchan. She quickly arranged the betrothal of nineteen-year-old Lord James to the little girl, and he was given possession of the lands of her earldom of Buchan.[29] However, long before young Christina was old enough to marry him, he fell in love with Lady Agnes Keith. He had converted to Protestantism in about 1555, when he openly went to hear John Knox preach at John Erskine of Dun's house, and he and the Earl Marischal were well known to each other.[30] When Mary of Guise lay dying in 1560, she asked the two of them to stay in Edinburgh Castle until the end came, and she dictated her will in their presence, making Marischal one of her executors, although he excused himself from the task once she was dead.[31]

According to Thomas Randolph, Elizabeth I's ambassador in Scotland, Lord James was rude, homely and blunt in manner but he had nevertheless been educated at St Andrews University and in France and he was much admired by many Scots as the man whom only an accident of birth had prevented from being king. Mary, Queen of Scots had, of course, known this brother since childhood, and it was he who had persuaded her to come back to Scotland. In her difficult situation as a Roman Catholic queen in a Protestant country she relied on him and on her secretary of state, William Maitland of Lethington. With their advice, she ruled at first with surprising success, accepting the Protestant settlement and trying hard to cultivate the friendship of Elizabeth I of England.

Lord James married within weeks of Mary's return. We do not know when he and Agnes first met, but on 24 October 1561 Randolph was reporting that the Earl Marischal's daughter had recently come to Edinburgh, and everyone was waiting to see what would come of 'the long love' between herself and Lord James.[32] Sure enough, the couple were married by John Knox in St Giles' Church on 8 February 1562. Mary, Queen of Scots had apparently drawn up the marriage contract, secretly created the bridegroom Earl of Moray and marked the wedding by giving a banquet afterwards at Holyroodhouse. Disapproving of lavish festivities on such occasions, Knox warned Lord James that if his support for Protestantism were seen to fall away afterwards, 'it will be said that your wife hath changed your nature'. This might have been taken for the sort of joke often made on such occasions, but Knox himself recounted his remark in all seriousness.[33]

At any rate, the marriage was a very happy one. The portraits of bride and groom, painted by Hans Eworth in London not long afterwards, show them in fashionable black garments with gold trimmings. Lord James has a large nose, a carefully trimmed moustache, a determined chin and a distinct resemblance to his royal father. Beneath the French hood which conceals most of her auburn hair, Agnes's face is long and oval, with large, wide-set dark eyes and a neat little mouth.[34] Soon after the wedding, the bridegroom's half-brother Robert Douglas married Moray's discarded fiancée, Christina, Countess of Buchan, occasioning an angry exchange of letters between Moray and his mother. Her side of the correspondence has not survived, but she evidently answered his criticisms of the match by telling him that if he was dissatisfied, it was his own fault for not marrying Christina himself. He retorted indignantly, 'I have indeed followed my heart's inclination in my marriage, and is provided by my sovereign'. Quite why he was so annoyed is not made plain, but perhaps he was afraid that he would lose the Buchan lands to Robert. He refused to give them up to his half-brother.[35]

The quarrel between mother and son soon passed, but a much more serious rift developed between the Earl of Moray and Mary, Queen of Scots when she married Lord Darnley. Moray rebelled against her in the Chaseabout Raid and then withdrew to England, where he sought the support of Elizabeth I. Until then, Mary and his wife had been the best of friends but now, of course, that must have changed. During his temporary exile, Moray relied on Agnes to look after his affairs, advising her to 'join with my mother and use her counsel . . . I pray you be blythe and praise God for all that he sends, for it is he only that gives and takes and it is he only that may restore again. Yours as ye know, James Stewart'.[36] In the early weeks of 1566, Agnes was staying at their house in St Andrews and there she received three sacks containing 3000 gold coins. This was intended as financial assistance for Moray and his friends from Elizabeth I. The transaction would hardly have endeared Agnes to Mary, Queen of Scots, who found out about it on the interception of the receipt Agnes tried to send to Randolph. When it was shown to Mary, she sent an indignant letter of complaint to Elizabeth.[37]

After the murder of Riccio, Moray was able to return to Mary's favour and when the Queen drew up her list of jewellery bequests that summer she indicated that 'Madame de Mora' was to have a set of jewels made up of gold paternoster beads filled with perfume and a fur with an enamelled gold head set with rubies and diamonds, while the Countess's baby daughter would receive several items including an emerald necklace. The daughter must have been Agnes's first child, and would be significantly named Elizabeth.[38] On the morning of Lord Darnley's murder in February 1567, Moray hastily withdrew from Edinburgh, making the excuse that he must visit his wife, who had just suffered a miscarriage. This may have been true, although his anxiety for her coincided rather neatly with his desire to distance himself from the events he almost certainly knew were to take place that night at Kirk o' Field.[39] Leaving Agnes behind in Scotland to deal once more with all his private business as his officially appointed commissioner and procurator, he travelled that spring to France and then on to England.[40] In August, after the abdication of Mary, Queen of Scots, he returned to Scotland. He saw Mary at Lochleven on 15 August, and a week later, to her great indignation, he was proclaimed Regent for her small son James VI.

It is a pity that we have so few details of Agnes's years as Lady Regent, which is what contemporaries called her, for this was very much a vice-regal position and Mary's bitter resentment of Moray's new role would have extended to include his wife. Agnes's short-lived second daughter, Annabel, was probably born during that time and, apart from supervising her family and her own household, the Lady Regent would have taken a leading role in all state ceremonial. No doubt with such public appearances in mind, in the autumn of 1567 she ordered from Alexander Clerk the tailor a gown bordered with lizard skin and another of figured velvet trimmed with sables.[41] It may well be that a later inventory refers to clothing she had worn during her husband's regency. Reposing in the great coffer at Dunottar in 1575, these garments are so grand that they must have been worn on state occasions. The seven gowns, for instance, are 'long tailed', in other words, had long trains, usually a sign of royal status. One of them was made of cloth of gold and others, in velvet, were crimson, purple and black, the colours usually favoured by royalty. There were elaborate skirts of satin and figured velvet, trimmed with silver and gold, some slashed to show the brightly coloured petticoats underneath, and the pairs of fashionable, detachable sleeves were also slashed and elaborately trimmed.[42]

Agnes's time as Lady Regent was, however, to be brief, for her husband was assassinated on 23 January 1570, shot as he rode through the streets of Linlithgow. Elizabeth I reportedly wept when she heard the news, saying that she had lost one of her best friends, but Mary, Queen of Scots rejoiced, all her former fondness for her half-brother long since dissolved by her conviction that he had deliberately set out to take her crown for himself. Indeed, she even declared that she would pay a pension to his assassin, James Hamilton of Bothwellhaugh.[43] On 14 February John Knox conducted Moray's funeral in front of a large congregation in St Giles', Edinburgh, where he had married Moray and Agnes just eight years earlier. The Reformers disapproved of fancy funerals and burials inside churches, but Moray was such an important figure that he was interred in a vault beneath St Anthony's Aisle.[44] On 20 February, Agnes commissioned two masons, Murdoch Walker and John Ryotell, to build a handsome stone tomb with an inscribed brass plate above her husband's burial place and then, seven months pregnant, she travelled north to her father's castle at Dunottar.[45] In early April, she gave birth there to a third daughter, Margaret. Her mother-in-law, after whom the baby was named, sent a letter to congratulate her, but they must both have been bitterly disappointed that the child was not a son.[46]

In his testament, dated at St Andrews on 2 April 1567, Moray had made Agnes his principal executor and, 'as long as she remains widow undeflowered', guardian of their eldest daughter Elizabeth, who by his death would become Countess of Moray in her own right. Should Agnes marry again or take up with another man, then his mother, Margaret Erskine, was to be guardian instead.[47] Agnes had already set about paying her husband's debts, a task which gave her much trouble.[48] An undated inventory of her jewels preserved among the papers of her early widowhood reveals something of her attempts to assemble money to pay off the debts. William Duncan in Dundee lent her 600 merks and was given for surety 'the belt chain which my lord himself gave me', along with another gold belt and an enamelled 'garnishing of gold'. Alexander Stewart of Kelso took in pledge a belt and a gold chain, the parson of Duffus lent the Countess 200 merks and in return was holding an enamelled gold neck chain of hers while James Keith lent her 500 merks, receiving as surety 'my principal tablet set with diamonds'.[49]

It was probably in this same context that the inventory of Agnes's long-tailed gowns and her fancy skirts was made, not that they were pawned, but because her garments were impounded by her husband's creditors. Her situation was further complicated when Mary, Queen of Scots from her captivity demanded the return of the jewels she had left behind when she fled to England. These had fallen into the Regent Moray's hands and she had been enraged to learn that by this time he had sold the famous pearls to Elizabeth I. Convinced that his widow must have the rest, Mary insisted that they should be handed over at once, but Agnes strongly denied having any in her possession, and repeated her denial when the Regent Lennox tried to claim them for James VI.[50]

Evidently foreseeing further trouble, Agnes urged Elizabeth I to ask that 'the Queen of Scotland should at all times hereafter accept Agnes and her children into her favour and be to them in all times coming their protector, so that they could peacefully enjoy their inheritance, untroubled by any legal actions'. Many people at that time still imagined that Mary would be restored and so this was a sensible enough precaution, but it seems unlikely that Elizabeth ever passed on this request. Even so, Agnes once again turned to Elizabeth when in 1573 she became involved in a dispute with the Regent Morton about property belonging to her children. 'I will submit me in all things to the will and determination of . . . the Queen's Majesty of England,' she instructed her agent to tell the English ambassador, 'for I am assured her highness will not suffer the posterity of [him] that was her servant [to] be utterly wrecked, but will be their maintainer and defender in all their just actions and affairs.'[51] For her part, when Mary drew up an unfinished testament in February 1577 she stated categorically that Moray's daughters could not inherit his title and that the earldom should revert to the Crown. This did not happen. Agnes's eldest daughter Elizabeth continued as Countess of Moray, and when in 1580 she married James Stewart, the eldest son of Sir James Stewart, Commendator of Inchcolm, he was given the title of Earl of Moray in her right.[52]

Devoted as she had been to her husband, Agnes did not remain a widow. Early in 1572 she became the wife of a childless widower, Sir Colin Campbell, Lord of Lorne, half-brother and heir to the 5th Earl of Argyll.[53] He must have been her own choice, for widows were generally free to marry whom they pleased and a woman of her strong character was certainly not going to be pushed into a union she did not want. Her first husband and the 5th Earl of Argyll had been close friends and Agnes and Colin had very likely known each other for years. For his part, he knew that he would soon succeed the ailing Earl, but he had no children to follow him and so he needed to marry again.[54] The following autumn Colin inherited the Argyll titles and estates,[55] and Agnes styled herself 'Countess of Argyll and Moray'. Apart from occasional visits to the Moray castle of Darnaway and her family home at Dunottar Castle, she now spent most of her time at her second husband's houses in Dunoon and Stirling and in the lodgings they rented in Edinburgh. They had three children, Archibald, born in 1575, Colin and Agnes.[56]

A determined and meticulous organiser, Agnes ran the Moray estates for her young daughter as well as her own household and her surviving correspondence gives ample evidence of her capability. One of her hectoring letters to Alexander Stewart, the Darnaway chamberlain, met with the blunt response, 'Your ladyship sees the small mote in my eye and oversees [overlooks] the great animal in other men's eyes',[57] but she was generally treated with the greatest deference. Her eldest brother, William, Master of Marischal, wrote to her affectionately as 'Dearest and best beloved sister', but her other siblings and her daughters were more circumspect and used the accepted forms of the time, addressing her politely as 'Madame', signing themselves 'Your Ladyship's most loving and humble sister', 'Your Ladyship's most humble and obedient daughter at command' and so forth. Her eldest, Elizabeth, always sent her letters 'To my most special lady and mother, my Lady Countess of Argyll and Moray'.

The Earl of Argyll died on 10 September 1584 at Darnaway and, four years later, Agnes fell ill at her Edinburgh lodging. Despite the attentions of Thomas Dickson the apothecary, Gilbert Primrose, surgeon and Mr John Craig, doctor of medicine, she died on 16 July 1588. Her testament lists her eighteen servants and two chamberlains, and gives the value of her estate as £11,314:6:8, with £1968:6:8 owed in debts.[58] She was buried in Edinburgh, in St Giles' Church, beside her first husband, the Regent Moray.[59] In 1850, at the request of his descendants, the vault was opened to see if his remains could be located, for many burials had been disturbed during the early nineteenth-century restoration of what was now the Cathedral and his handsome stone monument had been destroyed, only the brass plate engraved by James Gray the goldsmith remaining. Three lead coffins were found in the vault, one on top of the other. The upper two were of a later date and there was no sign of the Regent's coffin, but the lowest of the three contained the body of a middle-aged woman. She had been embalmed, and her body was in a good state of preservation, the red hair still intact. It seems likely that these were the remains of Agnes, Countess of Argyll and Moray. The coffin was carefully replaced and a small plaque was put on the wall above, recording her burial there.[60]

Any preconceptions we may have about the deep divide between Roman Catholics and Protestants in post-Reformation Scotland are challenged by the fact that women like Jean, Countess of Argyll, Annabella, Countess of Mar and Agnes, Countess of Moray were able to enjoy the Queen's favour and have amicable relationships with her. The 1560s were, of course, a period of transition. The change in the country's official religion was very new and many of the Protestants Mary met were recent converts, who had been brought up as Catholics. It is sometimes inferred from the Queen's acceptance of Protestant friends, relatives and attendants that she simply did not care about religion, but that was not so. It was more that she was a realist. Whether or not she envisaged the eventual re-conversion of her realm, she knew that if she were going to rule over Scotland she would have to deal with a large number of people who had left the Roman Catholic Church and her natural friendliness probably made it easier for her to interact with Protestants and Catholics alike.

Notes

1. *Inventaires*, p. xlii, n.1
2. *Scots Peerage*, i, 25
3. Dawson, *Politics of Religion*, 19–20
4. *Treasurer Accounts*, vii, 120, 477
5. *Ibid.*, vii, 148, 156, 187–8, 319; NAS, Exchequer Accounts, E34/23
6. Dawson, *Politics of Religion*, 19–20
7. *Ibid.*, 27
8. Knox, *History*, ii, 71–4; Ridley, *Knox*, 424; McCrie, *Knox*, 196–7
9. Keith, *History*, iii, 266–7
10. *Inventaires*, 99–104, 107, 108, 113; Peter D. Anderson, 'James V, mistresses and children of (act.c.1529–1592)', *Oxford Dictionary of National Biography*, Oxford University Press, 2004 [http://www.oxforddnb.com/view/article/69935, accessed 20 December 2004]
11. *CSP Foreign, 1566–82*, 142; Lynch, 'Queen Mary's Triumph', 1–21; Dawson, *Politics of Religion*, 31

12. Dawson, *Politics of Religion*, 28–9
13. *Treasurer Accounts*, xii, 87
14. Dawson, *Politics of Religion*, 31–2
15. *CSP Scot.*, iii, 314
16. *Clan Campbell Letters, 1559–1583*, 164
17. *CSP Scot.*, iv, 500–1, 583, 593; NAS, Mar and Kellie Muniments, GD124/5/152; Dawson, *Politics of Religion*, 33
18. Dawson, *Politics of Religion*, 33–4
19. *Scots Peerage*, i, 343
20. *Ibid.*, i, 25
21. *Ibid.*, v, 613–5. This title was previously held by Moray.
22. *Inventaires*, 105, 106, 108
23. *Scots Peerage*, vi, 615–6
24. *Lettres*, ed. Labanoff, v, 56
25. *Scots Peerage*, v, 615; Carleton Williams, *Anne of Denmark*, 52–71
26. *Scots Peerage*, i, 369–70
27. Moray Muniments, Box 15/1a, Bundle 1/96
28. *Ibid.*, Box 15/1a, Bundle 2/295
29. *Scots Peerage*, i, 269
30. Mark Loughlin, 'Stewart, James, first earl of Moray (1531/2–1570)', *Oxford Dictionary of National Biography*, Oxford University Press, 2004 [http://www.oxforddnb.com/view/article/26479, accessed 18 November 2004]
31. Archives of the Ministry of Foreign Affairs, Paris, Angl. Reg., xv, ff.112–14
32. *CSP Scot.*, i, 563
33. *Diurnal of Occurrents*, 70; Knox, *History*, ii, 313–5; Lee, *James Stewart, Earl of Moray*, 98
34. Portraits by Hans Eworth, in a private Scottish collection
35. *Registrum Honoris de Morton*, 9
36. *Ibid.*, 14–15
37. *Lettres*, ed. Labanoff, i, 317–20, 326–9
38. *Inventaires*, 100, 104–5, 108
39. Fraser, *Mary, Queen of Scots*, 296; Loughlin, *op. cit.*, 7
40. Fraser, *Sutherland Book*, i, 113
41. Moray Muniments, Box 15/1b, Bundle 1/7
42. Moray Muniments, Box 15/1b, Bundle 4/569
43. *Lettres*, ed. Labanoff, iii, 346–56
44. *CSP Scot.*, iii, 83–4
45. Lees, *St Giles', Edinburgh*, 381–2

46. *Registrum Honoris de Morton*, i, 45; Moray Muniments, Box 15/1a, Bundle 352
47. *Registrum Honoris de Morton*, i, 17
48. Moray Muniments, Box 15/1a, Bundle 1/47
49. *Ibid.*, Box 15/1a, Bundle 1/10
50. *Treasurer Accounts*, xii, 229; Moray Muniments, Bundle 2/248
51. *Ibid.*, Box 15/1a, Bundle 1/96, 98–102
52. *Lettres*, ed. Labanoff, iv, 361; *Inventaires*, p. xxxix, n.3
53. Moray Muniments, Box 15/1a, Bundle 3/344; *Scots Peerage*, i, 345
54. Moray Muniments Box 15/1a, Bundle 4/508
55. *Genealogical Deduction, Rose of Kilravock*, 264
56. *Scots Peerage*, i, 345
57. Moray Muniments, Box 15/1b, no. 1095
58. *Letters to the Argyll Family*, 79–87
59. *Lees, St Giles', Edinburgh*, 370
60. Laing, 'Notes', *Proceedings of the Society of Antiquaries*, i, 191

7

Aunt and Mother-in-Law:
The Countess of Lennox

One of the most significant female relationships Mary, Queen of Scots had was with Margaret Douglas, Countess of Lennox, her aunt who was also to become her second mother-in-law. The Countess lived in England for most of her life and is known in that context as Henry VIII's niece, and as an inveterate schemer who was constantly plotting the restoration of Roman Catholicism in England after the Reformation. Her links with Mary are sometimes overlooked. The two never seem to have met but, according to Mary herself, it was the Countess who influenced one of the most fateful decisions of her life, her choice of Lord Darnley as her second husband.

The Countess's background was complicated and her childhood disturbed. Her mother was Margaret Tudor, the volatile and impetuous daughter of Henry VII of England. In 1503, when she was still a child, the Princess became the bride of James IV of Scotland, a man almost twice her age. He was killed at the Battle of Flodden ten years later, leaving her as Regent for their young son, James V. However, with what was regarded as indecent haste, she soon afterwards met and married the young and personable Archibald Douglas, 6th Earl of Angus and the Scottish nobles promptly informed her that by taking another husband she had forfeited the regency. This precipitated a political crisis and, after a bitter power struggle, she decided to flee south to her brother Henry VIII. To her chagrin, her husband refused to cross the border with her, so she left him behind and rode into Northumberland.[1] She was heavily pregnant with his child, and as she passed near Harbottle Castle her labour pains began. Her alarmed escort took her to the castle where, after a difficult confinement, she gave birth to a daughter whom she called after herself. She then continued her journey with the baby and when they arrived in London little Margaret was placed in the royal nurseries at Greenwich Palace with her cousin Princess Mary (the future Mary I), Henry VIII's daughter. [2]

Henry VIII had been none too pleased by his sister's sudden arrival, for he wanted her in Scotland, where she was supposed to further his policies, and so in 1517 he insisted that she go back north. This she did, taking her daughter with her, and was reunited with her husband. However, during one of their frequent, violent quarrels, Angus snatched the little girl from her arms and carried her off. Over the next few years he took her to France, England and then back to Scotland again. Infuriated by the discovery that he had a long-term mistress, Queen Margaret managed to divorce him in 1527 and he left Scotland because he was facing a charge of treason. His twelve-year-old daughter went with him, but his peripatetic existence was no life for a child and eventually it was arranged that she should stay permanently in Princess Mary's household at Beaulieu.[3]

From that time onwards, Margaret was a favourite of the English royal family. Henry VIII treated her indulgently, sending gifts of ermine-trimmed gowns, black velvet hoods and lengths of dress material 'for the use of our dearest niece, the Lady Margaret Douglas', while Princess Mary became her close friend. Margaret had her own retinue, and over the years she became lady-in-waiting to Henry VIII's rapidly changing succession of wives.[4] During this period Henry considered various possible husbands for her, but monarchs were never eager to see close relatives marry and have heirs who might compete for their throne and so no husband was found for her. Margaret was, however, attractive, accomplished, and flirtatious. A Holbein miniature now believed to be of her shows a self-possessed young woman with a bejewelled outfit and a beguiling, sidelong gaze.[5] When she became secretly engaged to Anne Boleyn's uncle, Thomas Howard, Henry was furious and imprisoned her in the Tower. When she had an affair with Katherine

Howard's brother Charles, her uncle angrily placed her under house arrest, first at Syon and then in Norfolk, where Thomas Cromwell, the King's chief minister, reproved her for 'over much lightness', warning her to 'beware the third time'.[6]

Most young women of Margaret's status could have expected to marry at twelve or thirteen but it was not until she was twenty-seven that Henry VIII let her take a husband. It was by now the summer of 1543, the Scots had repudiated the marriage arranged between his son, Prince Edward, and Mary, Queen of Scots, and the Regent Arran, whom Henry had thought to be on his side, seemed to have gone over to the French. Henry needed to find a new Scottish ally and he decided to cultivate Arran's greatest rival, Matthew Stewart, 4th Earl of Lennox. The Hamiltons and the Stewarts of Lennox had been hereditary enemies for several gener-ations. As descendants of James II of Scotland, they both had a claim to the Scottish throne. Handsome and sophisticated, Lennox had been brought up by an uncle in France but he had been lured back to Scotland with promises that Mary of Guise might marry him. When these proved to be illusory, he turned to England, demanding the hand of Henry's niece as the price of his support.[7]

Henry was doubtful at first. It was all very well to enlist Lennox as an ally, but did he really want to welcome him into the English royal family? He suspected that Lennox was playing a double game, was actually still loyal to France, and so he temporised, insisting that the couple meet in person before any contract between them could be arranged. When Lennox eventually decided that there was nothing left in Scotland for him and fled south, he was allowed to meet Margaret and they unexpectedly fell in love with each other.[8] Their wedding took place at St James's Palace, London, on 6 July 1544, in the presence of Henry VIII and the entire Court. Princess Mary marked the occasion by giving the bride a selection of valuable gems including a gold brooch set with a large sapphire and other enamelled jewels depicting stories from the Bible.[9] Lennox became a naturalised Englishman and Henry VIII, in an expansive mood, not only settled on the couple properties in London and Yorkshire, but reputedly told Margaret that if his own children were to die, he 'should be right glad if heirs of her body succeeded to the Crown'.[10]

He also promised to make Lennox Lord Governor of Scotland instead of Arran, and so Lennox spent the first months of his marriage leading north a series of unsuccessful naval expeditions aimed at dislodging his rival. The Scots retaliated on 1 October 1545 by having him forfeited for treason.[11] Hardly had the Earl and Countess recovered from this not unexpected blow when, the following month, their first-born son Henry, Lord Darnley died in infancy.[12] Margaret was pregnant again, however, and on 7 December 1545 she gave birth to another boy, a second Henry, Lord Darnley. This baby survived.[13]

Even so, the family's troubles continued, as Henry VIII's reign drew to a close. He cut Margaret out of his will because of her refusal to break with the Roman Catholic Church, as he had done, and his death in early 1547 was another blow, because he was succeeded by his earnestly Protestant son, Edward VI. Margaret, a devout Roman Catholic, knew that she was no longer welcome at Court and so she and her husband retired to Temple Newsam, their home near Leeds. In the months that followed, the house became a centre for Roman Catholic plotting in England.[14] One of Margaret's few visits to London during those years came when her sister-in-law, Mary of Guise, visited the city briefly on her way back to Scotland from France in November 1551. Margaret escorted her to Westminster to meet the King and sat next to her at a state banquet on 4 November.[15] Did the two women speak proudly about their young children, Mary of Guise's daughter Mary, Queen of Scots and Margaret's son Lord Darnley? Perhaps, but Margaret almost certainly took the opportunity of complaining about her father's decision to bequeath his titles and estates not to her but to his younger brother, Sir George Douglas.[16]

In the summer of 1553, Edward VI died of tuberculosis, and Princess Mary succeeded to the throne. Margaret and her family immediately hurried to Court and the Queen welcomed them gladly, assigning to them luxuriously furnished apartments in the Palace of Westminster, making Lennox Master of the Hawks and showering them with gifts. There were two cloth-of-gold gowns for Margaret, along with a gold belt set with rubies and diamonds and a large, pointed diamond, probably for a ring. Lennox was given Edward VI's best horse and young Lord Darnley, who was musical, received not only three suits of clothing but Edward's lutes. Most gratifying of all, Mary announced that Roman Catholic Margaret should have precedence over her own younger half-sister, Protestant Elizabeth. Roman Catholics regarded Elizabeth as illegitimate, for they did not recognise her father's marriage to her mother, Anne Boleyn.

When Mary I married Philip II of Spain at Winchester Cathedral in July 1554, Margaret was one of the two ladies-in-waiting who carried her train,[17] not in the least dismayed by what could have been a severe setback to her own hopes. After all, if Queen Mary had children, Margaret and her son would be displaced from their position in the line of succession. Margaret knew, however, that Mary was almost too old for childbearing and in such poor health that conception seemed unlikely. Her marriage therefore posed little threat and Margaret continued to plan for the day when her son would, through her, inherit the throne of England. His glittering future seemed assured and in 1555, when he was nine, his proud parents commissioned the leading artist Hans Eworth to paint his portrait. The resulting picture shows a boy with short, fair hair and an innocent expression, clad in fashionable black doublet, hose and cloak.[18]

Not only did his mother want to show off his handsome appearance. She also made sure that he received an education suitable for a future king. He studied Latin with his tutor John Elder, a learned and ambitious canon from Caithness, and learned to write in an amazingly regular italic hand. Like his parents, he spoke Scots, English and French and, along with his academic studies, he was taught to play the lute and to sing and dance. He grew gratifyingly tall and strong, became a splendid horseman and loved hunting and hawking. Margaret had high hopes that Mary I would actually nominate him as her successor and her ambitions did not end there. Persistent rumours claimed that the Countess of Lennox's heart was set on marrying him to Mary, Queen of Scots, in this way uniting Scotland and England after Mary I's death.[19]

In 1556, when she was forty-one, Margaret gave birth to her youngest son, Charles, but of all her eight children only he and Darnley would survive early childhood. The following year she was mortified when her father the Earl of Angus died, leaving his titles and estates not to her but to his nephew, David, son of his dead brother Sir George Douglas. In spite of this, she defiantly began signing her letters 'Margaret Lennox and Angus'. In 1558, another of her dreams seemed to dissolve when Mary, Queen of Scots was finally married to the Dauphin. Worse still, Mary I failed to name Darnley as her heir, and when she died in November 1558 she was succeeded by Elizabeth I after all.[20] Margaret began telling everyone that she herself was the rightful queen and Elizabeth retaliated by trying to have it proved that, as the child of divorced parents, Margaret was illegitimate. Margaret retorted that she had been born in England and so she could not be ruled out as an alien, like that other candidate for the crown, Mary, Queen of Scots.[21]

Despite these unedifying exchanges, Margaret set out to win Elizabeth's favour while at the same time doing everything she could to keep in touch with Mary, Queen of Scots. Indeed, she moved from Temple Newsam to Settrington House, one of the other Lennox properties, which was only a few miles from Bridlington Bay. Merchant ships regularly sailed from there to trade with Dieppe, and travellers could be bribed to carry messages to the French Court. Shortly after her father's death, Margaret sent Lord Darnley's tutor, John Elder, to France to see Mary, Queen of Scots. This move was probably inspired by Margaret's desire to wrest the earldom of Angus from her cousin and see Lennox restored to his Scottish estates.[22] Mary allowed Elder an audience with her, but if he did pass on these requests, neither of them was granted.

Never one to give up, Margaret tried again when Henri II died in 1559. This time she sent thirteen-year-old Lord Darnley himself to the French Court, in the strictest secrecy and accompanied by Elder. He was to congratulate Mary on her husband's accession to the French throne and deliver a letter from Lennox, asking to be restored to his Scottish estates. Mary rejected this petition, but to soften the blow, she invited Darnley to attend François II's coronation and gave him 1000 crowns. Disappointing though this response was, Margaret was still thinking ahead and she had hugely ambitious ideas. In February 1560 she confided to the Bishop of Aquila that, should Mary, Queen of Scots die without sons, she herself and Lennox would be put on the Scottish throne by the French. Lennox, whom a contemporary described as being 'wholly governed by his wife', was apparently happy to go along with her plans, but the impetus was entirely hers.[23]

That autumn, everything changed with the death of François II. Suddenly, Mary, Queen of Scots was available. Margaret immediately sent Darnley to her niece with her condolences and when she knew that Mary was leaving France, she threw herself into a determined campaign. Mary later told Elizabeth I in a memorandum that, from the moment she arrived in Scotland, the Countess of Lennox urged her to marry Lord Darnley. Before that, she said, she had never given a thought to him or indeed to the Countess, for there were other far greater candidates for her hand, which was true.[24] In another, undated memorandum, Mary said that the Countess plied her with messages, letters and tokens urging her to marry Darnley and was never done pointing out that he was of the royal blood of both England and Scotland, was (in her opinion) the heir to Mary's throne, bore the popular name of Stewart, was of the same religion as Mary herself and would always treat her with respect.[25]

Casting caution aside, Margaret was now telling people openly that Darnley would marry Mary, and saying that they would not only rule Scotland together but would replace Elizabeth on the throne of England. These were treasonable words and, since the Lennox household was a nest of spies, both English and French, they soon reached Elizabeth's ears. She summoned the family to London. Lord Darnley managed to escape to France but his father was imprisoned in the Tower and his mother and two of her younger children were sent to live in the custody of Sir Richard and Lady Sackville at Sheen. Margaret was accused of saying that she was the rightful heir to the English throne, engaging in the 'secret compassing of marriage betwixt the Scottish Queen and her son', carrying on illicit correspondence with foreigners, especially French and Spanish, and courting the favour of Mary, Queen of Scots. She and her husband denied everything and they were eventually released in February 1563.[26] Darnley, who had presumably been staying with his father's relatives at Aubigny, returned to London,[27] where his parents defiantly commissioned an impressive full-length portrait of him with his little brother Charles by his side.[28]

Somehow or other, Margaret had managed to ingratiate herself with Elizabeth I once more and in July 1563 an observer, noting this, added, 'My Lord Darnley, their son and heir, is also a daily waiter [at Court] and playeth very often at the lute before the Queen, wherein it should seem she taketh pleasure, as indeed he plays very well'.[29] All three accompanied Elizabeth on her summer progress that year and the Queen was even persuaded to give Lennox permission to travel to Scotland in pursuit of the restoration of his estates. However, her Scottish correspondents warned Elizabeth that while he was there he would undoubtedly try to marry Darnley to Mary, Queen of Scots and so she cancelled his journey.

No doubt as a result of his wife's urgings, the Earl was finally allowed to travel north, making an impressive entrance into Edinburgh on 22 September 1564, after an absence of nearly twenty years. Sumptuously attired, he rode down to the Palace of Holyroodhouse with twelve velvet-clad horsemen in front of him and thirty attendants in grey livery behind him. Mary, Queen of Scots received him graciously and he presented her with letters from Elizabeth I urging his restoration.[30] Mary was reluctant to comply. She feared that his return would stir up trouble among her lords in general and the Hamiltons in particular but, in an effort to please Elizabeth, she gave him back his earldom on 16 October 1564, and arranged a public reconciliation between him and the Duke of Châtelherault.[31]

Meanwhile, in London, Margaret's plans were making equally good progress. Elizabeth really seemed to have taken to Lord Darnley and in October 1564 he carried the sword of state in front

1. *Mary of Guise* attributed to Corneille de Lyon (Scottish National Portrait Gallery)

2. *Antoinette de Bourbon, Duchess of Guise* by Léonard Limosin (Musée Condé, Chantilly © Photo RMN – © Gérard Blot)

3. *Catherine de Medici* by Corneille de Lyon (Château de Versailles ©
Photo RMN – © Daniel Arnaudet)

4. *Anne d'Este, Duchess of Guise* by an artist of the French School
(Musée Condé, Chantilly © Photo RMN – © Rights Reserved)

5. *Guillemette de Sarrebruche, Duchess of Bouillon* by Jean Clouet (Musée Condé, Chantilly © Photo RMN – © Harry Bréjart)

6. *Lady Agnes Keith, Countess of Moray* by Hans Eworth (In a private collection)

7. *Lady Margaret Douglas, Countess of Lennox* (The Royal Collection © 2006 HM Queen Elizabeth II)

8. *Lady Jane Gordon, Countess of Bothwell* by an unknown artist (Scottish National Portrait Gallery)

9. *Elizabeth Talbot, Countess of Shrewsbury* (Bess of Hardwick) by an unknown artist (National Portrait Gallery, London)

10. *Elizabeth I of England* in about 1588, attributed to George Gower
(National Portrait Gallery, London)

11. Monument to Elizabeth and Barbara Curle, St Andrew's Church, Antwerp (© IRPA-KIK, Brussels)

of her at the ceremony when her favourite Lord Robert Dudley became Earl of Leicester. When Elizabeth teasingly asked the Scottish ambassador, Sir James Melville, what he thought of the new Earl, he made a diplomatically evasive reply, but she persisted. 'Yet you like better of yonder long lad,' she remarked archly, pointing at Darnley. Melville knew she was hinting that the boy might make a suitable husband for his own Queen, and he replied tartly that 'no woman of spirit would make choice of such a man that was more like a woman than a man, for he was very lusty, beardless and lady-faced'. Perhaps there was already gossip that he was bisexual.[32]

Sir James might not have been impressed with Darnley, but he later described Margaret as 'a very wise and discreet matron'[33] and when he returned to Scotland he agreed to carry with him a selection of gifts with which she hoped to bribe influential figures. Mary, Queen of Scots herself was to have a fine diamond ring, a clock, a richly ornamented mirror and 'a marvellous fair and rich jewel'.[34] It has been suggested that this may have been the famous Lennox Jewel, the heart set with a large sapphire and enamelled with a variety of intricate symbols and inscriptions whose meaning would have been clear to the recipient but many of which remain mysterious for us today. The notion that the jewel was a present for Mary is an enticing one, but is not really very likely. A heart jewel of that kind was invariably a gift between lovers or husband and wife. The enamelled decoration, of course, complicates matters. Much of the symbolism is religious, some of the inscriptions appear to relate to now unclear political ambitions, but the lover's knot and two clasped hands on the back of the winged heart, with the inscription 'Death shall dissolve', are surely tokens of affection.[35] Margaret and her husband are always said to have been deeply in love and his letters to 'My sweet Meg' or 'My good Meg' are unusually affectionate for the time.[36]

Whatever the explanation of the Lennox Jewel, Margaret continued her campaign of trying to convince Mary that Darnley was the only man for her and she finally managed to extract permission from Elizabeth I to allow him to travel to Scotland, ostensibly to join his father for a period of three months.[37] On 10 February 1565 he crossed the border and on 17 February he and Mary met for the third time. Sir James Melville, who was there, remembered afterwards that she 'took well with him and said that he was the lustiest and best-proportioned long man that she had seen'.[38] Well instructed by his mother, Darnley went out of his way to please her, and Mary soon convinced herself that he was the solution to the problem of whom she should marry. Were she to take him as her husband, Elizabeth I would approve, she felt sure. Darnley had accomplished his mission, and when his three months were over, he refused to return south.

By this time, Elizabeth's advisers had convinced her of the danger of allowing the marriage of two people who both had claims to her throne. When her peremptory orders to Darnley and his father to come back at once were ignored, she instructed the Countess of Lennox to remain in her chamber at Whitehall and in June transferred her to the Tower. According to the Spanish ambassador, Da Silva, there was much public resentment of her imprisonment, for she was held in high esteem and even Protestants were strongly attached to her. From her all too familiar prison, Margaret sent an avalanche of letters to William Cecil and the other leading English statesmen begging for her release. Mary, Queen of Scots joined in, writing to Elizabeth with the same request, but to no avail. The Countess remained incarcerated in the Tower and the Lennox estates in England were confiscated. When an official inventory of their goods at Temple Newsam was made, an ornate canopy for a bed was found, significantly bearing the arms of England.[39]

Prisoner or not, Margaret must have been overjoyed when word came that, despite all Elizabeth I's remonstrations, Mary, Queen of Scots had married Lord Darnley in a Roman Catholic ceremony on 29 July 1565, in her private chapel at Holyroodhouse.[40] Among those present was the bridegroom's proud father. The following day, Darnley was proclaimed King of Scots. Elizabeth I was not the only person to be annoyed by these events. The Earl of Moray disliked Darnley intensely, and Mary heard rumours that he was plotting to kidnap him and his father and send them forcibly back to England. She summoned Moray to appear before her and when he ignored her commands, she raised an army and rode out against him, Darnley at her side, splendid in a suit of gilded armour.

Taking a circuitous route, Moray and his friends managed to elude her and finally slipped over the border into England. What came to be known as the Chaseabout Raid had been frustrating, but Mary and Darnley were enjoying an all too brief honeymoon period and by the end of the year there was further exciting news for Margaret. On 19 December 1565, her husband was able to send her a letter telling her, 'My Meg, we have to give God most hearty thanks for that the King our son continues in good health and liking, and the Queen great with child, God save them all, for the which we have great cause to rejoice more. Yet of my part, I must confess I want and find a lack of my chiefest comfort, which is you . . .'[41]

The following February, Mary was concerned to learn that 'my mother-in-law' was ill and in great pain,[42] but despite all pleas on the prisoner's behalf, Elizabeth I remained unforgiving. As a result, the Countess languished in the Tower throughout Mary's marital problems, when Darnley, immature and jealous, allowed himself to be used by his wife's enemies against her, when David Riccio was murdered in her presence, when Prince James was born and finally when Darnley perished at Kirk o' Field. William Cecil's wife Mildred and Lady William Howard broke the dreadful news to Margaret. They unwittingly compounded her distress by telling her that Lennox had been murdered too. So great was her shock that Dr Huick, the royal physician, had to be summoned, along with the Dean of Westminster. A few hours later Cecil hurried to the Tower to assure her that Lennox could not have been killed, for he had been in Glasgow all the time. While her husband remained in Scotland, urging Mary, Queen of Scots to prosecute Bothwell for Darnley's murder, Margaret was allowed to move to less strict imprisonment at Sheen.[43]

Despite Mary, Queen of Scots' assurances to her father-in-law that those responsible for the murder of Darnley would receive 'condign punishment', Bothwell, the man generally assumed to be guilty, was acquitted and on 19 April 1567, Lennox left Scotland

and hurried south to join his wife. Nicholas Throckmorton visited them on 1 July and told Cecil, 'My Lady wept bitterly and My Lord sighed deeply. Surely Her Majesty must have some commiseration of them, if only for her own service'. Grudgingly, Elizabeth granted them the dilapidated royal palace of Coldharbour, but although she eventually allowed them to draw the revenues from their Yorkshire estates, she remained deeply suspicious of them and kept their properties in her own hands.[44] Inconsolable, the Earl and Countess in January of the following year commissioned the large painting now in the Royal Collection attributed to Lieven de Vogeleer and known as *The Memorial of Lord Darnley*. One of its many Latin inscriptions explains that they ordered the work to be done because they were now advanced in years (he was forty-nine, she fifty) and if they died before their grandson James VI grew up, they wanted him to have a constant reminder of 'the barbarous murder of the late King, his father, till it should please God to permit him to avenge it'.

The painting shows them in what must be the royal chapel at Holyroodhouse. Darnley's lifelike effigy in gilded armour lies upon his tomb, to the right of an altar, and in the foreground kneel the infant King, the Earl and Countess of Lennox and their younger son, Charles. A small vignette in the lower left corner shows Mary, Queen of Scots surrendering at Carberry Hill to her lords, who bear a banner depicting Darnley's corpse, with the words 'Judge and revenge my cause, O Lord'. Further calls for vengeance appear on scrolls emerging from the mouths of the family. 'Hear, O Lord and avenge the innocent blood of the King my Father, and defend me, I beseech thee, with thy right hand,' cries the infant James VI, a plea echoed by his grandparents and his uncle. In addition, a lengthy inscription hung on the chapel wall specifically implicates Mary, Queen of Scots. Referring to Darnley, it says, '. . . he was cut off, O hard fate! Inhumanly murdered, Queen Mary, his wife, also conspiring his death'. A paper pinned to the wall describes Henry, late King of Scotland as having been barbarously murdered with his trusty servant, by Bothwell and his confederates, 'the Queen his wife also being privy and consenting to it, which Queen, soon after the murder of her most loving and faithful husband, married the said Bothwell'. These lines naming Mary have been obliterated in the Royal Collection painting, but they can still be read in another version in a private collection.[45]

There were many in Scotland who would have agreed heartily with the sentiments expressed, and on 13 May of that same year, Mary, Queen of Scots was defeated at the Battle of Langside. Three days later, she fled across the Solway into England. When they heard the news, the Earl and Countess of Lennox hurried to Court and threw themselves on their knees before Elizabeth I, begging for justice. The Countess's face was 'all swelled and stained with tears' and her cries were so vociferous and her weeping so prolonged that Elizabeth lost patience and sent the agitated couple away.[46] News of this audience filtered through to Mary, Queen of Scots, who wrote an indignant letter to Elizabeth, complaining that the Countess had been allowed to see her whereas she herself had been denied access. All Lady Lennox's accusations against her were false, Mary said, and she offered to tell her so in Elizabeth's presence. Needless to say, she received no reply to this suggestion.[47]

Time passed, Mary remained in captivity, and Margaret worked hard yet again to reinstate herself in Elizabeth's favour. The murder of the Regent Moray early in 1570 sent her into a panic about the safety of James VI and, terrified that Elizabeth might decide to release Mary, she plied Cecil with letters insisting that her guilty daughter-in-law must remain a prisoner in England. That summer there was talk of Lennox arranging to bring his grandson south, to be raised there. Mary, Queen of Scots heard the rumours, and wrote at once to the Countess. She had no desire to see her son fall into the hands of Elizabeth I, and indeed she harboured the ambition over the years that he should be sent to Spain, to be brought up as a Roman Catholic. She and her mother-in-law had not communicated for some years, not since the murder of Darnley, but she was desperate to find out more about what was being planned.

Beginning her letter in tones of reproachful indignation, she blamed her enemies for stirring the Countess up 'against my innocency' and declared that Margaret had not only 'condemned me wrongfully but so hated me, as some words and open deeds has testified to all the world a manifest misliking in you against your own blood'. Had it not been for this, she said, 'I would not have omitted thus long my duty in writing to you, excusing me of these untrue reports made of me'. Nevertheless, she hoped in time to make her innocence known. She then referred to the plan to move James into England. 'I would be glad to have your advice therein, as in all other things tending him,' she said.[48] Margaret's response was to write to Cecil on 8 September 1570, condemning Mary as 'the only means' of the murder of Darnley.[49]

Margaret then urged Elizabeth to persuade the Scottish lords to appoint Lennox to the regency in Moray's place. It is a measure of her influence that Elizabeth agreed. Lennox duly travelled north, but Margaret was ordered to stay at the English Court as a guarantee of his good faith. Safely installed in his new position, he sent all his official letters to Elizabeth through his wife, telling her, 'I cannot well commit the handling of those matters, being of such weight, to any other than yourself, neither am I assured if other messengers should be so well liked of, nor if the personages with whom you have to deal would be so plain and frank with others as they will be with you'.[50] They never saw one another again. On 4 September 1571, he was assassinated, shot in the back during a skirmish at Stirling. He managed to ride into the castle, exclaiming, 'If the babe [James VI] be well, all is well', but he died shortly afterwards, telling those present to 'remember my love to my wife Meg, whom I beseech God to comfort'. He was buried in the castle's Chapel Royal, and when word reached London four days later, Elizabeth I herself seems to have broken the news to the Countess.[51]

For the second time, Lady Lennox's life was shattered by a terrible tragedy, but on 4 October she was able to write to the new Scottish Regent, the Earl of Mar, speaking of her mournful widowhood and her concern for her little grandson, and in November Elizabeth thanked Mar for his kindness to 'our right dear cousin, the Lady Margaret, Countess of Lennox'.[52] That same month, saying she had recently awakened herself from her grief, Margaret asked

Cecil to take her sole surviving son, Charles, into his household, for 'he is somewhat unfurnished of qualities needful, and I now a lone woman am less able to have him well reformed at home than before'. Cecil made the excuse that he already had about twenty young noblemen being educated in his house, and instead he appointed a Protestant tutor for Charles, no doubt suspecting that the boy would have reported to his mother everything that was going on in the Cecil household.[53]

During her years of widowhood, Margaret effected a truly surprising rapprochement with Mary, Queen of Scots, the woman she was convinced had murdered her elder boy. Quite how their reconciliation came about is not clear but it must have been the result of messages carried between them by trusted emissaries. She excused herself to Mary for having believed the worst by claiming that other people had deliberately convinced her of Mary's guilt, but could she really have accepted Mary's determined protestations of innocence after all that had gone before, or was Margaret yet again engaged in the duplicitous plotting for which she was famous? Whatever lay behind their sudden friendship, Elizabeth was, not unnaturally, alarmed when she heard about it. When the Countess in August 1573 asked permission to go north to her house at Settrington in Yorkshire, Elizabeth immediately sprang to the conclusion that she would try to see Mary on the way. She warned Margaret not to go near Chatsworth, where Mary was being held, saying that if she did, people would think that she was plotting with the Queen of Scots.

Reporting this conversation, Margaret alleged that she answered robustly, asking Elizabeth 'if she could think so, for I was made of flesh and blood, and could never forget the murder of my child', to which the Queen replied, 'Nay, by her faith she could not think that ever I could forget it, for if I would I were a devil'.[54] In the end, Mary, Queen of Scots and Margaret did not meet. However, there was further trouble for Margaret when she did make the journey north the following year, taking her son Charles with her. He met and fell in love with the Countess of Shrewsbury's daughter, Elizabeth Cavendish. Their mothers arranged their marriage and

Elizabeth I was furious when she heard that they had gone ahead without her permission. Charles was too close to the throne to be allowed to marry anyone of his own choice.

Elizabeth summoned the two Countesses to Court and sent them both to the Tower of London. A prisoner once more, Margaret seems to have felt a sense of shared adversity with Mary, Queen of Scots, not only sending her a series of friendly letters but working a little square of lace with fine thread and some of her own white hairs. A few months later, Margaret was released, but concern for their 'peerless jewel' James VI strengthened her bond with Mary and their correspondence continued, Margaret signing herself 'Your Majesty's most humble and loving mother and aunt'.[55] Her son Charles and his wife Elizabeth Cavendish had a daughter in the autumn of 1575, whom they named Arabella. Mary, Queen of Scots was, of course, the baby's aunt by marriage, and she sent her a gift which the Countess acknowledged in a letter of 10 November 1575, thanking her 'for your good remembrance and bounty to our little daughter'.[56] Charles died of tuberculosis the following year, and his earldom passed to a male relative. Her last child gone, Margaret concentrated her ambitions on little Arabella and renewed her efforts to claim her own father's estates. She enlisted Mary's help, and when Mary drew up her unfinished will in 1577, she restored to 'My Aunt Lennox' her right to the earldom of Angus.[57] Later that year, Mary expressed strong satisfaction that the Countess was now not only opposed to James VI being brought to England but had come to realise the perfidy of the Regent Morton, her own longstanding enemy.[58]

Margaret was by then living permanently at Hackney, and from there she sent James gifts of hawking gloves and books, mostly about history and current affairs. She had for some time been suffering from 'the colic', which might have been a digestive problem or even heart trouble and she died suddenly on the evening of 9 March 1578. Amidst inevitable rumours of poisoning, she was buried in Henry VII's chapel in Westminster Abbey at Elizabeth I's expense.[59] Writing on 2 May to James Beaton, Archbishop of Glasgow, Mary, Queen of Scots told him that

'Madame the Countess of Lennox, my mother-in-law' was dead. 'This good lady was, thank God, very well disposed to me these five or six years past when we corresponded with each other,' she said, 'and she admitted in letters written in her own hand, which I have kept, the wrong she had done me.' Margaret had said she now realised that her accusations against Mary had been based on wrong information and she disavowed the legal actions that were being taken in her name. Mary was perfectly ready to blame Elizabeth I and her Privy Council for having misled the Countess deliberately.[60]

When Mary's belongings were seized at Chartley in 1586, among them was the little lace square 'worked by the old Countess of Lennox when she was in the Tower' and an ivory miniature of her.[61] The fact that she had kept those tokens seems to indicate that, on Mary's part at least, there was some genuine warmth towards her aunt in spite of all that had gone before. Whether or not that arch-plotter the Countess of Lennox was merely counterfeiting friendship towards the woman she regarded as her son's murderer is a matter for speculation. In pursuit of her dynastic ambitions she seemed able to set aside the memory of repeated incarceration in the Tower by her Tudor relatives and time and again she cultivated Elizabeth I, who had been such a source of grief to her old friend, Mary I. She was therefore perfectly capable of pretending to feel fond of Mary, Queen of Scots in case Mary should ever be restored to her throne. If she did, however, genuinely come to believe in Mary's innocence, then that says much about what really happened at Kirk o' Field on the night of 9 February 1567.

Notes

1. Strickland, *Queens of Scotland*, i, 2–8, 15, 26–40; Macdougall, *James IV*, 113–14, 263–76; Marshall, *Scottish Queens*, 85–9; Buchanan, *Margaret Tudor*, 12–13, 54–7; Perry, *Sisters to the King*, 10–11, 15, 21–2
2. *LPFD, Henry VIII*, ii, part 1, 271, 273–4, 277; Strickland, *Queens of Scotland*, i, 110–36; Marshall, *Scottish Queens*, 90–2

3. Fraser, *Douglas Book*, ii, 289

4. Schutte, *Countess of Lennox*, 25–38

5. In the Collection of HM Queen Elizabeth II at Windsor Castle. See James, 'Two miniatures re-identified'

6. Fraser, *The Lennox*, i, 427

7. Fraser, *Douglas Book*, ii, 263; *State Papers, Sadler*, i, 227; *Historie, Pitscottie*, ii, 16–18; Fraser, *The Lennox*, i, 364–7; Schutte, *Countess of Lennox*, 79–96; Martienssen, *Queen Katherine Parr*, 160

8. Schutte, *Countess of Lennox*, 79–96; Martienssen, *Queen Katherine Parr*, 160

9. Madden, *Privy Purse Expenses*, 172, 175

10. Strickland, *Queens of Scotland*, ii, 320

11. Marcus Merriman, 'Stewart, Matthew, thirteenth or fourth earl of Lennox (1516–1571)', *Oxford Dictionary of National Biography*, Oxford University Press, 2004 [http://www.oxforddnb.com/view/article/26497, accessed 7 March 2005]

12. Strickland, *Queens of Scotland*, ii, 293

13. Schutte, *Countess of Lennox*, 107; Bingham, *Darnley*, 38

14. Schutte, *Countess of Lennox*, 111, 135; Bingham, *Darnley*, 46–7

15. *Journal of King Edward's Reign*, 50–2; Schutte, *Countess of Lennox*, 117–18; Fraser, *The Lennox*, i, 428

16. Fraser, *Douglas Book*, ii, 281, 291, 323–5

17. Bingham, *Darnley*, 55–6; Fraser, *The Lennox*, i, 428; Schutte, *Countess of Lennox*, 130; Ridley, *Elizabeth I*, 54

18. Scottish National Portrait Gallery, PG2471

19. Bingham, *Darnley*, 60–1; Elder, *Copie of a Letter*, unpaginated

20. Bingham, *Darnley*, 62–3

21. Schutte, *Countess of Lennox*, 124–8

22. Fraser, *The Lennox*, i, 433; Schutte, *Countess of Lennox*, 138

23. Strickland, *Queens of Scotland*, ii, 336, 363, 369; Fraser, *The Lennox*, i, 469; Fraser, *Mary, Queen of Scots*, 118; Schutte, *Countess of Lennox*, 156; Bingham, *Darnley*, 71–2

24. *Lettres*, ed. Labanoff, iv, 33

25. *Ibid.*, i, 297

26. Schutte, *Countess of Lennox*, 161–2

27. Bingham, *Darnley*, 76–8

28. In Collection of HM Queen Elizabeth II at the Palace of Holyroodhouse

29. Schutte, *Countess of Lennox*, 182

30. *Ibid.*, 182–4

31. *Lettres*, ed. Labanoff, i, 232–6, 242–3; *The Lennox*, i, 393
32. Melville, *Memoirs*, 35
33. *Ibid.*, 40
34. Schutte, *Countess of Lennox*, 185–6; Guy, *My Heart is my Own*, 198–9, 529
35. *The Art of Jewellery in Scotland*, 17 (with colour illustrations); Tait, 'Historiated Tudor Jewellery', 226–45; Hackenbroth, *Renaissance Jewellery*, 291–3; Scarisbrick, *Tudor and Jacobean Jewellery*, 84; Scarisbrick, *Jewellery in Britain, 1066–1837*, 29, 105
36. Haynes, *Burghley State Papers*, 443; Fraser, *The Lennox*, ii, 448
37. Elizabeth's motives are more fully discussed in Chapter 12
38. Melville, *Memoirs*, 45
39. Crossley, 'A Temple Newsam inventory', 91–100
40. *Lettres*, ed. Labanoff, vii, 51; Schutte, *Countess of Lennox*, 195–6
41. Haynes, *Burghley State Papers*, 443
42. *Lettres*, ed. Labanoff, i, 313
43. Fraser, *The Lennox*, i, 447; Schutte, *Countess of Lennox*, 207–8
44. Fraser, *The Lennox*, i, 448
45. Vertue, 'Observations on a Picture', 103–27; Millar, *Tudor, Stuart and early Georgian Pictures*, 75–7
46. Strickland, *Queens of Scotland*, ii, 423
47. *Lettres*, ed. Labanoff, ii, 102–3, 106
48. Fraser, *The Lennox*, i, 448–9
49. *Ibid.*, i, 449
50. *Ibid.*, i, 448
51. *Ibid.*, i, 416, 448–9, 453
52. *Ibid.*, i, 453
53. Schutte, *Countess of Lennox*, 222–3
54. Fraser, *The Lennox*, i, 455–6
55. Durant, *Bess of Hardwick*, 90; Lovell, *Bess of Hardwick*, 242–4
56. *CSP Scot.*, 1574–80, 202
57. *Lettres*, ed. Labanoff, iv, 360
58. *Ibid.*, iv, 397–8
59. Fraser, *The Lennox*, i, 466
60. *Lettres*, ed. Labanoff, v, 31
61. *Ibid.*, vii, 243

8

The Countess of Bothwell and Lady Douglas

The Countess of Lennox was a powerful influence in the life of Mary, Queen of Scots and the fact that the two were eventually reconciled after the murder of Lord Darnley is endlessly intriguing. It also gives rise to speculation about the attitude and reactions of that other woman who played a significant role in Mary's marital career, Lady Jane Gordon, first wife of the Earl of Bothwell. Born in 1545, three years after the Queen, Jane was the daughter of Mary's most powerful Roman Catholic subject, George Gordon, 4th Earl of Huntly. He owned vast tracts of territory in Aberdeenshire, Banffshire and Angus and he was extremely wealthy. In 1530 he married Lady Elizabeth Keith, daughter of William, 3rd Earl Marischal, and they made their principal residence at Strathbogie Castle in Aberdeenshire. It was there that they brought up their nine sons and three daughters.[1]

Perhaps in response to this ever-growing family, Huntly rebuilt the castle during Jane's childhood and furnished it with all the latest luxuries. There were gilt leather hangings and tapestries on the walls, beds with silk and velvet curtains, chairs with velvet cushions and tables with velvet covers. When he received visitors, Huntly sat in his hall beneath a quasi-regal crimson satin cloth of state embroidered with gold. After all, he was a grandson of James IV and he had royal blood in his veins even though his mother had been the King's illegitimate daughter. His wife was equally proud of her status and on at least one recorded occasion, appeared before the Queen accompanied by a large retinue. A strong and forceful woman, the Countess was rumoured to consult witches during time of crisis.[2]

When Mary, Queen of Scots returned to her native country, Huntly, her first cousin, expected to be her principal adviser. He also expected her to restore Roman Catholicism to Scotland and, so it was said, was prepared to raise an army in that cause. Mary, of course, had other ideas, preferring to pursue her policy of religious toleration and relying instead on Lord James Stewart and William Maitland of Lethington for advice. To add to Huntly's simmering resentment, in 1562 Mary bestowed the earldoms of Mar and Moray on her half-brother, Lord James. She kept this secret at first because she knew that Huntly had been administering those territories and would bitterly resent Lord James being given a power base in his own part of the country. Inevitably, rumours began to fly about and matters went from bad to worse when one of Huntly's sons, Sir John Gordon, was not only imprisoned for attacking another man in the centre of Edinburgh but was suspected of plotting to abduct the Queen with a view to marrying her either himself or to one of his relatives.[3]

Sir John somehow managed to escape and made for his father's lands. Hearing the news, Mary decided that the time had come to show her Protestant subjects that she was willing to punish even her most powerful Catholic supporters if they broke the law. She and Lord James marched north with the royal army. When they reached Aberdeen, Lady Huntly arrived to plead for her son's life. It was on that occasion that she was attended by an impressive retinue, and it has been suggested that her youngest daughter was very likely to have been with her, in which case it was the first meeting between Jane and Mary, Queen of Scots, the Earl of Bothwell's two successive wives.[4] Vociferous though the Countess was, she did not succeed in making the Queen change her mind and Mary told her that Sir John must hand himself over before his situation could be discussed. She then made public her gift to Lord James of the two earldoms, and ordered Huntly himself to surrender. Lady Huntly promptly requested a second audience, but Mary refused to see her, whereupon the Countess went home and urged her husband to march against the Queen, which he did.[5]

The two armies met at Corrichie, where Huntly's force was

defeated. He and two of his sons, the fugitive Sir John and seventeen-year-old Adam, were captured. On the point of being led before the Queen, Huntly, who was grossly obese, suffered a catastrophic stroke or heart attack and fell from his horse, dead. Three days later, Sir John was executed. Mary watched until she collapsed in tears and had to be carried away. Huntly's embalmed body was taken to Edinburgh and there he was tried for treason in the Queen's presence, his coffin placed upright so that it looked as though he were standing before his judges. His corpse was condemned, attainted and forfeited.[6] Afterwards, Mary allowed his family to take the body back for burial in Elgin Cathedral. The Duke of Châtelherault then pleaded for the life of Huntly's heir, Lord George Gordon, who was married to his daughter Anne, and Mary spared the young man's life and that of his brother, the teenage Adam.

She did not intend the Gordons to languish in disgrace forever, and by 1565 the Dowager Countess of Huntly along with the George's wife and Jane were all at Court and on surprisingly good terms with the Queen.[7] How these women reconciled themselves to the brutal events of 1562 is difficult to imagine. Of course, in a hierarchical society people were expected to obey their monarch, no matter how exalted they thought themselves, and 'Old Lady Huntly' (the Dowager Countess) and her female relatives seem to have been willing to submit in the hope that the family titles and estates would eventually be restored. At a more personal level, it can only be supposed that Mary put aside the recollection of the Countess's pugnacious advice to her husband and exercised her famous sympathy and charm to help ease their feelings of shock and grief.

However it came about, Old Lady Huntly, George's wife Young Lady Huntly and Lady Jane were frequently at Mary's side in the mid-1560s. It is often said that they were ladies-in-waiting. This is not certain, because they do not appear on the list of people dining as members of the royal household. It could be that they were officially in attendance but had their own domestic arrangements, or it may simply have been that they were there as courtiers, often in the Queen's company because she knew them and was showing the rest of the Court that she did not hold a grudge against the Gordons. At any rate, all three ladies were intended recipients of Mary's jewellery bequests in 1566, a sure sign of favour. Anne, indeed, was the only Hamilton on the list. Jane was to have a head-dress set with rubies, pearls and garnets.[8]

Old Lady Huntly was now energetic in her efforts on the Queen's behalf. On the night of David Riccio's murder she was the only woman allowed to stay with Mary, who was held prisoner in Holyroodhouse in danger of her life. The following day Lady Huntly offered to smuggle in a rope ladder so that the Queen could escape through a window. Mary, who was five months pregnant, declined, but Lady Huntly went on suggesting other schemes until Lord Lindsay finally sent her away. Not to be deflected, she then managed to smuggle a letter to her eldest son, ordering him to wait at Seton the following night to be there to receive Mary when she escaped. After that, we have no further evidence of her relationship with Mary, Queen of Scots, nor do we know her date of death.[9]

Mary had restored George to the title of Earl of Huntly in 1565, although he was not given back his lands. Like his close friend James, 4th Earl of Bothwell, he had become a Protestant. The women of the family remained staunchly Roman Catholic[10] but in 1566 the Queen arranged for Jane's marriage to a Protestant. Privately, Jane had fallen in love with Alexander Ogilvy, Laird of Boyne in Banffshire, whom she had probably known from child-hood, but Mary had someone else in mind for her. Bothwell, the Queen's loyal supporter, was in financial difficulties and needed a wealthy wife. If Jane and her mother were reluctant, and they may well have been, it was no doubt pointed out to them that Jane's marriage to the Earl would be a further step towards her family's complete rehabilitation.

Since Jane's great-aunt, Margaret Gordon, had married Patrick, 1st Earl of Bothwell, there was a delay while a papal dispensation was acquired, but in the meanwhile the marriage contract was drawn up 'with advice and express counsel of our sovereign lady,

Mary, Queen of Scotland', and she was the first to sign the document.[11] The wedding took place on 24 February 1566. At Bothwell's insistence, it was a Protestant ceremony, conducted by Jane's uncle, Alexander Gordon, Bishop of Galloway. The bride wore a wedding dress of cloth-of-silver lined with taffeta, the material having been provided by the Queen, who gave a lavish banquet after the ceremony, followed by five days of tournaments and jousting.[12] A pair of oil on copper miniatures, only one and a half inches in diameter, painted that same year by an unknown artist, shows Bothwell in a yellow doublet, with dark hair, a drooping moustache and a distinctly wary expression while Jane looks calmly from her little portrait, her hair drawn back under her French hood, her long, oval face framed by the high, frilled edge of her fashionable chemise.[13] Her disappointed suitor, Alexander Ogilvy, became the husband of Mary Beaton of the Four Maries two months later, this match also arranged by the Queen.[14]

Mary was not acting in a particularly insensitive fashion when she made these marriages. Status and property were what mattered to aristocratic families, and it was hoped that affection would grow between the married couple as the months went by. What is interesting is that Bothwell was able to insist on a Protestant ceremony even though most of his future in-laws were Catholic and the Queen had expressed the wish that this should be a Catholic wedding. Perhaps we overestimate the strength of religious feeling in sixteenth-century people. Not everyone was as fervently devoted to their particular form of worship as Antoinette de Bourbon or John Knox and, then as now, for many, worldly motives were paramount. Probably most of those present at Jane's marriage took a cynical view, believing the match to be perfectly appropriate in that, regardless of how the ceremony was conducted, it brought the groom the money he needed and the bride the title of Countess.

Bothwell gave almost all Jane's dowry of £8000 Scots to his creditors so that he could redeem the lands of Crichton, surety for some of his many debts. These were now to form Jane's jointure. The couple settled at Crichton Castle and in June 1566 Bothwell gave his wife the life-rent of the lands and house of

Nether Hailes. According to the later evidence of one of their servants, he and she lived 'friendly and quietly together, like a man and wife as the saying is', but she must have known that he was a notorious womaniser and his ambition, combined with Queen Mary's unhappiness in her marriage to Darnley, would have dramatic consequences for them all.[15]

By the following year, Bothwell had decided to discard his wife. He was not by any means the first married Scottish nobleman to declare his willingness to abandon wife and children in order to marry a queen. Indeed, more than twenty years earlier Bothwell's own father, Patrick, the 3rd Earl, had been rumoured to be about to divorce his wife so that he could marry Mary of Guise.[16] In the aftermath of Darnley's murder, people began to say that Mary, Queen of Scots and Bothwell were lovers and had conspired together to kill her husband. Ignoring these accusations, Mary seems to have turned to Bothwell as a strong protector who would lend masculine authority to her decisions while he, seeing his chance, was determined to be her next consort. He proposed to her, not once but several times after Darnley's death, and when she refused him, he persuaded a group of leading men to sign the so-called Ainslie Bond, declaring him to be innocent of the murder and recommending him to Mary as a husband. Eight bishops, ten earls and eleven lords signed.

Even so, Mary hesitated, for she knew very well that marriage to the principal suspect would seem like an admission of her own guilt. However, towards the end of April, matters were seemingly taken out of her hands when he intercepted her as she rode back to Edinburgh from visiting her son in Stirling, took her to Dunbar Castle and, according to Sir James Melville who was with her entourage, he raped her. Most historians think that the alleged abduction could only have taken place with her collusion but whether she realised that he actually intended to have intercourse with her is open to doubt. She said afterwards, 'Albeit we found his doings rude, yet were his answer and words but gentle'. After that, she had to marry him and did, in a Protestant ceremony at Holyroodhouse.[17]

None of the nobles who urged Mary, Queen of Scots to marry Bothwell appears to have given any thought to his wife and, reading the contemporary accounts, it almost seems as though she was completely irrelevant to what was going on. Similarly, we have no indication of Mary's attitude towards Jane at this point. It could be that she was selfishly indifferent to Jane's feelings in the matter. That would have been uncharacteristic, but at this time of crisis her customary sympathy for the women she knew may have been swept aside by other considerations. Would she have broken up a Roman Catholic marriage without a thought? Perhaps not, but on the other hand Jane was her subject, and subjects were expected to give way to the needs of the monarch. Whatever Mary's attitude, any pangs of conscience she and others might have felt would have been eased if they knew that Jane was indifferent to her husband or actively unhappy as his wife. She had, after all, been in love with someone else, and she may have been only too glad to be rid of Bothwell.

Whatever her motivation, Mary, Queen of Scots, having arranged the marriage in the first place, was now involved in ending it. If either of the couple was going to sue for divorce, it had to be Jane, for it was Bothwell who was the adulterer. He had no grounds for suing her. On 26 April 1567, two days after Bothwell's alleged abduction of the Queen, Jane raised an action for divorce in Edinburgh's Protestant Commissary Court on the grounds of his alleged adultery with Bessie Crawford, one of her serving maids. Even the most indignant of wives would hardly have gone to law so swiftly unless she had been forewarned of what was about to happen. The likelihood is that she and the Queen and Bothwell agreed on their course of action during the foregoing weeks. The Regent Moray and his friends would later claim that it was Jane's brother, the Earl of Huntly, who persuaded her to sue for divorce. He was now high in the Queen's favour. She had made him Chancellor of Scotland the previous year, parliament had newly given him back his lands and on the very same day, 19 April 1567, Huntly and his friends signed the bond urging Mary to marry Bothwell.[18] But why did Jane seek a Protestant rather than a Roman Catholic divorce?

The answer lies in the marriage laws of the time. The Roman Catholic Church recognised only one ground for divorce and that was adultery. Jane could have sued Bothwell in the Roman Catholic Commissary Court on the pretext of his adultery with Bessie Crawford, but even had she been successful, she would only have been granted a divorce *a mens et thoro* (of bed and board). This meant that she and Bothwell would have been allowed to live apart, but the legal ties of their marriage would not have been dissolved. Bothwell would have forfeited his wife's dowry but neither he nor Jane would have been free to marry again. Because of the less than complete severance offered by divorce, a decree of nullity was the preferred path to freedom sought by people wanting to rid themselves of a partner in order to remarry and such a decree was relatively easy to obtain. Since so many men and women in a small country like Scotland were distantly related to each other, it was simple enough to argue that bride and groom were within the forbidden degrees but had only newly realised it because the relationship was remote. Jane knew, however, that she could hardly seek a decree of nullity, when she and Bothwell had obtained the necessary dispensation allowing them to marry.[19]

Bothwell himself did not care what stood in his way. The Queen, however, was apparently determined to do everything possible to convince everyone that he was free to marry her and so, in pursuit of this plan, she persuaded him to seek to have his marriage annulled in Archbishop Hamilton's recently restored Roman Catholic Commissary Court. Jane was cited to appear on 5 May before the judges, in St Giles' Church, Edinburgh, where the case was being heard. She did not come in person, but the lawyer acting for her presented himself on 6 May and on the following day Bothwell was granted his annulment on the grounds of consanguinity.[20] Jane and Bothwell must have agreed to suppress the original dispensation and indeed so must the Queen, for she would almost certainly have known of its existence.[21] Mary and Bothwell were then married on 15 May 1567 and she dispatched the Bishop of Dunblane to the French Court with the news, telling him that if anyone questioned the legality of the ceremony he was to explain that the bridegroom's previous marriage had been annulled because the couple had been within the forbidden degrees. Elizabeth I was to be given the same information.[22]

Jane is said to have had some correspondence from Bothwell soon after his second wedding, protesting that he was still fond of her, but if any such letters existed, they have vanished.[23] Not so the famous dispensation. In the nineteenth century it was found by the historian John Stuart among the Sutherland Archives at Dunrobin Castle, where Jane later lived.[24] Considering how many of the papers of the time have vanished, and how many people wished the vital dispensation to be suppressed, how did it come to survive? The answer can only be that Jane preserved it as evidence that her marriage to Bothwell had been perfectly valid. Did this mean that she had been reluctant to end it?

Apparently not. In the summer of 1567, when Bothwell was still in Scotland, she left Crichton Castle to travel north to her childhood home at Strathbogie. Passing through Edinburgh on the way, she called on her cousin Agnes Keith, Countess of Moray and, according to Elizabeth I's envoy Sir Nicholas Throckmorton, 'She hath protested to the Lady of Moray in this town that she will never live with the Earl Bothwell nor take him for her husband'.[25] Now Agnes must have known that her own husband and his friends, determined to discredit Mary's marriage to Bothwell, were saying that his divorce had been illegal. Was Agnes warning her cousin that this might happen, that in changed circumstances he might even try to make Jane come and live with him again? Was Jane's protest wrung from her because she had come to hate him? We know nothing about the rest of their conversation, so it is impossible to say, but that could have been why Jane was so anxious to keep the dispensation hidden. Why, then, did she not destroy it altogether? That would have been safer, but John Stuart reached the conclusion that she preserved it carefully because, as proof that she was still married to Bothwell, it allowed her to draw her jointure revenues, which indeed she did until her death long years afterwards. Considering that her dowry had paid for the retrieval of the jointure lands from Bothwell's creditors in the first place, the money was doubly hers.[26]

The main players in Jane's marriage soon became disenchanted with the Earl of Bothwell. Mary herself was said to have been in floods of tears soon after her wedding, regretting the Protestant ceremony, hating her husband's brusque behaviour. They parted at Carberry Hill when she surrendered to the Protestant lords and he rode off to look for help, and by 1569, Mary, now a prisoner in England, had decided to divorce him. She wanted to start an action in Scotland before John Hamilton, Archbishop of St Andrews or any other competent judge on the grounds that her marriage to him had been illegal. Stating the following year that she had asked the advice of 'the greatest clerks, best learned and expert doctors in divine and human laws as we could have in divers countries', she went on to say that they had informed her that her 'pretended marriage' with Bothwell was in no way lawful because, among other reasons, 'he was before contracted to another wife and he not lawfully divorced from her'.[27]

Jane's brother, the 5th Earl of Huntly, once Bothwell's close friend, declined to give him any help when he arrived at Strathbogie as a fugitive, allegedly remarking later that he hoped Bothwell's attempts to raise an army would fail, 'so that the Queen and his sister might be rid of so wicked a husband'. Huntly was not only with Mary at Hamilton when she escaped from Lochleven but after her defeat at Langside he continued to act as her lieutenant in the north of Scotland. Not until 1573 did he accept the authority of James VI.[28] Jane's own attitude towards Mary in all this is elusive, but it is perhaps not without significance that when she decided to marry again, her second husband was a strong supporter of the Queen.

On 13 December 1573, at the age of twenty-eight, Jane became the wife of eighteen-year-old Alexander Gordon, the Roman Catholic 12th Earl of Sutherland. Rumours from the continent suggested that Bothwell was dead, and although he actually lived for another five years, Jane must have believed them and felt free to take a new husband. They settled at Dunrobin Castle in

Sutherland, his ancestral home, and because his health was poor, Jane ran his estates with notable efficiency and placed her famous dispensation among his archives. They were married for twenty-one years and had seven children, two of whom died in infancy.[29] The Earl himself died in 1594 and five years later Jane married again. Her third husband was none other than Alexander Ogilvy of Boyne, the man she had loved thirty-five years earlier. He was a widower now and they signed their marriage contract on 10 December 1599. They were together for less than ten years, but even after his death Jane did not enjoy the luxury of retirement. Her eldest son, the 13th Earl of Sutherland, died in 1615, and she found herself running the Sutherland estates once more and bringing up her grandson, the 14th Earl.[30]

Historians at one time believed that Jane was a Protestant, like Bothwell, but now it is generally agreed that she remained a Roman Catholic throughout her life, and indeed when she had her portrait painted in widow's clothes, she was pointedly shown holding a large and noticeable rosary.[31] In her latter years she was often in trouble with the local presbytery, who accused her of harbouring Jesuit priests. Indeed, she was excommunicated by the minister of Golspie, Alexander Duff, when she was eighty-one years old. She finally died at Dunrobin on 14 May 1629 after a long illness and was buried in Dornoch Cathedral beside her second husband. She was, said her son Robert, 'a virtuous and comely lady . . . of great understanding, above the capacity of her sex'.[32] In marrying Bothwell in the first place and then in ending her marriage to him, Jane had twice set aside her own feelings in order to obey the Queen's commands and yet we have no evidence of hostility on her part towards Mary. It may simply be that her real reactions have gone unrecorded or that the evidence has been lost, but it nevertheless remains true that the Queen was able on various occasions to win over those who might have been expected to hate her.

A good example of this may be found in Mary's dealings with the women in whose custody she lived when she was imprisoned in Lochleven Castle after her surrender at Carberry Hill. She was sent there because the castle was in the hands of the Earl of Moray's widowed mother, Margaret Erskine, Lady Douglas. Margaret was the daughter of John, 5th Lord Erskine, one of the childhood guardians of Mary, Queen of Scots. In 1527 she had married Sir Robert Douglas of Lochleven, but three or four years after that she became the mistress of James V. Perhaps he had not been her only lover, for the King's friend, Sir David Lindsay of the Mount, used her as the model for Dame Sensuality in his famous play, *The Satire of the Three Estates*. However, he also told James that she was 'the lady that loved you best' and the King seems to have returned her affection.

His affairs were usually of brief duration, but his attachment to Margaret continued and in 1531 or 1532 their son, Lord James Stewart, future Earl of Moray, was born. By 1536 the King was trying to persuade the Pope to annul Margaret's marriage to Douglas so that he could marry her himself. The Pope refused, the King went on to marry Princess Madeleine and then Mary of Guise, and Lord James lost his chance of being declared legitimate and the heir to the Scottish throne.[33] Margaret, for her part, had to remain with her husband at Lochleven, bringing up their six children while Lord James was educated at St Andrews along with the King's other illegitimate sons. Sir Robert Douglas was eventually killed at the Battle of Pinkie in 1547.

James V was dead by that time and Margaret did not marry again, but ran his estate for her eldest son, William, and continued the work at Newhouse, the modern home she and her husband had been building on the shores of Lochleven.[34] Although Mary of Guise might have been expected to look askance at Margaret Erskine, a receipt of 29 January 1550 records the payment on her behalf of 300 crowns she owed Margaret. This could have been in the context of some sort of provision James V had made for his former mistress or for his illegitimate son, but at any rate Mary honoured the debt.[35]

Time passed, Mary, Queen of Scots returned, and in the early years of her personal reign, when she was on good terms with the Earl of Moray and his wife, she had a harmonious relationship with his family too. Margaret Erskine's brother, Arthur Erskine of Blackgrange, was said to be Mary's favourite equerry and it was no doubt she who arranged Arthur's marriage in 1562 to her maid of honour, Magdalene Livingston.[36] There were always rumours, of course, that Margaret was intensely jealous, believing that her own son, Moray, should have been ruling Scotland instead of Mary, but the Queen's meeting with John Knox about the Countess of Argyll's marital problems came during a stay she made at Lochleven, a place she is unlikely to have visited had she been on bad terms with its *châtelaine*.

When she was taken to Lochleven Castle as a prisoner, Mary deliberately cultivated a friendly relationship with Margaret and her household, the English ambassador Sir William Drury commenting that she had 'drawn divers to pity her who before envied her and wished her evil', the Regent's mother for one. The two women were even glimpsed strolling together in the castle garden.[37] Did Margaret perhaps reminisce about James V, the father Mary never knew? The Queen was also on friendly terms with Margaret's daughter-in-law, Agnes Leslie, wife of Sir William Douglas, despite the fact that Agnes came from a strongly Protestant family. Her father, George Leslie, was 4th Earl of Rothes. Her eldest brother Norman and her uncle John Leslie of Parkhill had taken part in the assassination of Cardinal Beaton in 1546 and her brother Andrew, 5th Earl of Rothes was another enthusiastic supporter of the Reformation. Agnes was told to sleep in the same bedchamber as Mary when the Queen arrived at the castle, in part jailor, in part attendant, and there was probably soon a sympathy between them for they were both pregnant. When Mary lost the twins she was carrying, Agnes possibly helped to nurse her.[38] In the end, it was Agnes's brother George Douglas and their cousin Willie who helped Mary to escape.

During that strange interlude, longstanding affections had somehow been resumed and new friendships made. Embarrassment, anger but perhaps some relief must have been the reaction of the women of the Douglas family when they realised that their royal prisoner had gone, but any sympathy they felt for Mary must surely have vanished when the Regent Moray was assassinated in

Linlithgow in 1570 and she reportedly rejoiced at his death. His mother, Margaret Erskine, died two years later on 5 May 1572[39] but her daughter-in-law, Agnes, Lady Douglas, lived on at Lochleven, raising five sons and seven daughters and looking after the estate when political events sent her husband into exile. Two years after his return home in 1586, he inherited the title of Earl of Morton and she became his Countess. Their marriage of over fifty years lasted until his death in 1606. She survived him, but her own date of death is unknown.[40]

Notes

1. *Scots Peerage*, iv, 536–9
2. Sanderson, *Mary Stewart's People*, 36
3. Fraser, *Mary, Queen of Scots*, 194–5; Hay Fleming, *Mary, Queen of Scots*, 307, n.35; 309, n.41, n.42
4. Sanderson, *Mary Stewart's People*, 36
5. *RPC*, i, 219–20; *CSP Foreign*, Elizabeth, v, 319, 329–30, 360–1, 386
6. Allan White, 'Gordon, George, fourth earl of Huntly (1513–1562)', *Oxford Dictionary of National Biography*, Oxford University Press, 2004 [http: // www. oxforddnb. com / view / article / 11034, accessed 16 September 2005]; *CSP Foreign*, Elizabeth, v, 399, 421–2; vi, 381; Fraser, *Mary, Queen of Scots*, 196–200; Herries, *Memoirs*, 66; *Diurnal of Occurrents*, 74–5; *APS*, ii, 573, 577
7. Fraser, *Mary, Queen of Scots*, 201–3
8. *Inventaires*, 119
9. Nau, *History*, 4; Fraser, *Mary, Queen of Scots*, 254–5
10. Sanderson, *Mary Stewart's People*, 37
11. Stuart, *Lost Chapter*, 5–6, 93–4; Hay Fleming, *Mary, Queen of Scots*, 453, n.76
12. *Inventaires*, 162; *Historie*, Pitscottie, ii, 570; Sanderson, *Mary Stewart's People*, 38
13. Scottish National Portrait Gallery, PG869 and PG870
14. See Chapter 9; Stuart, *Lost Chapter*, 6
15. Stuart, *Lost Chapter*, 5–7, 84–103; Sanderson, *Mary Stewart's People*, 38
16. *Historie*, Pitscottie, ii, 15–16
17. Melville, *Memoirs*, 64
18. Donaldson, *First Trial of Mary, Queen of Scots*, 181

19. Nau, *History*, pp. clxiii–clxvi; *CSP Foreign, Elizabeth*, viii, 198; Stuart, *Lost Chapter*, 21–3, 32; Hay Fleming, *Mary, Queen of Scots*, 453 n.73–6

20. Stuart, *Lost Chapter*, 19–20, 90–3

21. Marshall, *Virgins and Viragos*, 39

22. Donaldson, *First Trial of Mary, Queen of Scots*, 66; Stuart, *Lost Chapter*, 26–30

23. Stuart, *Lost Chapter*, 32–3

24. Sanderson, *Mary Stewart's People*, 41

25. Stuart, *Lost Chapter*, 48

26. *Ibid.*, 47

27. *Ibid.*, 41–2; Hay Fleming, *Mary, Queen of Scots*, 454; *National MSS of Scotland* (Edinburgh 1870), iii, 59

28. Fraser, *Mary, Queen of Scots*, 337; Stuart, *Lost Chapter*, 50–2

29. Fraser, *Sutherland Book*, i, 123, 127, 131, 142, 168; NLS, Adv. MS., 313/910. 1592, 1593, 197, 3323; Sanderson, *Mary Stewart's People*, 42- 51

30. Sanderson, *Mary Stewart's People*, 45–6

31. In a private Scottish Collection and reproduced as the frontispiece to Stuart, *Lost Chapter*

32. Fraser, *Sutherland Book*, i, 168

33. *Scots Peerage*, v, 609–10; Peter D. Anderson, 'James V, mistresses and children of', *Oxford Dictionary of National Biography*, Oxford University Press, 2004 [http://www.oxforddnb.com/view/article/ 69935, accessed March 2005]; Sanderson, *Mary Stewart's People*, 55–6

34. *Scots Peerage*, vi, 369

35. *Registrum Honoris de Morton*, i, 7

36. *Scots Peerage*, v, 611

37. Sanderson, *Mary Stewart's People*, 59; *CSP Foreign, Elizabeth*, viii, 349–50, 363; Donaldson, *All the Queen's Men*, 64

38. Sanderson, *Mary Stewart's People*, 56

39. *Scots Peerage*, v, 612

40. Margaret H.B. Sanderson, 'Leslie, Agnes, countess of Morton', *Oxford Dictionary of National Biography*, Oxford University Press, 2004 [http://www.oxforddnb.com/view/article/70475, accessed July 2005]

9

The Four Maries

The most famous attendants of Mary, Queen of Scots were, of course, the Four Maries, who went with her to France as children in 1548, came back with her to Scotland as young adults in 1561 and remained with her until dramatic events, marriage and, in one instance, ill health finally ended their active service with her. The notion of these small girls and their long loyalty has caught the public imagination, albeit sometimes in a confused way. People often imagine that the term 'The Four Maries' was coined for them because of a supposedly remarkable coincidence that they all had Mary as a first name. There was actually nothing unusual in that, for they were born in the 1540s when Scotland was a Roman Catholic country and it was common practice to call a daughter after the Virgin Mary. Moreover, previous Scottish queens are known to have had attendants called 'maries', a term which John Jamieson, the nineteenth-century lexicographer, linked to the Icelandic word 'maer', meaning a virgin or maid.[1]

There has also been considerable misunderstanding about the identity of the Four Maries. Ask anyone who they were and you are liable to be told, usually after some hesitation, that their names were Mary Beaton, Mary Seton, Mary Carmichael and 'some other Mary'. Quite often, the respondent will sing a line or two of the song remembered from childhood which supplies the information. This was the ballad 'Marie Hamilton', which tells an apocryphal tale of one of the maids of honour of Mary, Queen of Scots who supposedly had an affair with Lord Darnley and then drowned the resulting illegitimate child.

Arrested and tried for the murder, she went to the gallows with the words:

> Yestreen the Queen had four Maries,
> This night she'll ha'e but three,
> There was Marie Seaton and Marie Beaton,
> And Marie Carmichael and me,

the 'me', of course, being Mary Hamilton herself. It was Sir Walter Scott who originally published the ballad in his *Minstrelsy of the Scottish Border* in 1802–3. He knew that there was no such person as Mary Hamilton in the household of Mary, Queen of Scots, but he believed that the story had its origins in an incident which features in John Knox's *History of the Reformation*. Knox recounted with relish how one of the Queen's women was executed for murdering the illegitimate child she had with a royal apothecary.

Charles Kirkpatrick Sharpe, the famous antiquarian who had passed on the ballad to Scott in the first place, thought it more likely that the tale derived from events at the Court of Peter the Great. Mary Hamilton, a Scotswoman who had gone to Russia, had an affair with the Tsar and then murdered not only the baby she and Peter had but also her two other illegitimate children. She was executed on 14 March 1719. Wherever the story really came from, it became extremely popular despite the fact that, in 1905, Thomas Duncan published a scholarly article in the *Scottish Historical Review*, pointing out that the tale of infanticide had nothing whatsoever to do with the Four Maries of Mary, Queen of Scots. The tragedy had such a hold on the public mind that even today many people are convinced that it really happened and that Mary's childhood companions included a Mary Carmichael and a Mary Hamilton. In fact, the Four Maries were Mary Fleming, Mary Seton, Mary Livingston and Mary Beaton.[2]

Mary Fleming always heads the list of Maries, for she was the cousin of Mary, Queen of Scots, being the fifth daughter of Lady Fleming, the Queen's aunt and governess.[3] Mary Seton was also from an old aristocratic family. She was the only daughter of

pearl belt and a black and white enamelled gold necklace. She, Mary Seton and Mary Beaton were also to have ruby rings as keepsakes to remind them of the Queen.[11]

By that time, two of the four Maries had married, with Mary, Queen of Scots taking the traditional royal role and making all the arrangements. The first bride was Mary Livingston, who may well have had a hand in the choice of her husband, since he was not an important member of the aristocracy but a younger son. John Sempill was the second son of Robert, 3rd Lord Sempill, a conservative Roman Catholic who had been a firm supporter of Mary of Guise and was now an energetic adherent of Mary, Queen of Scots herself. Because he had been born in the south, of an English mother, John's contemporaries, including the Queen, teasingly referred to him as 'the Englishman', while John Knox called him 'the Dancer' and alleged in an unpleasant innuendo that the marriage was hurried through because the bride was pregnant. There is no evidence for this, and in fact the preparations were made in the usual way with both French and English dispatches mentioning them two months in advance. Thomas Randolph, Elizabeth I's ambassador, noted that the Scottish Queen had arranged the match, endowed the couple with land and intended to have the ceremony at Court.[12]

The Queen signed the contract on 3 March 1565, named the wedding day and gave a dowry of £500 a year in land, augmented by a further 100 merks a year and 1000 merks in cash supplied by the bride's brother, William, 6th Lord Livingston. She had already supplied one pound eight ounces of silver for Mary Livingston's wedding gown, she paid for the lavish banquet which followed the marriage ceremony three days later, on Shrove Tuesday,[13] and she gave the young couple a magnificent scarlet velvet bed fringed and bordered with embroidered black velvet, its curtains lined with scarlet taffeta.[14] Three days after the wedding, they received a grant of lands in recognition of their services.[15] Probably the following year, 'Mademoiselle de Semple', as she was now styled in the household accounts, gave birth to a son, who was named James, after the Queen's own child. Indeed, Prince James, himself still a baby, was the godfather. Young James Sempill was educated by George Buchanan along with the Prince, and in adult life would become James VI's agent in London, the King rewarding him on one occasion with 'a jewel of great beauty and value' which had belonged to Mary, Queen of Scots.[16]

After the murder of Lord Darnley, Mary Livingston's father-in-law changed sides, allied himself to the dead man's father, the Earl of Lennox, and commanded the vanguard of the army opposing the Queen at Carberry Hill. Apparently unaffected by his change of allegiance, Mary Livingston was with the Queen that day, she and Mary Seton pressing protectively close behind her as she was taken ignominiously back to Edinburgh. Lord Sempill was one of those who signed the act authorising the Queen's imprisonment at Lochleven but his son John was involved in some of the early attempts to rescue her from there.[17] Mary Livingston remained in Scotland with her husband during the Queen's long imprisonment. In 1573 she was alleged still to have in her possession some of Mary's jewels and other belongings.[18] Her husband was involved in a conspiracy to assassinate the Regent Morton in 1577 and, confessing his part in the plot, was sentenced to death. However, he was reprieved and released after a short imprisonment. He died soon afterwards, on 25 April 1579. Mary Livingston lived until 1585.[19]

The second Marie to marry was Mary Beaton, who in the spring of 1566 became the wife of Alexander Ogilvy of Boyne. This was an interesting match, because Ogilvy was the man loved by Lady Jane Gordon before she married Bothwell. It was the Queen who arranged Ogilvy's marriage to Mary Beaton, which took place two months after Bothwell's wedding.[20] Interestingly, when the Queen listed her jewellery bequests that year, she had intended bequeathing half of her Greek and Latin books to Mary Beaton.[21] Ogilvy remained a firm supporter of Mary, Queen of Scots and was captured at the Battle of Langside.[22] Like the other married Maries, Mary Beaton remained in Scotland when the Queen fled south. One writer has suggested that she might have been responsible for forging the Queen's writing in the notorious Casket Letters, produced by the Earl of Moray in an attempt to implicate Mary in Darnley's murder. Allegedly written by her, they appeared to prove that the Queen was guilty but they are known to us only as copies. The original letters have vanished so it is impossible to tell what the handwriting was like but there is no evidence at all that Mary Beaton had anything to do with them. Even if she and the Queen did have similar writing, this was hardly surprising since they both used the italic hand they had been taught in France.[23] Mary Beaton disappears from the records after 1568, and all we know is that she survived the Queen by ten years, dying in 1597. As we have seen, two years after that, her widower married the woman he had loved in his youth, Lady Jane Gordon, by now the divorced wife of James, Earl of Bothwell and the widow of Alexander, 12th Earl of Sutherland.[24]

The third and final Marie to marry was Mary Fleming. Because of their blood relationship, she had always been particularly close to Mary, Queen of Scots. A few weeks before she left France in 1561, the Queen bestowed upon her the wardship of the lands belonging to the late Henry Drummond of Riccarton, along with the marriage of his son Henry Drummond.[25] This did not imply that Mary and Drummond had any intention of marrying. It was simply a financial gift. When she was back in Scotland again, the Queen's secretary, William Maitland of Lethington, was strongly attracted to Mary Fleming and he wrote at this time that love was the 'most singular remedy for all diseases in all persons'.[26] He was not a romantic youth, however. A widower with at least one daughter, Marion Maitland, he was about eighteen years older than Mary Fleming and because of political complications it took a long courtship before their marriage was arranged.

Variously characterised as Scotland's Machiavelli and 'The Chameleon', because of his readiness to change sides, Maitland had openly converted to Protestantism in 1559 and his greatest ambition was to see Scotland and England united. As a result, he was often ambivalent about the policies of Mary, Queen of Scots, acting as one of her principal advisers during her first years back in Scotland but disapproving strongly of the Darnley marriage and involving himself in the Riccio murder. However, he and the Queen were reconciled in 1566, paving the way for his marriage to Mary

Fleming, which Mary, Queen of Scots may well have seen as a means of attaching him more firmly to herself.

Their wedding finally took place at Stirling on 6 January 1567, the bridegroom's old friend Sir William Kirkcaldy of Grange commenting wryly that the bride was as suitable to be Lethington's wife 'as I am to be Pope'.[27] During the last months of the personal reign of Mary, Queen of Scots, Maitland managed to support both her party and that of the lords who opposed her. He played a prominent part in setting up the Earl of Moray as Regent for the young James VI,[28] but either because of his long former service with the Queen or because of his wife's influence, when Mary, Queen of Scots was held prisoner at Lochleven he seemingly sent her a gold jewel with the figure of Aesop's lion trapped in a net which is being gnawed by a mouse, with the words 'He who has spirit enough will not want force' engraved on it in Italian.[29] At the same time, the Queen was in touch with his wife, telling Lady Lethington to send her a gown and various other clothes.[30]

Maitland was with the Regent Moray just before the Battle of Langside and took part with him in the first trial of Mary, Queen of Scots at York, but after that he favoured a plan for the Queen to divorce Bothwell and marry the Duke of Norfolk, something Moray opposed. From then onwards Maitland supported Mary, Queen of Scots, joining Sir William Kirkcaldy of Grange who was holding Edinburgh Castle for her. By this time, Maitland was gravely ill with a wasting disease which rendered him unable to walk. His wife, who had been bringing up their two children, James and Margaret, at Lethington Tower (now Lennoxlove) near Haddington, joined him and remained devotedly at his side. He was taken prisoner when the castle fell to Mary's enemies in 1573 and was moved to Leith where he died on 9 June, some said by his own hand. When nothing was done about burying him, Mary Fleming presented a petition to the Lords of the Congregation begging them 'that his body should not be dishonoured by maltreatment' but her plea was ignored and it was only when she wrote to William Cecil pleading that the corpse should not be propped up at his posthumous trial for treason that her request was granted.[31]

A month later, Mary Fleming was ordered by the Regent Morton to appear at Holyroodhouse and produce any jewels which had been the property of Mary, Queen of Scots.[32] When she was in Leith after the fall of Edinburgh Castle, the Laird of Grange had reportedly asked her to hand over a ruby and diamond chain belonging to the Queen, but she 'altogether refused to deliver it' and was now ordered to hand over it and any other items within six days under pain of rebellion, for they were the property of James VI.[33] Her loyalty to her royal mistress was as strong as ever and in 1581, when Mary Seton retired from her service, Mary, Queen of Scots wanted Mary Fleming to replace her, but this did not happen. Possibly Elizabeth I refused to allow it,[34] or it may have been that Mary Fleming had by this time married her second husband, George Meldrum of Fyvie, and did not want to leave her family. She is believed to have died in about 1600.[35]

Mary Seton, the only one of the Maries to remain unmarried, served Mary, Queen of Scots devotedly for thirty-five years. After the murder of Lord Darnley, when the Queen spent some days at Seton Palace recovering from the shock, Mary Seton was her bedfellow, and when the Protestant lords rebelled after the Queen's marriage to Bothwell, Mary Seton rode with her to the confrontation at Carberry Hill.[36] She stayed with her during her imprisonment at Lochleven, and played an important part in her escape. While Mary, Queen of Scots disguised herself in an old red kirtle and a shabby cloak and was rowed to safety, Mary Seton who, like the Queen, was very tall, put on one of her black gowns, pretended to be her and earned enough time for her to get away. No reprisals seem to have been taken against Mary Seton, and after the Battle of Langside and the Queen's flight south, she was able to join her at Carlisle.[37]

On 26 June 1568, Sir Francis Knollys told William Cecil that Mary, Queen of Scots had six women attendants, 'although none of reputation but Mistress Mary Seton, who is praised by this Queen [Mary] to be the finest busker, that is to say, the finest dresser of a woman's head of hair that is to be seen in any country, whereof we have seen divers experiences since her coming hither'. He added admiringly that, on the previous day, she had arranged a curled *perruque* on the Queen's head, and every other day 'she hath a new device of head-dressing, without any cost, and yet setteth forth a woman gaily well'.[38] Her attentions must have played a considerable part in raising the Queen's morale. The following March, when the Queen was in the keeping of the Earl of Shrewsbury, Mary Seton and Lady Livingston were said to be constantly sitting with her and Lady Shrewsbury, planning the needlework with which they all passed the time.[39]

In the late 1560s, Mary Seton was courted by Christopher Norton, the younger son of Sir Richard Norton of Norton Towers. He and she devised a plan for the Queen to escape, but when he took part in the Northern Rebellion with his father, uncle and six brothers in 1569, he was captured and executed.[40] The following summer, Mary Seton fell ill, causing her mother to write a letter to Mary, Queen of Scots asking anxiously about her and begging the Queen to take good care of her. She had allowed her daughter to share the Queen's hardships, she said, something she would have done for no one else and, in return, she asked only for the friendship the Queen had promised, and consideration of the long, affectionate and most humble services she and her daughter had given Mary of Guise and Mary, Queen of Scots herself.[41]

Fortunately Mary Seton recovered, and when Andrew Beaton succeeded his brother John as master of the household to Mary, Queen of Scots in 1572, he fell deeply in love with her. Andrew was a real asset to the retinue, drawing designs for the Queen's needlework, inventing amusing nicknames for the Earl of Shrewsbury's servants and ordering little gifts for Mary Seton. Another of his brothers was James Beaton, Archbishop of Glasgow, Mary, Queen of Scots' ambassador in France, and on one occasion he urged the Archbishop 'for God's sake' to see to the dispatch of a silk hanging he himself had ordered for Mary Seton, along with a watch Mary, Queen of Scots had commissioned for her.[42]

Unfortunately for him, Mary Seton viewed his advances with more dismay than enthusiasm. On 12 January 1577 Mary, Queen of Scots wrote to tell the Archbishop that, in keeping with her promise, she had spoken three times to 'our girl', who protested at great length that Andrew was not good enough for her, and reminded the Queen of the criticism levelled at Mary Livingston and her sister Magdalene when they married beneath them. Mary Seton also said a great deal about a vow of chastity she had taken. Brushing aside the vow 'upon which I place no value', the Queen reminded Mary that it was her duty to obey her good mistress, who was acting in place of her mother. Even then, 'our girl' made difficulties, in the end only agreeing with reluctance that if 'the doctors' found that the vow could be set aside, then she would accept Andrew. Delighted with this ray of hope, 'our man' set off for Paris, possibly to consult the experts at the Sorbonne, but he died of smallpox on 5 November 1577 on his way back and Mary, Queen of Scots had to write to the Archbishop of Glasgow offering her sympathy and expressing her regret that it was no longer possible for her to make this marriage alliance between his family and that of Lord Seton.

This brief correspondence is instructive. The Queen's light-hearted, ironic tone is entirely characteristic of her, and it is notice-able that Mary Seton, although her servant, felt able to offer all manner of objections to the proposed match, even accusing the Queen of too much partiality towards Andrew and making her promise to pass on her objections to the Archbishop. Mary did not scold her, as she might have done, but responded with whimsical kindness combined with determination and a realistic under-standing of how to progress the plan, her own motive being to please the Archbishop, who was not concerned with the feelings of those involved but was eager to make a marriage alliance for his brother with a very important Scottish family.[43]

There was no more talk of a marriage for Mary Seton after that. In 1581 she was speaking of retiring from the Queen's service because of poor health and she finally withdrew in September 1583. She could not return to Protestant Scotland, of course, and so she travelled to France with another of the maids of honour, possibly Marie Courcelles, and made her way to Rheims, finding shelter in the Abbey of Saint Pierre-les-Dames, where Renée de Lorraine, aunt of Mary, Queen of Scots, was abbess.[44] There she spent the rest of her days, outliving Mary, Queen of Scots by nearly thirty years. A few of her letters from that period survive, and in one of them, written on 21 October 1586, she told Monsieur de Courcelles, the French ambassador, 'It is nearly twenty years since I left Scotland and in that time it has pleased God to take the best part of my relations, friends and acquaintances, nevertheless I presume there remain still some who know me, and I shall be obliged by your remembering me to them as occasion may serve'. She then went on to say that she was 'in extreme pain and distress at the news which has reached here of a fresh trouble which has fallen on the Queen my mistress'. She had no time to elaborate, but she was referring to the discovery of the Babington Plot and this is the closest we come to learning at first hand how the surviving Maries felt about the last months of Mary, Queen of Scots.[45]

In 1602 Mary Seton, lying ill in bed in an upper chamber in the Abbey of St Pierre, made her testament. She had few resources, but she left money to endow Masses for the souls of herself and Mary, Queen of Scots, and to her two servants, bequeathing all her moveable goods to Dame Margaret Kirkcaldy, a nun in the abbey. Dame Margaret was probably the widow of Sir William Kirkcaldy of Grange. Everything arranged, Mary Seton then recovered from her illness and on 7 June that same year she revoked the will she had made.[46]

Eleven years after that, she was visited by James Maitland, the only son of Mary Fleming and William Maitland of Lethington. A Roman Catholic, he was living on the continent. Passing through Rheims, he stopped at the abbey and found 'Mistress Mary Seton' now 'decrepit and in want', living on the charity and courtesy of the abbess. He wrote a letter urging James VI to bestow some small pension upon her in recompense for her honourable and godly behaviour and her long years of service to Mary, Queen of Scots, his majesty's mother. The King's reply is not recorded.[47] On 6 April 1615 Mary Seton wrote to thank a relative in England for having helped with some business, in a postscript sending the greetings of Dame Margaret Kirkcaldy, who had by now become Abbess of Saint Pierre. That is Mary Seton's last known letter. She had asked to be buried in the abbey when she died, and we can presume that her wishes were followed.[48]

Notes

1. Jamieson, *Dictionary of the Scottish Language*
2. Duncan, 'The Queen's Maries', 362–71; *Scottish Ballad Poetry*, 318–23
3. Ruble, *Première jeunesse*, 282; *Foreign Correspondence, 1548–57*, 223
4. *Scots Peerage*, viii, 585
5. *Ibid.*, v, 437–8
6. Donaldson, *All the Queen's Men*, 60; Seton, *Family of Seton*, i, 140
7. Adhémar and Moulin, *Cabinet des Estampes*, no. 543
8. *Ibid.*, no. 110
9. Fraser, *Mary, Queen of Scots*, 188–91; *Inventaires*, 151; *CSP Scot.*, i, 683; ii, 8
10. *CSP Scot.*, i, 688
11. *Inventaires*, 116, 120; 113, 118; p.xxxi, 111, 113, 116–7, 120–1
12. Rosalind K. Marshall, 'Sempill, Robert, third Lord Sempill (c.1505–1573x6)', *Oxford Dictionary of National Biography*, Oxford University Press, 2004 [http://www.oxforddnb.com/view/article/25074, accessed 20 December 2004]; *Scots Peerage*, vii, 538–43; Duncan, 'The Queen's Maries', 370; *CSP Scot.*, i, 204; ii, 113
13. Fraser, *Mary, Queen of Scots*, 224; *Scots Peerage*, v, 437; *Treasurer Accounts*, xi, 347; Seton, *Family of Seton*, i, 31; *CSP Foreign, Elizabeth*, vii, 277
14. Seton, *Family of Seton*, i, 31
15. *RSS*, v, part i, 1953, 9 March 1565
16. Stephen Wright, 'Sempill, Sir James (1566?-1626)', *Oxford Dictionary of National Biography*, Oxford University Press, 2004 [http://www.oxforddnb.com/view/article/25073, accessed 30 December 2004]; *RPC*, vi, 533–4
17. Rosalind K. Marshall, 'Sempill, Robert, third Lord Sempill (c.1505–1573x6)', *Oxford Dictionary of National Biography*, Oxford University Press, 2004 [http://www.oxforddnb.com /view /article/25074, accessed 20 December 2004]; *Scots Peerage*, vii, 538–43; Duncan, 'The Queen's Maries', 370–1
18. *Inventaires*, p. clviii
19. *Scots Peerage*, v, 438
20. Sanderson, *Mary Stewart's People*, 38–9; Duncan, 'The Queen's Maries', 370
21. Ruble, *Première jeunesse*, 131; *Foreign Correspondence, 1548–57*, 312 and

312 n.1; Duncan, 'The Queen's Maries', 365; *Inventaires*, 117, 119, 124

22. Duncan, 'The Queen's Maries', 370; *RSS*, v, part ii, 239
23. Fraser, *Mary, Queen of Scots*, 408
24. Sanderson, *Mary Stewart's People*, 34–54
25. *RSS*, v, part i, 194
26. Public Record Office, SP52/10/21
27. *Scots Peerage*, viii, 541; *CSP Scot.*, i, 622
28. Mark Loughlin, 'Maitland, William, of Lethington (1525x30–1573), *Oxford Dictionary of National Biography*, Oxford University Press, 2004 [http://www.oxforddnb.com/view/article/17838, accessed 30 September 2004]
29. Nau, *History*, 58–9
30. *Lettres*, ed. Labanoff, ii, 64
31. Mark Loughlin, 'Maitland, William, of Lethington (1525x30–1573), *Oxford Dictionary of National Biography*, Oxford University Press, 2004 [http://www.oxforddnb.com/view/article/17838, accessed 30 September 2004]; Duncan, 'The Queen's Maries', 367
32. *Treasurer Accounts*, xii, 355
33. Thomson, *A Collection of Inventories*, 193–4; *RPC*, ii, 246; *Scots Peerage*, viii, 541; *Inventaires*, p. clvii
34 *Lettres*, ed. Labanoff, iv, 222; Seton, *Family of Seton*, i, 144
35. *Scots Peerage*, viii, 541
36. Seton, *Family of Seton*, i, 136–7
37. *Ibid.*, i, 137–8
38. *Ibid.*, i, 139
39. Durant, *Bess of Hardwick*, 63
40. Seton, *Family of Seton*, i, 139
41. *Ibid.*, i, 143–4
42. *Ibid.*, i, 140
43. *Ibid.*, i, 141–4; *Lettres*, ed. Labanoff, 341–4
44. Seton, *Family of Seton*, i, 144–5
45. *Ibid.*, i, 146
46. *Ibid.*, ii, 958–65
47. *Ibid.*, i, 149
48. *Ibid.*, i, 150

10

The Scottish Retinue

The general perception of the Court of Mary, Queen of Scots during her personal reign is that she was surrounded by empty-headed, flirtatious Frenchwomen who had come over to Scotland with her in 1561. John Knox certainly gives that impression in his *History of the Reformation*. The very sight of Mary's female retinue annoyed him and he had no hesitation in declaring that, although the Queen behaved with suitable gravity when she attended meetings of her Privy Council, 'how soon that ever her French fillocks [wanton young women], fiddlers and others of that band got the house alone, there might be seen skipping not very comely for honest women'.[1]

Nor was he slow to criticise the attendants to their faces. After one of his notorious confrontations with the Queen in 1563, he berated a group of fashionably clad women sitting in her outer chamber with the words, 'O fair ladies, how pleasing were this life of yours if it should ever abide and then in the end that we might pass to heaven with all this gay gear. But fie upon that knave Death, that will come whether we will or not!' When that happened, he said, 'the foul worms will busy with this flesh, be it never so fair and so tender', and they would be unable to take with them their gold, their trimmings, their tassels, their pearls and their precious stones.[2] Knox did not record the ladies' reaction to this unsettling harangue, but he would have been equally disapproving when he heard about them dressing up in fancy costume for various masques in the French style.[3]

How accurate was Knox's assessment of Mary's retinue? Certainly the Queen was young – only eighteen when she came back to her own kingdom – and she and her women no doubt enjoyed dancing, chatting, playing cards, riding and otherwise diverting themselves, but were the attendants really all youthful Frenchwomen? In France, the numerous ladies-in-waiting had been leading members of the aristocracy whose right it was to serve. Did this mean that Mary's Scottish retinue was similarly drawn from the wives of important Scottish lords? There is no complete and comprehensive record akin to the 1560 list of attendants in France,[4] but there are some sources of information. The household books for 1562, for instance, note the tables at which members took their meals.[5] It is not clear if these monthly lists are complete, for it is possible that some of the ladies-in-waiting might have eaten in their own homes with their own families. This is rather unlikely, however, given the public formality of meals at Court. Moreover, the number of ladies and maids of honour mentioned does suggest that all or most of them were there, apart from the occasional absentee.

Looking at the household book for July 1562, we find that there were sixteen tables, the fourth occupied by nine ladies-in-waiting. Seven of them had already been in the Queen's service. There were, of course, the Four Maries, now promoted from their previous position as maids of honour. The other three ladies were French. These were the Dame de Péguillon, Cobron and Fonterpuy, the latter also elevated from her former position as maid of honour.[6] What had motivated these young women to leave their native land and travel to a country generally regarded by the French as distant, cold and barbarous? The decision must have been fairly straightforward for the Dame de Péguillon, since her husband and son, both in the household, were going too, and her other children were grown up, with lives of their own. The other two ladies-in-waiting were young and unmarried. Personal loyalty to Mary no doubt played an important part in their decision, and they probably hoped to find suitable Scottish husbands. Long and dangerous though the voyage to Scotland was, there were constant comings and goings between the two Courts and they knew that if they were homesick or if some family crisis required their presence, they could return to France, which is what they eventually did.

The final two ladies-in-waiting were older women, the mothers of Mary Seton and Mary Beaton. Both were Frenchwomen married to Scots and both had served Mary of Guise. Mary Seton's mother, Marie Pierres, Madame de Briante, had originally come to Scotland with Mary of Guise in 1538 and it was the Queen who had arranged her wedding the following year to George, 4th Lord Seton, a widower with eight children.[7] During the ten years of their married life they had two sons, Robert and James, as well as their daughter Mary.[8] Lord Seton died on 17 July 1549 and by the end of 1554 his widow had married Pierre de Clovis, Seigneur de Briante. He was a nephew of Jacques de la Brosse, former French ambassador to Scotland and an old friend of the Guise family. By 1559 the Seigneur de Briante was seeking a position in the household of Mary, Queen of Scots but his wife's name does not appear on the lists until 1562.[9]

From then onwards, Madame de Briante features from time to time in the Lord Treasurer's accounts, that same year receiving no fewer than sixty-five ells of white and ten ells of red taffeta at the royal expense, possibly for the use of the Queen. Two years later, she was given two ells of linen to be lining for little sleeves for Mary and, in February 1565, a hat was bought for Madame de Briante herself, from a merchant named John Adamson.[10] The following year she features in the Queen's dispositions of jewellery as the intended recipient of a pair of amethyst bracelets.[11] Her loyalty was never in doubt. While she was still married to Lord Seton she had written an undated letter warning Mary of Guise of unsubstantiated rumours of a plot by the Regent Arran and the Council to seize Mary, Queen of Scots. Her husband had told her he did not think there was any real danger, and he was right.[12] Two decades on, in 1567, she was with Mary the morning after Darnley's murder, solicitously giving her a fresh egg to eat.[13] She did not join her in England but, in August 1570, the month after her husband's death, she wrote a long letter to the imprisoned Queen from Dunkeld, where she had gone to be present at a gathering of Mary's friends, she said. This letter was intercepted and she and her son Robert were imprisoned and their goods seized. However, they were set free not long afterwards.[14]

In the autumn of 1574, Madame de Briante returned to France, to sue her brother-in-law for payment of her jointure, and the Queen did her best to help. Mary wrote to her ambassador, James Beaton, Archbishop of Glasgow, about this, urging him to do all he could, and told him to ask the Cardinal of Lorraine and her other relatives to give assistance too. If Madame de Briante had to travel to Paris for her lawsuit, Mary wrote, the Cardinal should let her lodge in one of his houses, for 'she is a good and virtuous lady and former servant of the late Queen my Mother and of me, and her daughter always did me most agreeable service'. The following February she wrote another letter to Beaton on behalf of 'the good Lady of Seton'.[15] After that there is no further mention of Madame de Briante until her death in 1576.[16]

Madame de Briante must have been about thirty years older than Mary, Queen of Scots, and the final lady-in-waiting on the 1562 list, 'Madame de Cricq', was of the same generation. She was Jeanne de la Rainville, wife of Robert Beaton of Creich and mother of Mary Beaton of the Four Maries. Rainville is in Lorraine, and so it seems likely that she had connections with the Guise family. She had certainly been a member of the household of Mary of Guise and undoubtedly came to Scotland with her. References to her are fleeting, but her husband was one of those who were in the supper chamber with Mary, Queen of Scots on the night that Riccio was murdered and, had Mary died giving birth to Prince James, Jeanne would have received a bequest of a pair of cornelian bracelets and a small ruby ring.[17] She had her own servants, a man and a woman, and was still in Mary's household in 1566–7, receiving 300 livres a year.[18] Her date of death is unknown.

What, then, can we conclude about the ladies-in-waiting during the early part of Mary's personal reign? There were far fewer of them than there had been in France, a mere nine compared with the former twenty-seven, but this was not surprising in a much smaller country. They were also younger, for seven of the nine were seemingly unmarried and would have been in their late teens or early twenties, whereas at least half of the twenty-seven ladies-in-waiting in France had been over forty. Interestingly, they were also of lower status. Mary Fleming was the Queen's cousin and Mary Seton was the daughter of an important lord, but there was no one to compare with the Duchess of Montpensier or Constable Montmorency's wife. In other words, the retinue lacked any mature, high-ranking relatives or friends to give advice in awkward situations.

When she was in France, Mary had ten maids of honour, four of them Scottish and six of them French. In Scotland in 1562, the sixth table accommodated seven maids of honour and their governess. Claude de Pons, Demoiselle du Mesnil no longer occupied that position. She was probably in her sixties, if not older, and she had evidently decided to stay on in France. She had been replaced by Mademoiselle de la Souche. This lady's exact identity is uncertain. In the 1530s, Mary of Guise employed as governess of her maids of honour Renée d'Avantigny, Mademoiselle de la Touche.[19] Also in the household at that time were a carver named Urbain de la Touche and a maid of honour called Françoise de la Touche, both of whom had been recommended by the Cardinal of Lorraine.[20] Renée's husband died in September 1548, deeply in debt as a result of being a prisoner in England. Home again in France, she wrote to Mary of Guise begging for money and for a position in the household of Mary, Queen of Scots.[21] She does not seem to have received any appointment at that time, but it is tempting to wonder if she could possibly be the Demoiselle de la Souche who fourteen years later was the governess of the maids.

There is no mistaking the letter S which begins the name 'Souche' in the 1562 household books, nor can the T at the beginning of Renée's surname be mistaken. However, given the coincidence of such similar names and positions, it is not beyond the realms of possibility that 'De la Touche' and 'De la Souche' were variants of the same name. Whatever the connection, if any, the Queen gave Mademoiselle de la Souche a black satin robe with long sleeves in May 1563, and in 1566 intended leaving her a chain enamelled white and red. She was still at her post on 2 April 1567, and makes her last appearance on a 1573 list of Mary's attendants and pensioners, by which time she would almost certainly have been back in France.[22]

The seven maids of honour in the charge of Mademoiselle de la Souche were all new to the household, apart from Mademoiselle de

Rallay, who had been with Mary in France, and only two of them seem to have been Scottish. Both Scots were sisters of members of the Four Maries. One was Mary Livingston's sister Magdalene, and the other was Mary Beaton's sister, Lucrece. Magdalene was next in age to her sister Mary in the large Livingston family,[23] and on 7 January 1562, within months of joining the royal household, she married the Queen's favourite equerry, Arthur Erskine of Blackgrange, younger brother of John, 1st Earl of Mar. Mary gave her a handsome wedding present and in her 1566 disposition of jewellery meant to leave her no fewer than seven items, including a necklace, a long chain and a watch set with a dozen rubies and two great sapphires, a pearl hanging from it.[24] This was a sure sign that Magdalene was high in the Queen's favour and, that same year, she and her husband were given the lands of Cromar in Aberdeenshire.[25]

Arthur was another of those who were with the Queen in the little supper chamber at Holyroodhouse on the evening David Riccio was murdered and Magdalene remained in Mary's household until 1567. She and Arthur had no children, and he died some time before mid-January 1570.[26] Magdalene remained a widow for seven years, until she married a widower, Sir James Scrymgeour of Dudhope, becoming stepmother to his young children, a small son and two daughters.[27] When Mary, Queen of Scots heard the news she was disgusted. 'The marriage of Magdalene Livingston displeases me greatly,' she told the Archbishop of Glasgow, ordering him not to send the gift she had ordered for Magdalene some months previously, at least not until she could discover further details about the marriage. Later, when Mary Seton was trying to fend off attempts to marry her to Andrew Beaton, she reminded the Queen of the criticism Magdalene Livingston had attracted when she married a man of lower standing than herself.[28] Mary's surviving correspondence does not mention her again.

The other Scottish maid of honour in 1562, Lucrece Beaton, was the daughter of Jeanne de la Rainville and the younger sister of Mary Beaton. In 1566 her wages were 200 livres a year, and the Queen intended leaving her an enamelled chain with a large cipher at the end of it.[29] When Mary fled to England, Lucrece stayed behind and it was probably then that she married her own first cousin once removed, David Beaton of Melgund, son of the famous Cardinal David Beaton. He was an older man, divorced from his first wife and, whatever the Queen thought of that match, her surviving correspondence makes no mention of it. Lucrece and her husband had one son, David, and three daughters. David Beaton of Melgund probably died in the winter of 1592–3[30] and by 1599 Lucrece had married Andrew Wishart of Mylneden.[31] She must have been in her fifties by that time but they lived together for the next twenty years and more, until his death in September 1622.[32] Lucrece made her will on 29 November the following year, and probably died not long afterwards.[33]

The family connections of Magdalene and Lucrece are well known, but much more elusive are the next four maids of honour. Mademoiselle Thore features variously in the accounts as 'Torrie', which sounds Scottish, and 'Thore', which seems French. She would have been favoured with an enamelled gold chain and a matching edging had the Queen died in 1566[34] and when she married in August that same year, Mary supplied her with the materials for a violet velvet gown lined with violet taffeta and trimmed with gold.[35] Whoever she was, she had left the household by 1566–7. Equally mysterious is Mademoiselle Thou. We do not know her first name, either, but she could well have been a relative of Christophe de Thou, First President of the Parlement of Paris. He had at least two daughters, one of whom, Anne, in 1566 married Philippe Hurault, Count of Cheverny and later became a lady-in-waiting to Catherine de Medici.[36] Another of Mary's maids, La Sauvaige, was probably a relative of Adrian Sauvaige, one of her butlers of the kitchen vessels.[37] As for 'Grisel', none of the other maids was referred to by her first name and it may be that the actual reading of the rather cramped writing in the household books is 'goisel', which could have made her a daughter of Pierre de Joisel, Seigneur de Bettoncourt, one of Mary's masters of the household.

Finally, there was Rallay, who had been one of Mary's chamberwomen in 1555 and, as we have seen, was later termed by the Queen 'as good a servant as it is possible to wish for'.[38] She seems to have had charge of various personal items belonging to her mistress, for from 1561 to 1565 she received cloth to make into a cover for the Queen's mattress and a bag for Mary's rings and belts, an ell of linen to make sacks to put papers in, cloth to put round the Queen's coifs and collars and more to make ties for her wigs.[39] In December 1561 Mary gave orders that she was to receive two fur scarves which had belonged to Mary of Guise, one a marten and the other an ermine, both decorated as was the fashion with enamelled heads and paws, their collars studded with gems and pearls.[40] It is not altogether certain whether this was a gift or whether she was to look after the scarves for the Queen, but she certainly received presents of a robe of black damask with great sleeves from Mary in May 1563 and a bed the following year.[41] By this time, her annual salary had risen to 200 livres.[42]

It is not known where Rallay was during the tumultuous months of 1567–8, but it seems as though she went home to France at about that time. Certainly during 1573–4 Mary made many requests for a passport for her to come to her, emphasising her age and honesty, saying that she could serve and keep the Queen company in her chamber 'as she did during my youth' and remarking that if only Rallay could make the journey she could bring with her a maid who could help Mary to design and carry out new needlework.[43] It seems as though the request must have been granted, and that she brought with her a relative named Renée Rallay 'alias Beauregard', for in the testament she drew up in February 1577, Mary bequeathed 100 crowns 'to Beauregard, to take her back to her country' and in August that year Gilbert Curle, her secretary, told Andrew Beaton that he had passed on the latter's good wishes not only to Mary Seton but to 'Mademoiselle de Rallay, your valentine of last year'.[44] This surely applied to the younger Rallay rather than to the long-serving and by now undoubtedly mature maid.

On 6 September 1585 from Tutbury Mary, having described the horrors of life in that semi-ruinous castle, declared, 'I have lost my good Rallay, who was one of the principal consolations of my captivity', and hoped that the Countess of Atholl might come to replace 'Seton and my good Rallay'.[45] It is not clear whether Rallay had died or retired to the continent. However, 'Rallay alias Beauregard' remained with her, for when the Queen's goods were listed at Chartley in July 1586, her bedcurtains, table carpet and needlework were said to be in the care of her French gentlewoman of the chamber, 'Mademoiselle de Beauregard'. It was Renée de Beauregard who bore Mary's train at her trial at Fotheringhay,[46] and afterwards had in her custody various garments and items of jewellery belonging to the Queen.[47] Presumably Renée went back to France when the maids of honour were allowed to leave.

In France, six chamberwomen had been attached to Mary's household, but in Scotland in 1562 there were no fewer than fourteen of them, sharing the same table. Eleven are not named. It is simply noted that three served the Queen herself, three worked for the maids of honour, and the Dame de Péguillon, Madame de Briante, Madame de Cricq (Creich), Mademoiselle de la Souche and Mademoiselle Cobron had one each. In addition to the anonymous eleven, there were Hambal, La Jardinière and her governess. All we know of Hambal is that she features on the 1562 lists, but La Jardinière and her governess are much better documented and indeed very interesting, for La Jardinière was a dwarf. It is well known that kings and queens often had dwarves in their retinues, and in fact the dwarves in Catherine de Medici's troupe were sumptuously dressed and had their own household of attendants. Her particular favourite, Catherine La Jardinière, apparently accompanied her everywhere in the mid-1560s.[48] Mary, Queen of Scots' dwarf must have been someone different, however, although no doubt a close relative of Catherine La Jardinière. Her first name was Nicole. In the late 1540s, Mary of Guise had employed an attendant called 'Jardinier', who was given thirty livres to go to France, perhaps with Mary, Queen of Scots.[49] This might even have been Nicole.

Certainly in 1561 La Jardinière and her governess, Jacqueline, came to Scotland with Mary. Throughout the Queen's personal reign they feature in the household accounts as the recipients of bedding and clothing.[50] Occasionally, La Jardinière appears as 'Nicole, the Queen's fool'. Canvas for her palliasse was supplied in September 1561, Jacqueline was given a blue velvet bonnet for her in 1563 and in February 1564 she was to have a new dress with yellow and violet trimmings.[51] After Mary's imprisonment at Lochleven, the Regent Moray seems to have taken over responsibility for Nicole and Jacqueline. He gave £10 to pay the debts of 'Critoflat, keeper of the Queen's fool' (this must have been Jacqueline's surname), so that she could visit France. On 10 January 1568 Nicole herself received forty shillings by his special command and other disbursements followed. On 3 January 1570 a tailor was paid £3:10/- for making her two gowns, two hoods and four pairs of hose and finally, on 1 August 1570, Nicole received £15 for her journey back to France.[52]

Members of the household naturally came and went, and there were no doubt greater changes among the female attendants, for they were inclined to leave when they married and had children. Some of the other lists of tables and household accounts reveal the names of those not specified in July 1562: a maid of honour called Ros,[53] Marna the chamberwoman,[54] Wardlaw, Françoise[55] and Marie Courcelles. Marie had come to Scotland with the Queen and remained in her service until 1567, receiving sixty livres a year along with bedding and items of clothing.[56] She was with Mary during her Lochleven imprisonment, but when the Queen escaped, she stayed behind on the island with Mary Seton.[57] There is no mention of her after that, apart from the fact that she features on the 1573 list of Mary's servants and pensioners as receiving 200 livres a year, and, as we have seen, it has been suggested that it was she who travelled to Rheims with Mary Seton in 1583.[58]

During the early years in Scotland, light-hearted gaiety must often have marked the atmosphere, and the various household and treasurer's accounts give us an occasional glimpse of the way of life of the women attendants. Some had their own servants, male and female, and most had chambers in the royal palaces. We know this because they were provided with heating and lighting for their rooms, in the form of coal and candles. As for food, the yearly calendar was divided into flesh days and fish days, no meat being eaten on Fridays or during Lent. There were two main meals a day, dinner (at around noon) and supper, the food eaten at each being pretty much the same: soup, followed by a selection of boiled and roasted meats such as beef, mutton, veal and chicken on flesh days and an astonishing variety of fresh and salted fish and shell-fish on fish days. Figs, oranges, raisins, apples, pears, plums and nuts featured on the Queen's own table, according to season, and the ladies and maids probably had a good selection too.[59] Eggs appeared at supper only, French wine, milk and water were drunk with meals and there was always bread and butter.

We know that on special occasions such as weddings and banquets, there were elaborate entertainments. Masques had been performed at the Scottish Court since at least the early 1530s and so the festivities Mary had known in France were nothing new. It seems rather that their scale was more lavish than before, and of course John Knox was quick to condemn what he regarded as pagan excesses. For others, celebrations of this kind were a necessary part of Court life, to be enjoyed by those who took part as well as impressing visiting dignitaries. Such entertainments reached their high point in the triumph devised to celebrate the baptism of Prince James in 1566, with masques, decorated floats, fireworks and a mock attack on a fortress.[60]

The Scottish ladies did not, however, have the same level of education as their French counterparts. Elizabeth Keith, the old Countess of Huntly, could not write at all and signed the marriage contract between Bothwell and her daughter Jane with her hand 'led on the pen'.[61] Margaret Erskine's signature is a wild, illegible scrawl with the different parts of each letter scarcely joined together[62] but, in the next generation, Lady Moray's signature, 'Annas keyt', is that of someone who has been taught a neat, italic hand, while her sister Mary, Lady Calder does italic writing with elegant flourishes and her daughter Elizabeth has an equally accomplished style.[63] They all wrote in Scots, of course, not English. Whether any of them could speak foreign languages remains unknown, nor do we know if they read anything other than their Bibles or prayer books. Even so, they could merrily join in the ballets and the masques, enjoying the fun of dressing up, dancing and making speeches.

By the time of the Prince's baptism, however, the happy years were at an end and, in the months that followed, the Queen's attendants must have had to change from being vivacious participants in merrymaking to supportive companions in adversity. A list of the royal servants drawn up just four days after the murder of Lord Darnley lets us see who the Queen had with her in 1566–7.[64] Those mentioned were to be paid out of the revenues from her French jointure lands, obviously a way of safeguarding their position. It is likely that the list is therefore incomplete and that there must have been other servants paid from a different source.

There were now twelve ladies-in-waiting instead of nine, but only two maids of honour along with their governess compared with the former seven, and seven chamberwomen instead of fourteen. Moreover, not all the people on the list were actually present but were pensioners. For example, the very first ladies-in-waiting mentioned are Mary's grandmother, Antoinette de Bourbon, Dowager Duchess of Guise, Mahanet des Essartz, Dame de Curel who had departed in umbrage from the household as long ago as 1553, and the Dame de Péguillon, long back in France. The Four Maries, of course, were very much present on the 1566–7 list, as were the two mothers, Madame de Briante and Madame de Cricq. The Dame de Péguillon and Fonterpuy have vanished, having gone home, and the Demoiselle de Cobron has also disappeared. They had been replaced, however, and there are three new names, the most interesting being the lady noted down as 'Madame d'Astel', the recipient of no less than 500 livres a year, second only in the size of her remuneration to the Dowager Duchess of Guise with her 800 livres. Her name sounds French, but she was actually Mary, Queen of Scots' cousin, Margaret Fleming, Countess of Atholl, another daughter of Lady Fleming the governess.[65]

Margaret was by this time married to her third husband, John, 4th Earl of Atholl, having been twice widowed at an early age. By now she would have been in her early forties, and had a son and five daughters.[66] The Earl was a devout Roman Catholic and a strong supporter of the Queen. He had helped to defeat Huntly at the Battle of Corrichie and had promoted her marriage to Lord Darnley.

No doubt Margaret was on hand when Mary went hunting in the Forest of Atholl at his invitation. We do not know when she entered the household, but she apparently provided a unique service in 1566. Reputed to have 'the powers of incantation', she is said to have cast Mary's labour pains when she was giving birth to Prince James on to Margaret Beaton, wife of Arthur Forbes of Rires.[67]

The Earl of Atholl eventually changed sides, attending the coronation of James VI and being nominated as provisional Regent until Moray returned and took over. He was made Lord Chancellor in 1578, but died the following year.[68] Mary does not seem to have held his withdrawal of support against his Countess and, when he died, wrote sympathetically to his widow, addressing her somewhat confusingly as 'My good auntie'.[69] The Countess had married for the first time when Mary was still a very small child, and so the Queen probably always thought of her as belonging to the older generation.

Aunt or cousin, Margaret's loyalty to the Queen never seems to have wavered, and in 1570 a jewel sent by her to Mary was intercepted. It was set with gems and elaborately enamelled, with a maiden's head, the arms of Scotland, Mary in a royal robe and the significant inscription 'Fall what may fall, the Lion [of Scotland] shall be lord of all'.[70] Elizabeth I was said to be furious when it was brought to her, but since the Countess was in Scotland there was little she could do. However, she did not forget . Fifteen years later, in the summer of 1585, Margaret wrote to Mary saying that she and her young daughter would like to come to England to serve her. Mary was delighted with the offer, telling the French ambassador that it would be a great consolation to have such a lady with her, lacking, as she did, 'any company worthy of my rank'. She urged the ambassador to procure a passport for the Countess, and promised that the latter's retinue would be as small as possible.[71] However, Elizabeth I refused to allow Margaret to enter England and she was dead by 15 March 1587.[72]

Because of her family relationship with Mary, Queen of Scots, Margaret was a significant figure. The other two new ladies-in-waiting were not so prominent, and in fact we do not know the exact identity of one of them. 'Mademoiselle d'Asquin' was presumably the Marie Erskine who was left a belt of crystal and more than six other items in the 1566 disposition of jewellery.[73] She must have been a relative of the Mar family, but the appropriate Earl of Mar is not recorded as having either a daughter or a sister named Mary at that time. Of course, female members of sixteenth-century families are often omitted from peerages, but Mary could have been a member of a cadet branch.

The other new lady-in-waiting certainly had a longstanding family connection with the royal household. Jeanne Piédefer, Madame de Bettoncourt had come to Scotland as one of Mary of Guise's maids of honour.[74] Her parentage is not known, but Piédefers had been prominent in French public life for some time: in 1500 one of the clerks of the French King in the Chambre des Comtes had been Guillaume Piédefer and in 1546 Robert Piédefer was a counsellor in the Paris parlement.[75] It was no doubt Mary of Guise who arranged Jeanne's first marriage to Alexander, 5th Lord Livingston, a twice-married widower with nine children including Mary Livingston of the Four Maries.[76] Two undated letters sent to Jeanne still survive among the Balcarres Papers, giving us a momentary glimpse of her life. The first is from Captain de Faucher in Dumbarton, asking if she would like some of the fine cinnamon which had come in aboard a ship, and telling her that he has found a place where cress for salads grows. However, his recollection is that she prefers parsley. He addressed this helpful note to 'Madame my Valentine, Madame de Livingston'. The second letter is a chatty one from Françoise d'Alluye, writing from Joinville, where she was evidently in the suite of Antoinette de Bourbon. She thanked Jeanne for her letter, gave news of friends, wished that she could see her again to pour out all the latest gossip and ended by asking teasingly after 'the gentleman with the violet doublet'.[77]

Could she have been referring to Pierre de Joisel? Some time during the 1550s, Jeanne married again. Her new husband was Pierre de Joisel, Seigneur de Saint Rémy-en-Bouzemont and de Bettoncourt, one of the masters of the household to Mary of Guise.[78] He was always known by the name of his second lordship, but St Rémy-en-Bouzemont and Bettoncourt are both in Lorraine. As was customary, Jeanne kept her grander title, and an undated account records the Bishop of Ross paying 'Madame de Livingston' two Scots crowns which the Queen lost at cards with the Sieur de Bettoncourt.[79] After the death of Mary of Guise in 1560, Bettoncourt and his wife were given eighty livres by the Lord Treasurer.[80] We do not know if they then went back to France or stayed on in Scotland, but they were both in the household of Mary, Queen of Scots by 1566 and Jeanne features on Mary's roll of 1573 servants and pensioners.[81]

Setting aside the three pensioners on the 1566–7 list of ladies-in-waiting, only three were now French while the remaining six were Scottish, and it is interesting to speculate as to whether this trend towards Scottish attendants would have continued had Mary's personal reign lasted for longer. As for the maids of honour in 1566–7, Mademoiselle de la Souche was still at her post as governess, and of the only two maids named, one was French, the faithful Rallay, and one Scottish, Lucrece Beaton. Magdalene Livingston was married now and had probably retired to private life, while Mesdemoiselles Thore, Thou and La Sauvaige had very likely gone back to France. Grisel/Joisel has also disappeared. The suspicion that the 1566–7 list is not complete is confirmed by the mention of various other maids of honour in the household accounts and Lord Treasurer's accounts. In April 1567, for instance, 'Quelay', Elizabeth Preston and Barbara Sunderland [Sondrelan] were numbered among six maids who received linen for Communion and Barbara had been mentioned in the 1566 jewellery bequests as the recipient of some small items.[82]

Similarly, there are omissions in the chamberwomen, who now numbered seven instead of the previous fourteen. Marie Courcelles is still there and La Jardinière's governess is mentioned, but La Jardinière herself is not, although we know that she was still in Scotland and would surely have merited inclusion in the payments from the French jointure lands. Another notable omission is Margaret Carwood, who had entered the Queen's household in 1564. Not only was she still there, but she is reputed to have been

Mary's favourite chamberwoman. Margaret and her elder sister Janet were the daughters and heirs of William Carwood of that Ilk. After their father's death, they had trouble with John Fleming, illegitimate son of Malcolm, 3rd Lord Fleming and half-brother of Mary Fleming of the Four Maries. He allegedly held the sisters captive for several years in their home, Carwood House, near Biggar, instead of finding husbands for them as he should have done, having received the gift of their wardship and marriage. In September 1554 the girls were old enough to sue him in the Court of Session, and he boldly appeared in person to deny the charges. Unfortunately there is a gap in the Register of Acts and Decreets immediately after that and so we do not know how the case was decided.[83]

Deprived of a properly arranged marriage when she was in her teens, Margaret remained unmarried, and ten years later we find her in charge of the Queen's bedding and other furnishings.[84] Mary intended leaving a painting of herself, probably a miniature, garnished with a cross of five diamonds, and a couple of other small items of jewellery to 'Marguerite',[85] and it seems that the Queen took on the responsibility John Fleming had neglected, for she arranged Margaret's marriage to John Stewart. The wedding took place in February 1567 at Holyroodhouse, Margaret wearing a fashionable black velvet dress trimmed with gold. The Queen not only supplied the materials but gave the bride a very generous pension of 300 merks a year.[86] However, the atmosphere at the wedding must have been distinctly strained, for Lord Darnley had been murdered only two days before, and Mary had interrupted her official mourning to attend the wedding feast, something which was much criticised.[87] Within months, the Queen was a prisoner at Lochleven and nothing of Margaret's subsequent career is known.

Returning to the changes of personnel in the household, some new names have come in: Marie Gobelin, Anne l'Enfant, Pochomnères, the daughter of Monsieur Arnault, Helen Bog [Hélène Boc] and Catherine Bingueton, who was chamberwoman to the maids of honour. Probably these were not actually new arrivals but had been among the unnamed chamberwomen in the

1562 list. As usual, it is difficult to find details of these more lowly members of the household. We know only that Marie Gobelin and Anne l'Enfant were still on the list of attendants and pensioners in 1573. They were obviously French, and Marie might have been a relative of Claude Gobelin, who had been the first nurse of François II.[88] Anne may have had family connections too, for Michel l'Enfant was secretary and master of the household to the Cardinal of Lorraine before being secretary to Mary, Queen of Scots in 1562.[89] Pochomnères must have been the wife or daughter of one of Mary's two ushers of the chamber, Louis de Forestz, 'called Pochomnères', while Monsieur Arnault, the father of another maid, was probably Monsieur Arnault de Colomniers, one of the Queen's doctors.[90] Finally, Helen Bog was wife of Mary's master cook.[91]

Marie Gobelin, Anne l'Enfant, Pochomnères and Marie Courcelles were paid sixty livres a year, the others forty livres. With the probable exception of Helen Bog/Hélène Boc, all seven chamberwomen on the list were French, but this may have been because they were to be paid from the French jointure lands. Various other accounts supply additional names. The wife of Captain Hay was one of the Queen's chamberwomen in 1567, as were Margaret Fame and Marie McLeod, the only woman in the household with an obviously highland name.[92] Last of the female servants on the 1566-7 list is Marie Carre, washerwoman, who was probably a Scottish Mary Kerr. Finally, other sources inform us that there were three additional named women who were employed in special roles by the Queen. Margaret Asteane was Mary's midwife, given a black velvet dress in 1566 shortly before she delivered the future James VI, Margaret Tweedie was Mary's nurse and, as well as La Jardinière, there was in 1566 a female Scottish fool named Jane Colquhoun who wore the royal livery, a red and yellow gown, hose and coat paid for by the Queen.[93]

Having looked in detail at the structure of Mary's household, we can ask if our traditional notion that she was surrounded in Scotland by a group of young Frenchwomen is correct. Because the evidence is incomplete, it is difficult to say, but it seems that during her Scottish years Mary did employ twice as many

Frenchwomen as Scots in her household. This was not surprising. Naturally she had brought with her members of the retinue she had employed in France and their presence in Scotland was part of a continuing tradition. It is particularly interesting to note the presence of people like Marie Pierres and Jeanne de la Rainville, who had come in the retinue of Mary of Guise, married Scots, settled down, presumably became integrated into Scottish society but, once widowed, chose Frenchmen as their second husbands. That they had daughters who served the Queen is also typical, remembering that, at the French Court, the ladies-in-waiting and maids of honour were members of a complex network of friends and relatives.

Little is known about these women's private lives and personalities, but their devotion to the Queen is very evident. Some must have been closer to her than others, of course. The Four Maries had been with her since early childhood, as we have observed. Margaret Carwood was a favourite and the Countess of Atholl was a relative. Perhaps we can also find evidence about which of her ladies Mary particularly liked from the gifts she gave them. We have already noticed her intended dispositions of jewellery in 1566. An inventory of her clothing made in February 1562 indicates the expensive gowns and dresses she later gave away.

Predictably, the Four Maries figure prominently, especially Mary Livingston. She would have received a particularly generous series of jewellery bequests and during her period of service she was given more of the royal garments than anyone else – no fewer than eight items including a crimson satin dress trimmed with silver. Her sister Magdalene, as we have seen, would have had seven items of jewellery and did receive a crimson petticoat and sleeves as a wedding present. Mary Fleming, Mary Beaton and Mary Seton also benefited from the Queen's generosity with her wardrobe, as did her cousin the Countess of Atholl. Mademoiselle de Fonterpuy was given a crimson dress edged with gold and Nicole la Jardinière the dwarf became the owner of one of the unusually tall Queen's white dresses edged with white satin. She obviously could not wear it, but it would have been cut up and the material used either to make her an outfit or for some other purpose. Finally, the washer-woman's little daughter was given a white satin foreskirt, yet another indication of the kindly interest Mary, Queen of Scots took in the women who served her.[94]

Notes

1. Knox, *History*, ii, 25
2. Knox, *History*, ii, 82–4
3. *Diurnal of Occurrents*, 87; Marshall, '"This lady and princess is a notable woman"', 100; Carpenter, 'Performing Diplomacies', 194–225; Lynch, 'Queen Mary's Triumph', 1–21
4. Cf. Chapters 4 and 5
5. NAS, Exchequer Records, E33/6. The following analysis is based on E33/6/2
6. See Chapter 5
7. *Foreign Correspondence*, 1537–48, 245
8. *Scots Peerage*, viii, 583–5
9. Seton, *Family of Seton*, i, 128; *Lettres du Cardinal de Lorraine*, 370; *Two Missions of Jacques de la Brosse*, in Brosse, *Histoire d'un Capitaine Bourbonnais*
10. *Treasurer Accounts*, xi, 86–7, 349
11. *Inventaires*, 106
12. *Foreign Correspondence*, 1537–48, 246
13. Seton, *Family of Seton*, i, 128
14. *Ibid.*, i, 128–9; *Accounts of the Lord High Treasurer*, xii, 216
15. *Lettres*, ed. Labanoff, iv, 238, 269
16. Seton, *Family of Seton*, i,129
17. *Inventaires*, 106, 113
18. NAS, Exchequer Records, E33/6/2; Teulet, *Papiers d'Etat*, 121
19. *Foreign Correspondence*, 1537–48, xxxii
20. *Lettres du Cardinal de Lorraine*, 77–8; NLS, Balcarres Papers, Adv. MS., 29.2.5 f.17
21. *Foreign Correspondence*, 1537–48, 10–11
22. *Treasurer Accounts*, xii, 400; Lang, 'Household, 1573', 349
23. *Scots Peerage*, v, 437
24. *Lettres*, ed. Labanoff, iv, 389; *Inventaires*, 111, 117, 123, 138
25. *RSS*, v, part ii, 78
26. *Lettres*, ed. Labanoff, iv, 389

27. *Scots Peerage*, iii, 311–3; v, 439
28. *Lettres*, ed. Labanoff, iv, 323, 389
29. Teulet, *Papiers d'Etat*, 122; *Inventaires*, 119
30. NAS, Ogilvy of Inverquharity Muniments, GD205/19/lxiv (3)
31. NAS, Register of Acts and Decreets, C57/186 f.252r
32. NAS, Brechin Commissary Court, Register of Testaments, CC3/3/4, f.104
33. NAS, Miscellaneous testamentary documents, RH15/1/8: I am grateful to Dr Margaret Sanderson for drawing my attention to the Lucrece Beaton testamentary material
34. *Inventaires*, 118
35. *Treasurer Accounts*, xii, 19
36. *Lettres de Catherine de Médicis*, ix, 511; Anselme, *Histoire Généalogique*, viii, 799; *Lettres du Cardinal de Lorraine*, 265
37. NAS, Exchequer Records, E33/6
38. See page 52
39. *Inventaires*, 127–8, 135, 141, 145
40. *Ibid.*, 130, 131
41. *Ibid.*, 138, 144
42. Lang, 'Household, 1573', 349
43. *Lettres*, ed. Labanoff, iv, 84, 90, 107, 121, 158, 219
44. *Ibid.*, iv, 381
45. *Ibid.*, iv, 219, 223
46. Fraser, *Mary, Queen of Scots*, 509
47. *Lettres*, ed. Labanoff, vii, 259, 265, 270, 272
48. Frieda, *Catherine de Medici*, 179
49. NLS, Balcarres Papers, Adv. MS., 29.2.5 f.61
50. *Treasurer Accounts*, xi, 421, 442; *Inventaires*, 126, 127, 130, 137, 143, 144
51. *Inventaires*, 125, 142, 146
52. *Treasurer Accounts*, xii, 69, 182, 186, 208
53. *Inventaires*, 129; *Treasurer Accounts*, xi, 84
54. NAS, Exchequer Records, E33/6
55. *Inventaires*, 126, 132, 137, 143
56. Teulet, *Papiers d'Etat*, 121; *Inventaires*, 125, 127, 143; *Treasurer Accounts*, xi, 163, 240; xii, 401
57. Seton, *Family of Seton*, i, 138
58. Teulet, *Papiers d'Etat*, 121
59. NAS, Exchequer Records, E33/6/2
60. Carpenter, 'Performing Diplomacies', 194–225; Lynch, 'Queen Mary's Triumph', 1–21

61. Sanderson, *Mary Stewart's People*, 38
62. Moray Muniments, Bundle 352
63. Moray Muniments, Box 15, Bundle 2/307; Bundle 3/323
64. *Ibid.*, 121
65. *Scots Peerage*, viii, 540–611
66. *Ibid.*, i, 444; viii, 540–1
67. *Ibid.*, i, 444; Fraser, *Mary, Queen of Scots*, 149
68. *Ibid.*, i, 444
69. *Ibid.*
70. NAS, Mar and Kellie Muniments, GD124/15/5
71. *Lettres*, ed. Labanoff, vi, 202
72. *Scots Peerage*, viii, 541
73. *Inventaires*, 118, 120, 124
74. *Foreign Correspondence, 1548–57*, 209n.
75. Anselme, *Histoire Généalogique*, vi, 261
76. *Scots Peerage*, v, 436–9
77. *Foreign Correspondence, 1548–57*, 29–30, 298–9
78. *Scots Peerage*, v, 439; Francisque-Michel, *Les Français en Ecosse*, i, 534
79. NLS, Balcarres Papers, Adv. MS., 29.2.5 f.87
80. Francisque-Michel, *Les Français en Ecosse*, i, 534
81. Teulet, *Papiers d'Etat*, 349
82. *Treasurer Accounts*, xi, 400; *Inventaires*, 124
83. NAS, Register of Acts and Decreets, CS7/10, f.415v; *Scots Peerage*, viii, 5410
84. *Inventaires*, 147, 158; *Treasurer Accounts*, xi, 419, 432; xii, 12, 21, 31, 36, 46, 396, 397, 400
85. *Inventaires*, 123, 117
86. *Treasurer Accounts*, xii, 41; Donaldson, *All the Queen's Men*, 66
87. Fraser, *Mary, Queen of Scots*, 266, 307; Guy, *My Heart is my Own*, 317
88. Ruble, *Première jeunesse*, 25
89. *Lettres du Cardinal de Lorraine*, 547 n.1
90. Teulet, *Papiers d'Etat*, 126
91. Hay Fleming, *Mary, Queen of Scots*, 511
92. *Treasurer Accounts*, xi, 401, 350
93. Fraser, *Mary, Queen of Scots*, 266; *Treasurer Accounts*, xii, 7, 26
94. *Inventaires*, 72

11

Bess of Hardwick and the English Years

When Mary, Queen of Scots escaped from Lochleven Castle on 2 May 1568, she rode to Hamilton, gathered her supporters and on 13 May confronted her enemies once more, this time at Langside, near Glasgow. Watching the battle from a nearby hill, she realised that her forces were in disarray, mounted her horse and hurried down to encourage her soldiers. However, she found them quarrelling among themselves and, realising that all was lost, she fled. In a letter to the Cardinal of Lorraine a month later, she wrote, 'I have endured injuries, calumnies, imprisonment, famine, cold, heat, flight not knowing whither, ninety-two miles across the country without stopping or alighting, and then I have had to sleep upon the ground and drink sour milk and eat oatmeal without bread and have been three nights like owls', and all with no female for company.

Stopping at last, she held a council of war with Lord Herries and the others who were with her, telling them that she intended seeking the help of Queen Elizabeth I. They tried desperately to dissuade her, reminding her of the various Stewart kings, her ancestors, who had been held prisoner by the English in the past. They urged her to go to France instead but, by her own admission, she would not listen. Vowing to be back in Scotland by the end of August at the head of an army, she crossed the Solway Firth into England on 16 May 1568 with sixteen companions, confident that Elizabeth would help her to regain her throne. She was twenty-five years old. For the rest of her life, she would be a prisoner.[1] When she first realised that, instead of restoring her, Elizabeth intended to hold her captive, she was incredulous and indignant.

She was a queen, a monarch in her own right, and no one had any jurisdiction over her, she protested. Sir Francis Knollys, the Puritan gentleman Elizabeth I sent to interview her, was impressed in spite of himself, praising her intelligence, eloquence, courage and practical good sense. Victory over her enemies meant everything to her, he said, and indeed her thoughts and energies were all directed towards return to Scotland and restoration to her throne. She never did lose hope of regaining her freedom and throughout her long captivity, she always placed great emphasis on her royal status.

Given into the keeping of George, 6th Earl of Shrewsbury after her first trial at York, Mary was moved around his various residences, staying mostly at Sheffield. As the years went by, hope faded and her health steadily declined. She had long been troubled with a pain in her side, the result, it is now believed, of a duodenal ulcer, and in the damp, cramped quarters in which she was held she developed arthritis as well as suffering colds and fevers. Sometimes she was allowed to go out riding, sometimes she was even permitted to travel to the baths at Buxton in the hope of improving her health but, whenever a new plot to free her was revealed, the security around her was tightened, her movements were curtailed and her contacts with the outside world were severely restricted.

Mary first entered the custody of the Earl of Shrewsbury when she arrived at his depressing castle of Tutbury on 4 February 1569, and by 31 March he was telling William Cecil how she 'continueth daily to resort to my wife's chamber where, with the Lady Livingston and Mistress Seton, she useth to sit working with the needle in which she much delighteth and in devising works'. This was strictly against the instructions he had been given. At the very start, he had been warned that his wife was to see Mary only if the Queen were sick or should specifically ask to speak with her, and that 'very rarely'. The Countess of Shrewsbury, better known as Bess of Hardwick, was a strong-minded woman, however, and the Earl was powerless to prevent her from doing as she wished.[2]

Bess was about fifteen years older than Mary, red-haired, with a long nose and sharp, intelligent eyes. She came from a relatively humble background. Her short-lived father, John Hardwick, had been a member of the local gentry at Hardwick in Derbyshire. However, by a series of judicious marriages, Bess rose to be the second richest woman in England, or so it was said, the first being Queen Elizabeth herself. She had already been married three times and was the mother of eight children when in 1567 she married Shrewsbury, a widower with a grown-up family. She had also been for a time one of the gentlewomen of Elizabeth I's Privy Chamber just before Elizabeth came to the throne, but that had ended when the two quarrelled and Bess was dismissed. Her ambitions had not been dashed, however, and whereas for most people the custody of a royal prisoner was an intolerable financial burden and a source of constant anxiety, Bess saw it as a wonderful opportunity. Mary, Queen of Scots was Elizabeth's most obvious heir and so Bess set out determinedly to gain her friendship, with an eye to the time when Mary could be Queen of England.[3]

It was not so difficult. Even in such strained circumstances Mary was affable, outgoing and only too eager to have the company of someone who could tell her all about the personalities of the English Court: William Cecil, the Earl of Leicester and, most of all, Elizabeth I herself. Poring over engraved book illustrations, Mary and Bess found a shared love of symbolism and cunning devices which looked perfectly innocent at first sight but concealed all manner of subversive messages. Their professional embroiderers copied the designs on to canvas for them, and with relish they and their ladies set about sewing, for example, a large ginger cat with a small gold crown on its head (Elizabeth) looming threateningly over a small mouse (Mary).[4] As they sewed, they all chatted and Mary soon found that both Bess and her women had deliciously scurrilous tales to tell of Elizabeth, enhanced by wickedly amusing imitations.[5]

The tedium of daily life was relieved, and Mary was further diverted by the presence of two of Bess's small granddaughters. One was the orphaned Lady Arabella Stuart, who came to live with Bess in 1578 at the age of two and a half, when her other grandmother, the Countess of Lennox, died suddenly. Arabella's father had been Lord Darnley's younger brother, and so she was Mary's niece by marriage. Mary loved children, and whatever her feelings about Lord Darnley, she seems to have taken pleasure in the little girl's company. Certainly Mary joined Bess the following year in an ultimately unsuccessful attempt to extract from the Countess of Lennox's executor jewels left in trust for Arabella.[6] Another of Bess's granddaughters came to live in Mary's own household when she was very young. This was Bess Pierrepont, daughter of Frances Cavendish and her husband Sir Henry Pierrepont. Little Bess was one of Mary's many god-children and Mary would later describe how she was 'brought up [as] my bedfellow and at board ever since she had four years of age, so carefully and virtuously, I trust, as if she had been my own daughter'.[7]

As young Bess grew up, Claude Nau, Mary's secretary, fell in love with her and wanted to marry her. When the Pierreponts heard, they were horrified. They had allowed their child to live with the Queen of Scots in the hope of future honours and advancement. Her marriage to a mere secretary was not at all what they had in mind. Believing that Mary was encouraging the romance, they promptly asked her in July 1586 to send their daughter home. Mary was hurt. Perhaps disingenuously, she denied that she had tried to arrange any marriage, claiming that she had actually been trying to persuade Elizabeth I to take Bess into her household. 'To be plain,' Mary told a friend bitterly, 'I would be the rather quit of her, for that I see too much of her grandmother's nature in her behaviour every way, notwithstanding all my pains for the contrary, and therefore now would be sorry to have her bestowed upon any man that I wish good unto.'[8]

Her friendship with Bess of Hardwick had by this time come to a traumatic end. The sheer discomfort and tedium of being cooped up together was affecting everyone who shared Mary's imprisonment, and it was perhaps inevitable that two such strong-willed women would clash. Bess angered Mary by pressing Arabella Stuart's claims to the throne of England, doing everything she could to have her recognised as Elizabeth's heir. Mary was bound to object, for even if she herself did not live to succeed Elizabeth, then the throne should go to her son, James. The real trouble between the two women had, however, a different cause. The late marriage of the forceful Bess to the mild-mannered Shrewsbury had never been a happy one and Bess now decided that her husband and Mary, Queen of Scots were far too friendly. Shrewsbury had always got on much better with Mary than might have been expected, and Bess grew jealous.

Matters came to a head in the last weeks of 1583. Rumours were rife not only in London but abroad to the effect that Mary was having an affair with Shrewsbury and had actually borne his child. Mary was affronted when she heard what was being said. She was always extremely sensitive to any reflection on her honour and she could not rest until she found out who was responsible for such damaging stories. It was not long before she was told that the perpetrators of the calumnies were none other than Bess and two of her sons, Charles and William Cavendish. Mary poured out her rage in a series of letters to Michel de Castelnau-Mauvissière, the French ambassador in London, urging him to protest to Elizabeth I, while Shrewsbury, equally indignant, made his own complaints to the English Queen.[9]

Elizabeth I sympathised with the Earl, for she knew what Bess was like, but the matter dragged on and in November 1584 Mary, in a state of agitated despair, wrote a long and indiscreet letter to Elizabeth, repeating all sorts of unsavoury stories about the English Queen's alleged promiscuity. Bess had told her these tales, she said, adding that of course she had not believed them, but they showed the sort of woman Bess was. It was a measure of Mary's distress that, usually so urbane and broad-minded in those matters, she descended into such petty spite. Fortunately for her, Elizabeth apparently did not see the letter. Either Mary did not send it or Elizabeth's advisers suppressed it.[10] In the end, Elizabeth did intervene and by 1586 Mary was finally able to report that 'The Countess of Shrewsbury (I thank God) hath been tried and found to her shame in her attempt against me . . . The said lady upon her knees, in presence of the Queen of England and some principals of her Council, denied to her the shameful bruits [rumours] by herself spread abroad against me'.[11] Bess had been forced to swear that she and her sons had no reason for saying that Mary had any children after her arrival in England or had behaved other than a queen and a princess of her quality ought, in honour and chastity.[12]

Even after that, the irrepressible Bess tried to get in touch with Mary again, through Castelnau, the French ambassador, but Mary told him with dignity that there had passed between the Countess and herself such great and important occasions of enmity that there could be no talk of reconciliation without a really solid and very express assurance and proof of repentance. Even were that forthcoming, Bess's ingratitude and the terms she used could not allow Mary with honour ever again to have anything to do with such a wicked woman.[13] Shrewsbury and Bess had by now separated, he was replaced as Mary's custodian, and Mary and Bess did not meet again. Mary did, however, see Shrewsbury at her Fotheringhay trial and on 7 February 1587, as Earl Marshal of England, he arrived to tell her that she had been found guilty of treason and sentenced to death. He presided at her execution the following day, tears streaming down his face.[14] He died three years after that. Bess survived until February 1608, outliving Mary, Queen of Scots by more than twenty years.

Mary's long captivity was not spent in a prison cell, but the few apartments assigned to her in Shrewsbury's castles and then in the residences of her subsequent custodians must have seemed woefully inadequate to her after the spacious splendours of Fontainebleau, Amboise, Blois, Holyroodhouse and Linlithgow. Nevertheless, she insisted on displaying her cloth of state and maintaining her own retinue. Her defeated supporters were ready enough to join her in the early days and indeed, by September 1568, William Cecil was complaining that she had almost 140 people with her. By the following February, at the start of her time as Shrewsbury's prisoner, this number had been reduced to sixty, but even so Mary was forced to agree that half of those attendants should be sent away, leaving her with only thirty, not counting her women and the grooms of her stable. The numbers were cut yet again in May 1571, when the Duke of Norfolk, whom she had hoped to marry, was imprisoned and subsequently executed, and after the murder of French Protestants in the Massacre of St Bartholomew the following year, her train was reduced to a mere sixteen.[15]

As usual, most of the attendants were men, but what is noticeable about the women is the drastic reduction not only in number but in status. Mary Seton remained at the Queen's side until 1583, but the only other aristocratic lady in the household was Agnes Fleming, Lady Livingston, the Queen's cousin. Agnes had served her in France,[16] but after her marriage she had returned to Scotland. She and her husband William, 6th Lord Livingston lived with their family of five sons and two daughters at Callendar House, near Falkirk in Stirlingshire. Mary, Queen of Scots visited them there several times, notably with Lord Darnley in 1567 when she was bringing him back from Glasgow to Kirk o' Field. Lord Livingston was present at her marriage to Bothwell that same spring, tried in vain to negotiate her release from Lochleven, fought for her at Langside and rode with her to England, where Agnes joined them.[17]

Reporting to William Cecil on an audience with Mary, Queen of Scots, Nicholas White wrote on 26 February 1569, 'The greatest personage about her is the Lord Livingston and the lady his wife, which is a fair gentlewoman'.[18] A month later, Agnes was busy devising needlework with the Queen and Mary Seton.[19] In 1572 she was allowed to return to her children in Scotland, and there she actively engaged in passing on secret messages between the Queen's friends. When the Regent Morton discovered this, he imprisoned her in Dalkeith Castle, but she refused to divulge any information and after two months he released her.[20] Her husband died in 1592, but Agnes's date of death is unknown. They are said to have been buried together in Falkirk Churchyard.[21]

The year after Agnes left Mary's retinue, a 'Roll of servants of Mary, Queen of Scots' was drawn up, and it lists eight ladies-in-waiting. One was Mary Seton, at a salary of 400 livres a year, but the others do not seem to have been with the Queen at all and were really receiving pensions. The Dowager Duchess of Guise,

Mademoiselle de Curel and Madame de Péguillon feature although they were in France and Mary had not seen them for years, while Madame de Bettoncourt, Madame de Briante and Mary Beaton had been left behind in Scotland.[22] Her grandmother was to have 800 livres a year, Mary Beaton would receive 500, de Curel and de Péguillon 400 and Mesdames de Bettoncourt and de Briante 300 livres.

Mademoiselle du Verger, the eighth lady-in-waiting and the lowest-paid at 200 livres, was the wife of Gilles, Seigneur du Verger, one of the council which ran Mary's jointure lands in France.[23] In 1575, writing to James Beaton, Archbishop of Glasgow, Mary asked him to be her proxy as godmother to Monsieur du Verger's child.[24] If the baby was a boy, the Archbishop could choose whichever name he pleased, but if it was a girl, she should be called Antoinette, probably after Mary's grandmother. He was to be sure to remember the christening present too – a chain girdle or neck chain 'of reasonable price' would be the most suitable choice. Mademoiselle du Verger was a helpful contact, for in February 1580 Mary was telling Beaton that he need not trouble himself getting the linen, silk, thread and other necessities she had requested, since Mademoiselle du Verger was in the habit of buying such items for her.[25] It seems safe to conclude that Mademoiselle du Verger appears on the list because she undertook these useful commissions in France, not because she was personally in attendance on the Queen.

The maids of honour had likewise dwindled and there were only three of them now. Their governess, Mademoiselle de la Souche is mentioned but she, of course, had long since left the retinue, as had Lucrece Beaton and Marie Courcelles, whose whereabouts are uncertain. It is possible that Marie was with the Queen in England as a maid of honour, but there seems to be no documentary evidence. The third maid was Mademoiselle de Rallay, who did share Mary's captivity. Nine chamberwomen feature on the 1573 list. This is a very slight increase on the 1566–7 complement of seven, but once again it seems that previous employees are probably included. Marie Gobelin, Anne l'Enfant, Pochomnères and Hélène Boc (now recorded as 'Damoiselle Eleen Bog') may have been with Mary still, but it is more likely that they were elsewhere and were receiving pensions. La Jardinière's governess Jacqueline features but had certainly gone home. Four of the chamberwomen were new, or at least had not been mentioned by name before: 'Mademoiselle Jehanne de Kierie' [Jane Kennedy], Demoiselle Christine Hog, Marie Hanet and Marie Pages.

Jane Kennedy has sometimes been confused with Lady Jean Kennedy, daughter of Gilbert Kennedy, 3rd Earl of Cassillis, but Lady Jean married Robert Stewart, 1st Earl of Orkney, one of the Queen's half-brothers, and was mother of nine of his children. The Jane Kennedy who was Mary's chamberwoman may have been a member of a cadet branch of the Kennedy of Cassillis family, but her exact connection has not been discovered. She had joined the Queen's household in 1569 and she was to be with her to the end. According to Mary's unfinished testament of 1577, she was to receive 1000 francs.[26] During the last year of the Queen's life, Jane had charge of some of her jewels and silver plate, along with two gold looking-glasses, one incorporating a miniature of François II, and a selection of her garments – gowns, doublets, a petticoat, a cloak, waistcoats, caps and collars.[27]

After Mary was told by the Earl of Shrewsbury at Fotheringhay that she was to be executed the following day, she is said to have exclaimed to this favourite servant, 'Well, Jane Kennedy, did I not tell you this would happen . . . I knew they would never allow me to live, I was too great an obstacle to their religion'. That night when she lay down on her bed to rest, she asked Jane to read aloud to her from the Bible the story of some great sinner, and Jane chose the passage about the good thief.[28] At the execution, Jane was one of the two women allowed to accompany Mary on to the scaffold, where she helped her to take off her outer garments. Weeping, it was Jane who bound a white cloth embroidered with gold round Mary's eyes. After the Queen's funeral that summer, Jane followed her instructions and sought out the Countess of Arundel to give her one of Mary's rosaries, which is still preserved at Arundel Castle. She then went home to Scotland.

There, she had an audience with James VI and told him all that had happened. Not long afterwards she married Andrew Melville, who had been Mary's steward and was now master of the King's household. He was a Protestant, she a Roman Catholic, but their loyalty to the dead Queen had brought them together. In 1589, James VI chose Jane to be among the group of courtiers he was sending across the North Sea to bring back his bride, Princess Anne of Denmark. This was an honour for her, a recompense for her services to his dead mother but sadly, when Jane was crossing the River Forth from Burntisland to join the ship at Leith, her boat was in collision with another vessel and she and many of her companions drowned.[29] As for the other three chamberwomen on the 1573 Roll, nothing more is known of Marie Hanet but Christine Hog and Marie Pages are better documented, for they were the wife and daughter of another servant.

Sebastian Pages, better known as Bastian (a diminutive particularly popular in Lorraine), was one of the Queen's *valets-de-chambre*, a clever, amusing man who devised various masques including the one celebrating the christening of Prince James. He had married Christine Hog, one of the Queen's chamberwomen, on the morning of 9 February 1567, the very day of Lord Darnley's murder. Mary gave the bride as a wedding gift thirteen and three-quarter ells of black satin to be a wide-sleeved gown, along with velvet lining materials and thirty-two ells of green ribbon for a skirt and hood. She attended the wedding feast at noon and then later in the day she rode up to Kirk o' Field. She meant to spend the night there with Darnley but, as the evening wore on, someone reminded her of her promise to attend Bastian's wedding masque and she returned to Holyroodhouse. Four hours later, the town was shaken by the fateful explosion. Afterwards Bastian was imprisoned in Edinburgh Tolbooth on suspicion of complicity in the murder but he was later released and by the autumn of 1568, he and his wife were with Mary at Bolton.[30]

Telling the Archbishop of Glasgow in a letter dating from 10 September 1571 that Bastian was in her household, Mary described him as an invaluable servant who had come south at her request, 'where he and his wife serve me well and faithfully'. However, she was worried about their future for they had a young family and, although his friends had promised him advancement if he returned to France, he had no means of support should anything happen to the Queen. She therefore urged the Archbishop to find some source of income for him.[31] By 1586, Christine, her two daughters and her son were all listed as members of Mary's household and when there was talk of yet another reduction in the numbers, the English were reported to be hoping that if Christine were dismissed, Bastian would go too, 'wherein there were no great loss because he is cunning in his kind and full of sleight to corrupt young men'.[32] The family remained with Mary to the end, however, and she left Christine a pair of perfumed bracelets, a double ring and a white satin doublet. Bastian was to have 300 crowns, a gold jewel set with pearls and a sapphire, a little gold bird enamelled green, and a 'suit of savage attire' – possibly masquing costume or perhaps even highland dress, which is sometimes described in this way in contemporary accounts.[33]

The final chamberwoman on the 1573 list was Marie Pages, Christine and Bastian's eldest daughter. Marie was the Queen's god-daughter and she could have been no more than five, but perhaps she helped her mother with small tasks. She was recorded as receiving an annual salary of 100 sous at that time. Four years later, Mary intended leaving her 600 francs and, in her final will of 7 February 1587, bequeathed 2000 francs to her and recommended her to the Duchess of Guise, asking her to take Marie into her service.[34] During the last days at Fotheringhay, Marie had various belongings of Mary in her custody: an amber heart set in gold, a little gold crown of thorns, a small gold horseman and a miniature enamelled silver heart, a silver warming pan, a small silver box and some items of clothing including a black velvet gown and a taffeta hat.[35]

The very last female attendant on the 1573 list was Marie Carre the washerwoman, who may or may not have been with the Queen in England. Mary's laundry had by then become a matter of some concern because Elizabeth I insisted that her linen and that of her women should be inspected by the porters in the house before it went to be washed. This was a normal enough precaution, since jailors were always on the look out for letters or messages smuggled in or out among laundry. To Mary, however, the procedure seemed demeaning and in November 1571 she wrote to Catherine de Medici explaining what was happening and asking her to intervene. Surely, she said, Shrewsbury or his wife could lend her a laundress whom they trusted, so that the men did not have to handle her things. It is not known for certain if Catherine did make representations, but the later list of 1586 does include the names of English laundresses.[36]

This final list of Mary's servants was made at Chartley on 29 August 1586 by her last custodian, Sir Amyas Paulet, shortly before she was taken to Fotheringhay, and it records thirty-eight attendants, thirteen of them women.[37] There were no ladies-in-waiting or maids of honour but there were five gentlewomen of the Queen's chamber, two maidens who served the gentlewomen, Bastian's wife and two daughters and three laundresses. Their nationalities are noted alongside their names, with the Pages' daughters classified as Scots. Only one of the thirteen was French, Renée Rallay alias Beauregard. Four were English, Catherine Braye who was one of the gentlewomen's maidens and the three laundresses, Elizabeth Butler, Alice Sharpe and Alice Forster. The other eight were Scots.

Three of the five Scottish gentlewomen formed a tight little family group. 'Curle's wife', who heads the list, was Barbara Mowbray, wife of the Queen's secretary, Gilbert Curle. Barbara's father had been another of Mary's servants, John Mowbray, laird of Barnbougle, near Edinburgh, while Gilbert's father, an Edinburgh burgess, James Curle, had attended James V's Paris wedding to Princess Madeleine, later occupied the post of customs officer in the capital and was described by Mary in 1574 as a faithful servant. Gilbert's brother, James, was outlawed for being present at the Battle of Langside, while his sister Janet was married to Mary's Italian steward and purse-bearer, Timothy Cagnioli.[38] Together, they formed another of those familiar servant dynasties. Barbara Mowbray had joined Mary's household by the beginning of 1584 and her marriage to Gilbert took place the following year. The match was arranged by the Queen, who wrote that if she had done Gilbert some good by it, then he deserved it. Sir Amyas Paulet harboured dark suspicions that their wedding ceremony had been conducted by a disguised Roman Catholic priest.[39] Whatever the truth of that, Barbara and Gilbert went on to have a large family and we know that Jane Kennedy helped Barbara when she gave birth to one of her children at the beginning of 1587.[40] The Queen left Barbara a gold brooch depicting Aesop (or perhaps more correctly one of his fables) and two little rings, one of them set with a diamond.[41]

A month before Barbara's wedding, her sister Gilles Mowbray arrived in London, applied for a passport and was allowed to join the Queen's service.[42] She too was with Mary till the end, and at the time of the execution she had in her custody various personal items belonging to the Queen: a pair of gold bracelets, a crystal jewel set in gold and another jewel in the form of a little ox made of gold and enamelled red, along with 150 French crowns, a couple of black gowns, a kirtle, a cloak, a velvet hat, two pairs of virginals, a cittern and a velvet saddle.[43] In her final will on 7 February 1587, the Queen not only left Gilles the sum of 1000 francs but tried to make arrangements for her future, asking her own aunt, the Abbess of Saint Pierre-les-Dames in Rheims, either to find a good place for Mowbray or to keep her in her service for the honour of God.[44] Gilles had other plans, however, for she returned to Scotland and married Sir John Smith of Barnton.

As well as Janet Curle who married the banker, Gilbert Curle had another sister, Elizabeth, who also joined Mary's household and was to become one of her favourite women. On the eve of the execution, Mary bequeathed 2000 francs to her and it was Elizabeth who mounted the scaffold with Jane Kennedy, to help Mary to remove her gown before she knelt at the block.[45] Immediately after the execution, Elizabeth and the other women were locked in their chambers. They were allowed to attend one Requiem Mass the following morning, but although the Queen had begged for their release, they were held at Fotheringhay until 30 July, when they were taken to her funeral at Peterborough

Cathedral. Barbara and Elizabeth Curle, Gilles Mowbray, Jane Kennedy and Christine and Marie Pages walked in the procession and then stood to one side during the Protestant service. Some of the English ladies present came to embrace them afterwards, but when the rest of the congregation moved on to the funeral banquet in the Bishop's Palace, Mary's women wept in a separate room.[46]

They were not finally released for another two months, after which Gilbert and Barbara Curle and their eight children travelled to the continent. Elizabeth Curle went with them. Supported by money from Philip II of Spain, at Mary, Queen of Scots' request, they settled in Douai, eventually moving to Antwerp, where Elizabeth spent her last months in an impressive house with a large garden near St Andrew's Church.[47] Gilbert died in 1609, Barbara seven years later and Elizabeth in 1620. One of Gilbert and Barbara's sons, Hieronymous Curle, had entered the Church, becoming rector of the Scots College at Douai. He commissioned a fine black and white marble monument to his mother and his aunt, who were buried in St Andrew's Church. It can be seen to this day, high up on the wall, with its circular portrait on copper of Mary, Queen of Scots wearing her crown, and a Latin inscription proudly recording that Elizabeth Curle had received the Queen's last kiss.[48]

Some years earlier, in the first decade of the seventeenth century, Elizabeth Curle had decided to commission a large, full-length portrait of Mary, Queen of Scots. It is a striking image, portraying her as a martyr for the Roman Catholic faith and leaving all who saw it in no doubt as to those whom her faithful servant held responsible for her death. Mary stands on the scaffold in her familiar black dress and French hood, a large crucifix in her hand. To the right are two tiny background figures, one clasping her hands in anguished prayer, the other clutching a handkerchief. They are Elizabeth Curle herself and Jane Kennedy. Three Latin inscriptions tell how Mary, 'the Queen, the daughter, wife and mother of Kings', sought shelter with Elizabeth I but was instead held prisoner until 'by a dreadful sentence of the English council and by the command and perfidy of them and of Queen Elizabeth, her cousin, after 19 years' captivity, in an unheard of way, [she] was delivered over to be killed . . . '[49]

Notes

1. *Lettres*, ed. Labanoff, ii, 117
2. Durant, *Bess of Hardwick*, 61–2
3. Lovell, *Bess of Hardwick*, 1–210; Durant, *Bess of Hardwick*, 1–60
4. Swain, *Needlework of Mary, Queen of Scots*, 63–5, 75–8; Levey, *Elizabethan Inheritance*, 14–15
5. *Lettres*, ed. Labanoff, vi, 51–6
6. *Ibid.*, v, 104–5
7. *Ibid.*, v, 370; vi, 275–6
8. *Ibid.*, vi, 424–5
9. *Ibid.*, v, 389–90, 396–7, 402, 413, 425–9, 436–8, 462; vi, 45–6
10. *Ibid.*, vi, 51–6
11. *Ibid.*, vi, 305
12. *Ibid.*, vii, 168
13. *Ibid.*, vi, 342–3
14. Fraser, *Mary, Queen of Scots*, 530–47; Elizabeth Goldring, 'Talbot, Elizabeth [Bess of Hardwick], countess of Shrewsbury (1527?-1608)', *Oxford Dictionary of National Biography*, Oxford University Press 2004 [http://www.oxforddnb.com/view/article/26925, accessed 9 May 2004]
15. Lang, 'Household, 1573', 346–7
16. See p. 50
17. *Scots Peerage*, v, 439–43
18. Strickland, *Queens of Scotland*, vi, 354
19. Durant, *Bess of Hardwick*, 62. See p. 150
20. *Scots Peerage*, v, 441–2; *RPC*, ii, 220
21. *Scots Peerage*, v, 442
22. Lang, 'Household, 1573', 349–50
23. Greengrass, 'Mary, Dowager Queen of France', 177
24. *Lettres*, ed. Labanoff, iv, 269
25. *Ibid.*, v, 121
26. *Ibid.*, iv, 358
27. *Ibid.*, vii, 258–9, 262, 265, 267, 270
28. Fraser, *Mary, Queen of Scots*, 434, 532–4
29. *Ibid.*, 539–50; Stevenson, *Scotland's Last Royal Wedding*, 25

30. Fraser, *Mary, Queen of Scots*, 296–7, 338, 383; *Treasurer Accounts*, xii, 40; Teulet, *Papiers d'Etat*, 495
31. *Lettres*, ed. Labanoff, iii, 373. The letter is dated with the day and month. Labanoff supplies the year.
32. *Ibid.*, vii, 252
33. *Ibid.*, vii, 259–60, 265, 269
34. *Ibid.*, iv, 358; vi, 488, 491
35. *Ibid.*, vii, 259–60, 269
36. *Ibid.*, iii, 396
37. Fraser, *Mary, Queen of Scots*, 493–5
38. Durkan, 'The Library of Mary, Queen of Scots', 97, n.46; *RSS*, v, part i, 542; vi, 83; *Lettres*, ed. Labanoff, iv, 167
39. *Lettres*, ed. Labanoff, iv, 357; vi, 350
40. NLS, MS 3647.31, Letter of Sir Marmaduke Darell to Richard Bagot, 28 February 1587
41. Cf. p. 148; *Lettres*, ed. Labanoff, vii, 258
42. *Ibid.*, vii, 339
43. *Accounts and Papers relating to Mary, Queen of Scots*, 46
44. *Lettres*, ed. Labanoff, vi, 488, 491
45. *Ibid.*, vi, 488
46. Fraser, *Mary, Queen of Scots*, 533–47
47. Meulemans, 'Op zoek naar de woning', *passim*
48. Visschers, *Aenteekening*, 10–12
49. Marshall, 'Mary, Queen of Scots: a Flemish Connection', 43-7.

12

Elizabeth I of England

The relationship between Mary, Queen of Scots and Elizabeth I of England has been a subject of endless fascination not only for historians but for dramatists, historical novelists, television producers and film makers. The long hostility between Scotland and England and between England and France made tension between the two queens inevitable, and then there was the complicating factor of their family relationship. Both were descendants of Henry VII of England, Mary had been taught to believe that she had the greater right to the English throne, and the fact that she was Roman Catholic and Elizabeth was Protestant intensified the hostility between their supporters, if not between themselves. Then again there is the suspicion that, on Elizabeth's part at least, there was sexual jealousy between them.

Mary herself was well aware of the complexities of the situation. Conversing with Elizabeth's ambassador Thomas Randolph in February 1565, the month when Darnley came to Scotland, she alluded to the political difficulties, saying, 'How much better were it that we being two Queens so near of kin, neighbours and living in one isle, should be friends and live together like sisters, than by strange means divide ourselves to the hurt of both'. Yet this was no naive expression of unrealistic hope, for when Randolph replied with assurances of Elizabeth's good will, Mary answered, 'To say that we may for all that live friends, we may say and promise what we will but it will pass both our powers'.[1]

So what were the realities of their relationship? Elizabeth had been born on 7 September 1533, in what were widely perceived to be scandalous circumstances. Henry VIII had long been married to his faithful Spanish wife, Catherine of Aragon, but for the previous seven years he had been passionately in love with her sophisticated, French-educated lady-in-waiting, Anne Boleyn. Apart from his feelings for Anne, he desperately needed a son and heir but saw no likelihood of Catherine providing one. Over the years, she had given birth to four stillborn children, a daughter dead in infancy, and one surviving child, a girl, Princess Mary. Henry was desperate to end his marriage, but his situation was complicated by the fact that Catherine had a very influential relative. Her nephew was the Holy Roman Emperor, Charles V, and so foreign policy as well as dynastic considerations had to be taken into account.

Henry decided to argue that his marriage to Catherine should be declared null and void on the grounds that she had originally been the wife of his elder brother, Prince Arthur. When Arthur had died not long after his wedding, it had been arranged that Henry should marry his widow in an effort to preserve England's alliance with Spain. Canon Law forbade the marriage of a man to his brother's wife, but Pope Julius II had granted the necessary dispensation, allowing their wedding to take place. Now, however, Henry VIII declared that a marriage such as his was contrary to the law of God. No dispensation could change that, he said, and for good measure he claimed that in any case the papal dispensation had been invalid. His arguments were in vain. Clement VII had succeeded Julius as Pope by now and, apart from the fact that Henry's case was weak, Clement did not dare offend Charles V, who had sacked Rome in 1527. When, after lengthy and complicated discussions, it became clear that Clement never would annul the marriage, Henry decided to take matters into his own hands. A complete break with Rome was the only answer. In 1531 he made himself Supreme Head of the Church of England 'as far as the law of Christ allows'.[2]

Anne Boleyn told him in January 1533 that she was pregnant, he immediately married her in a quick, secret ceremony before dawn and Catherine of Aragon was informed that she was no longer Queen. In future she would be known as Dowager Princess of Wales and her daughter Princess Mary was declared illegitimate. At the end of May, Anne Boleyn was crowned, amidst lavish celebrations. She went into labour three months later and gave birth to a girl, whom Henry named Elizabeth, after his mother. At three months old, Elizabeth was given her own household and taken to live at the Palace of Hatfield. Her bitterly resentful half-sister, Mary, was brought there too, as one of her ladies-in-waiting.[3]

Henry's actions brought the Reformation to England, infuriated Charles V and offended Roman Catholics everywhere. For them, Catherine remained Henry's legal wife, Anne was no more than his concubine and Elizabeth was his bastard. When Anne failed to give him the son he desired, he accused her of adultery and had her executed for treason. The very next day, he was betrothed to one of her ladies-in-waiting, Jane Seymour. At only three years old, Elizabeth was far too young to realise what was happening, but her household was thrown into disarray and her father announced that she too was illegitimate, cutting her out of the succession. On 12 October 1537, Queen Jane gave birth to a son, the future Edward VI, but she died of septicaemia less than a fortnight later. Henry would marry three more times, but he had no further children.[4]

Brought up in the country in her own household, Elizabeth, a sharp, intelligent child, received an excellent education in the classics, French and Italian, and sent dutiful letters and gifts to her usually absent father. Henry VIII died on 28 January 1547, when she was thirteen, and was succeeded by his only son, Edward VI, an intelligent, promising boy who had developed a deep devotion to Protestantism. Roman Catholic Mary stayed away from his Court but Edward received Protestant Elizabeth graciously on her occasional visits to London. Her first realisation that her high position could bring unexpected dangers came when she went to live with her final stepmother, Katherine Parr, and Katherine's new husband, Thomas Seymour. He was personable, high-spirited and enjoyed teasing Elizabeth. She, now an impressionable teenager, responded eagerly. They flirted and his pregnant wife watched their boisterous fun with indulgent amusement until tragedy soon intervened. Katherine died after the birth of her daughter and before long Thomas was arrested for plotting to marry Elizabeth and overthrow his brother, the Duke of Somerset, who was ruling England as the young King's Regent. Found guilty, Thomas was executed on 20 May 1549 and Elizabeth narrowly escaped imprisonment.[5]

Worse was to follow. Edward VI contracted tuberculosis and died. He was succeeded by his devout half-sister, Mary, who promptly restored Roman Catholicism, declared her parents' divorce null and void and insisted that Elizabeth go to Mass. The following year, when Sir Thomas Wyatt rebelled against Mary, Elizabeth was implicated and sent to the Tower of London. Her prospects seemed bleak. Not only had her father executed her mother, but now her sister seemed intent on sending her to a similar fate. After two months it was decided that there was insufficient evidence to convict her of treason and she was transferred to Woodstock in Oxfordshire, where she was held under house arrest. There she had to stay for eleven months, finally owing her release to the intervention of Charles V's son Philip of Spain, who had married Mary I. There is no evidence that Philip had any fond feelings for Elizabeth. His motivation was entirely political. He knew that it was unlikely that he and Mary would have any children, for she was in very poor health. If Elizabeth were to vanish from the scene, then the person with the best claim to the English throne would be Mary, Queen of Scots, and she, of course, was the future daughter-in-law of his father's great enemy, Henri II of France. Philip therefore persuaded his wife to release Elizabeth.[6]

Mary I had fallen deeply in love with her husband and, eager to please him, she began to persecute her Protestant subjects, many of whom fled to the continent. Elizabeth considered doing so too when Mary tried to insist that she marry one of Philip's allies, Emmanuel Philibert, Duke of Savoy, threatening to send her to the Tower if she disobeyed. In a panic, Elizabeth asked the French ambassador whether she could flee to France. He replied tersely that if she hoped to inherit the throne of England she must stay where she was.[7] Mary I, meanwhile, was growing ever more unpopular and her personal life was in ruins. Her health was precarious, she suffered two false pregnancies and she constantly longed for the presence of her husband, who was spending almost all his time on the continent. At the beginning of November 1558, realising that she was dying, she sent word to Elizabeth that she would allow her to succeed to the throne provided she maintain the Roman Catholic faith and pay all her debts. Elizabeth agreed. Mary died on 17 November, Elizabeth became Queen and England was transformed into a Protestant country once more.[8]

Elizabeth's accession did not, however, go unchallenged. Henri II at once declared that Mary, Queen of Scots was the rightful monarch, Elizabeth an illegitimate usurper. When Mary attended the wedding of his daughter, Princess Claude, early in 1559, he ordered her servants to wear on their livery the arms of England quartered with her own. His great ambition was, he believed, about to be realised: the creation of what the French termed 'a Franco-British Empire'. He would rule France, Mary and his son would rule Scotland and England, and when he himself died they would reign over all three countries.[9] Meanwhile Mary of Guise in her dying months was trying in vain to stem the tide of the Reformation in Scotland. The French sent her reinforcements, and Elizabeth dispatched an army to help the Scottish Protestants. Worn out with the long struggle, Mary of Guise died on 11 June 1560. By the Treaty of Edinburgh, signed less than a month later, it was agreed that all foreign forces should leave Scotland and Mary, Queen of Scots and her husband would henceforth 'abstain from using or bearing the said title and arms of the kingdom of England or Ireland . . .' Mary, however, avoided ratifying the treaty and the battle lines were drawn.[10]

Mary was widowed later that year, and when she decided to return to Scotland in 1561, she sought a safe conduct from Elizabeth in case her ship was driven ashore in England by storms. Elizabeth flew into a rage and refused, because Mary had not ratified the Treaty of Edinburgh. 'I trust the wind will be so favourable as I shall not need to come to the coast of England,' Mary told Sir Nicholas Throckmorton, the English ambassador in Paris, 'but if I do, then, Monsieur l'Ambassadeur, the Queen your mistress shall have me in her hands to do her will of me, and if she be so hard-hearted as to desire my end, she may then do her pleasure and make sacrifice of me.' Mary always was fond of a dramatic turn of phrase, but on this occasion her words were to have a prophetic ring to them.[11]

In the past, Mary had been able to leave her relationship with Elizabeth to her father-in-law and then to her husband, but now everything had changed and the two queens were going to have to decide how to deal with each other. Suppressing as far as she could her alarm at the threat Mary posed, Elizabeth chose to adopt the lofty tone of an experienced monarch addressing a newcomer to the task, while Mary in her letters was all friendly civility. At the French Court there was nothing but contempt and dislike for the English Queen, but William Maitland of Lethington was urging Mary to pursue a policy of friendship with England. His great ambition was to see the two countries united – not as part of a Roman Catholic Franco-British Empire, of course, but as a Protestant kingdom, and only after Elizabeth's death. Mary must cultivate Elizabeth to this end.[12]

Mary had been taught to regard herself as the rightful Queen of England but she knew that she did not have the power to depose her rival and take the throne herself. Instead, she would content herself with official recognition as Elizabeth's successor. Various factors made her willing to play a waiting game. Elizabeth was making it clear to her own disconcerted parliament and advisers that she would never marry and have children. Mary I had said the very same thing, and there is little doubt that the sisters had been traumatised by their father's treatment of his wives. Mary I had changed her mind in the end, in the hope of re-establishing a Roman Catholic dynasty in England, but Elizabeth's personal aversion to giving herself into the power of any man strengthened her belief that it was impossible for a queen in her own right to find a suitable consort. In her sister's marriage to Philip of Spain she had already seen at close quarters how England's interests had been subordinated to that of another country, and she well knew that if she took the other possible course and chose one of her own subjects, she would not only be damaging her position by marrying beneath herself but she would stir up all manner of jealousies among her nobility.

If Elizabeth kept to her unconventional resolution, then Mary's place in the succession was almost secure. What was more, life expectancy in the sixteenth century was short. Accident, plague or smallpox might carry her off at any moment and so Mary believed that time was on her side. Again, much is usually made of the fact that she and Elizabeth were cousins, but they were not first cousins. Mary's father was the same generation as Elizabeth, his first cousin. To put it another way, Henry VII was Elizabeth's grandfather but Mary's great-grandfather. This may seem a trivial point and it is true that Elizabeth was only nine years older than Mary, but age gaps are more noticeable when people are young and how they are perceived is more important than the precise number of years involved. Mary was a child of six when flirtatious Elizabeth was rumoured to be the likely bride of Thomas Seymour, and when Mary returned to Scotland at nearly nineteen, Elizabeth was almost twenty-eight, long past the usual age for marriage.

On at least two occasions during her imprisonment, Mary would assure Elizabeth that she would obey her 'as a daughter does her mother' and 'as if she had the honour to be Elizabeth's daughter'.[13] This was not what Elizabeth wanted to hear, and presumably someone gave Mary a hint, for after that she referred to herself more acceptably as being like the English Queen's younger sister. Renouncing marriage, Elizabeth had deliberately created for herself the image of The Virgin Queen, perpetually young, perpetually beautiful, perpetually desirable. It was extremely difficult for a woman to rule over men in a male-dominated society, and that was Elizabeth's way of doing it. This did not mean that she was supremely confident. Rather the reverse was true, and her carefully assumed image was a veil for her insecurities. Determined to be the centre of attention, she was rarely at ease in her relationships with other women and there is no doubt that she was personally jealous of Mary, that statuesque, majestic younger woman, not only a queen but, until the death of François II, a cherished bride and so lavishly praised for her beauty and her charm.

Sir James Melville's *Memoirs* recount the entertaining conversations he had with Elizabeth when he was sent to London as Mary's envoy. Having dazzled him with the variety of her wardrobe, appearing in a different dress each day throughout his visit, Elizabeth took to questioning him about his own Queen's appearance. Was Mary's hair (dark auburn) or hers (reddish gold) the better colour? Which of them was the fairest? Gathering his diplomatic skills, 'I said she was the fairest queen in England and ours the fairest queen in Scotland'. She persisted, however, and when he answered that each was the fairest lady at her own Court 'and that Her Majesty was whiter but our queen was very lovely', she moved on to quiz him about their relative height. Which was the taller? He replied that Mary was. '"Then", saith she, "she is too high and that herself was neither too high nor too low."'[14]

Could Elizabeth ever have set aside her suspicions and decided that what was shared by two queens in their own right was far more important than what divided them? There were times when it seemed that she could, and Mary certainly believed it to be possible, convinced as she was that if only they could meet in person, she would be able to banish all Elizabeth's dark doubts. Sir William Cecil and the other English councillors seem to have thought so too, and that may well have been why they were so determined that such a meeting should never take place. Of course people tend to attribute far greater powers to their enemies than these foes actually possess, but there is no denying that while Elizabeth was prickly and imperious, Mary had inherited her mother's gift of empathy and her charm of manner. There is just a faint possibility that a personal encounter might have worked a miracle.

The fact of the matter was that both Elizabeth and Mary had ambivalent feelings towards each other. Elizabeth's suspicion and hostility were tempered by her recognition that Mary was a fellow monarch. That gave them a strong bond, for however threatening Mary might seem, Elizabeth had more in common with her than she did with William Cecil or Lord Robert Dudley or anyone else who was not a reigning king or queen. Each believed that she had been chosen by God to rule, and that placed them in a very special category. As for Mary, her contempt for the woman she considered to be Henry VIII's bastard was modified not only by her awareness of their shared sovereignty but by the nearness of their kingdoms and their family relationship, all features which she never tired of pointing out. In addition, while Elizabeth preferred men, Mary instinctively felt friendship for other women, and looked for it to be reciprocated. 'It is fitter for none to live in peace than for women,' she told Elizabeth, 'and for my part I pray you think that I desire it with all my heart.'[15] With her mother dead and so many of her friends left behind in France, she seems to have felt a perfectly genuine impulse of friendship towards her sister queen. Unfortunately, the amicable feelings experienced by both of them were soon minimised by the realities of sixteenth-century politics.

Mary's choice of husband was a matter of urgent concern from the moment that she was widowed in France and it was to lead to a deterioration in her relations with Elizabeth. When she came back to Scotland, Mary was still deep in negotiations to marry Don Carlos of Spain, something which both Catherine de Medici and Elizabeth I were desperate to prevent. In order to keep her negotiations secret, Mary had set up a secret correspondence with one of her Guise relatives, Anne, Duchess of Arschot, whom she addressed as her aunt. In fact this lady had been her mother's affectionate cousin, the daughter of Antoine, Duke of Lorraine. The Duchess was a friend of Antoine de Perrenot, Cardinal Granvelle, Philip II's chief minister in the Low Countries, and through him Mary sent Philip assurances of her desire to return Scotland to Roman Catholicism.[16]

In June 1563, Elizabeth I warned Maitland of Lethington that Mary would be her enemy if she married Don Carlos. If, however, she married someone of whom the English Queen approved, then Elizabeth would acknowledge Mary as her heir. That November, she advised Mary to marry an English nobleman and recommended

Lord Robert Dudley, the man generally believed to be her own lover. The Scots were affronted, Maitland gave Elizabeth a discouraging reply when she spoke to him about it, and Dudley himself was horrified. Historians have long been puzzled by Elizabeth's behaviour, suspecting her of cynical deception, but it remains possible that she was for a time convinced that a marriage between Lord Robert and Mary would solve all her problems. She could not marry him herself, but since he was completely loyal to her she might be able to control Mary through him, and he would certainly never allow his wife to try to gain the English throne. The thought that one of his children would eventually inherit her throne may even have comforted Elizabeth. In the end, of course, she could not bear to part with him and instead she offered Henry, Lord Darnley, no doubt at the instigation of his mother, the Countess of Lennox.[17]

Did the Countess's incessant urgings temporarily blind Elizabeth to the dangers of the match? Darnley was not the safe suitor Lord Robert would have been. He may have seemed to Elizabeth to be perfectly biddable and loyal but, like Mary, he was the great-grandchild of Henry VII and by marrying Mary he would be uniting their claims to the throne of England. Possibly Elizabeth, like Sir James Melville, thought Darnley effeminate and did not believe for a moment that Mary would contemplate marrying him. Whatever she felt for him personally, however, Mary was perfectly well aware of Darnley's dynastic significance and she imagined that by taking the man Elizabeth had offered she would please her. In the event, Elizabeth's reaction was very different. She summoned Darnley and his father back to London, and was both outraged and alarmed when they refused to obey. To her fury, Mary and Darnley then married.[18]

By the time that Mary became pregnant, her relationship with her husband had deteriorated dramatically but the fact that she had conceived considerably enhanced her prospects of gaining recognition as heir to the English throne. William Cecil had already warned that if Mary should marry and have a child, then the people of England, both Protestant and Catholic, would flock to her cause. At a banquet in Holyroodhouse in honour of visiting ambassadors,

Mary triumphantly if unwisely told the assembled company 'that there was no other Queen of England but herself'.[19] Her son James was born on 19 June 1566 and Elizabeth heard the news with a pang of regret. 'Alack, the Queen of Scots is lighter of a fair son and I am but of barren stock,' she is said to have exclaimed.[20] However, when Mary invited her to be the baby's godmother, she sent an unexpectedly lavish gift in the form of a solid gold font. That autumn, taken ill at Craigmillar Castle, Mary declared that if she were to die, she wanted Elizabeth to bring up her little son.

Elizabeth responded by suggesting that she and Mary sign a personal accord, agreeing that neither should do anything to harm the other. Elizabeth would then recognise Mary as her heir.[21] It seemed for a moment that a harmonious relationship was possible and Mary was enthusiastic, but dramatic events supervened. Darnley was assassinated at Kirk o' Field, and Mary was generally suspected of having been implicated in the murder. A month after the event, Elizabeth wrote to tell her, 'My ears have been so astounded, my mind so disturbed and my heart so appalled at hearing the horrible report of the abominable murder of your late husband and my slaughtered cousin that I can scarcely as yet summon the spirit to write about it'.

However, she went on, 'I must tell you boldly what I think about it, as I cannot hide the fact that I grieve more for you than for him. Oh Madam, I should neither perform the office of a faithful cousin nor an affectionate friend if I studied more to please your ears than to preserve your honour. Therefore I will not conceal from you that people for the most part are saying that you will look through your fingers at this deed instead of avenging it'. She would never harbour such suspicions herself, of course, for all the gold in the world, but she begged Mary to take action against the perpetrator of the crime, 'even him whom you have nearest to you if he was involved'. She meant, of course, Bothwell, and she added grimly that Mary should ratify the Treaty of Edinburgh at once.[22]

Mary did not like the tone of this letter and she did not tell Elizabeth when she married Bothwell. Of course the news soon reached London and Elizabeth's response was blunt. 'No good friend you have in the whole world can like thereof,' she told Mary, 'and if we should otherwise write or say, we should abuse you. For how could a worse choice be made for your honour than in such haste to marry such a subject who, besides other notorious lacks, public fame has charged with the murder of your late husband . . .' She was even more horrified, however, when she heard about the confrontation at Carberry Hill and Mary's imprisonment at Lochleven. Furious that any monarch should be treated in that way by her subjects, Elizabeth quickly sent Sir Nicholas Throckmorton north to try to obtain Mary's release on condition that she repudiated Bothwell.

'What warrant have they, in Scripture, as subjects, to depose their Prince?' she asked angrily, telling Throckmorton, 'Plainly denounce them that if they determine the deprivation of the Queen their sovereign lady of her royal estate, we are determined . . . that we will take plain part against them to revenge their sovereign, for an example to all posterity . . .' Of course she abhorred the murder of Darnley, she said, 'but 'we think it not lawful nor tolerable for them, being by God's ordinance subjects, to call her, whom also by God's ordinance is their superior and Prince, to answer to their accusations by way of force, for we do not think it consonant in nature the head should be subject to the foot'.[23]

When Mary refused to put Bothwell away because she was pregnant by him, Elizabeth told her that, if the worst came to the worst, she should abdicate in order to save her life. Any such abdication, extorted by force, was illegal and she could say so once she was safe. Mary followed this advice, was grateful for it, and signed the deed of abdication saying that it had no validity because she was being compelled to do it.[24] When Elizabeth heard that she had indeed been forced to take this step, she was outraged, and was only prevented from making war on the Scots when Cecil warned her that this would lead to Mary's certain death. Even so, her support during this crisis meant a great deal to Mary and it was what later encouraged her to ride into England after the Battle of Langside in 1568 rather than taking ship to France.

Time and again in subsequent years Mary would remind Elizabeth how she had come to England to throw herself into Elizabeth's arms, as she liked to put it, in the expectation that her principal friend would help her to regain her kingdom. She was desperate to speak to Elizabeth in person, tell her all that had happened, and explain that she was innocent of Darnley's murder. Elizabeth refused to see her. 'Oh Madam,' she wrote to her, 'There is no creature living more willing to hear such a declaration than me . . . But . . .' She could not possibly risk her own reputation. Once Mary was acquitted of murdering her husband, then she would hear what she had to say. Mary replied, 'When has a prince ever been blamed for listening to those who have been falsely accused?', but Elizabeth was adamant.[25]

William Cecil and the other privy councillors were all for handing Mary over to Moray so that he could go on ruling Scotland in the Protestant interest. Cecil's deep suspicion of Mary had been exacerbated by the report he had received from Sir Francis Knollys. 'This lady and princess is a notable woman,' Knollys had written. 'She seemeth to regard no ceremonious honour beside the acknowledgment of her estate regal. She showeth a disposition to speak much, to be bold, to be pleasant and to be very familiar. She showeth a great desire to be avenged of her enemies. She showeth a readiness to expose herself to all perils in hope of victory . . .' He had formed such a high opinion of Mary's shrewdness that he advised Cecil not to go on deceiving her about their intentions, since it might not be wise 'to dissemble with such a lady'.[26]

Elizabeth's attitude was rather different because, whatever she may have thought Mary had done, her instinct was still to protect a fellow monarch. The Scots had created a dangerous precedent by deposing their Queen who was of a different religion to themselves. Her own Roman Catholic subjects would be encouraged to follow this bad example. She felt impelled to restore Mary to the throne of Scotland but Cecil and her other privy councillors would not hear of it. In the end the uneasy compromise was reached whereby Mary would be held in the north of England until a public enquiry investigated both her part in the murder of Lord Darnley and the counter-accusations she was making against Moray and his friends.[27]

Throughout her imprisonment Mary was to pour out her feelings in long and passionate letters to her Guise relatives, her French friends, her Scottish supporters, to Elizabeth I and to Catherine de Medici. In the immediate aftermath of her arrival in England she had also sent a messenger to her childhood friend, Princess Elisabeth, Catherine's daughter, who was now Queen of Spain. At the end of September 1568 she received from Elisabeth what she described as amiable and comforting letters 'which seem sent by God for my consolation in the midst of the troubles and adversities which surround me'. No other correspondence between the two has survived, no hint of any letter since Elisabeth's departure for Spain. It seems likely, however, that they had kept in touch, for when she wrote back Mary begged Elisabeth's forgiveness for not having written during the tumultuous months of 1567–8. She continued her long letter with a discussion of the situation of Roman Catholics in England, noting: 'I have been offered many fine things to change religion, which I shall never do', and she urged Elisabeth to beg both Philip II and Charles IX of France to tell the Queen of England that she must be restored to her throne. If that could be achieved, then Mary would take up Elisabeth's kind offer to marry one of her little daughters to Prince James. Less than a fortnight after Mary wrote this letter, Elisabeth died in childbirth, but for years Mary clung to the hope of a Spanish marriage for her son.[28]

On 4 October 1568 the public enquiry into Mary's affairs opened at York, with Moray and Morton attending in person. Queen Elizabeth would take no part, preferring to distance herself from what was being done, not least because she recognised that she had no right to sit in judgment on another monarch. Mary was not allowed to be present either, much to her indignation. 'I am a free princess, having the imperial crown given me of God, and acknowledges no other superior,' she protested, but her objections were ignored and Moray produced the notorious Casket Letters which he said proved her guilt. In the end, the conference was moved to

Westminster, but its findings were inconclusive and on 10 January Cecil read out a statement to the effect that neither Mary's complaints against her subjects nor theirs against her had been proved.[29]

Moray and his friends were, however, allowed to return to Scotland, while Mary was moved into stricter captivity at Tutbury Castle. In spite of this, she remained convinced that if once she were returned to Scotland she could resume her reign despite the opposition of her rebels, for she, 'placed by God as head unto them, tends yet to do the office of a loving mother to our subjects'.[30] This was a constant theme in the long letters she wrote to Elizabeth and she had made it plain from the start that she would not accept life in captivity. 'If I shall be holden here perforce,' she had told Sir Francis Knollys, 'you may be sure then, being as a desperate person, I will use any attempts that may serve my purpose, either by myself or my friends.'[31] In the early days, rage and indignation were plainly evident in her correspondence. She was in touch with many of her Scottish supporters still and restoration seemed to her to be imminent. As the years passed and one bitter disappointment followed another, she lost her initial conviction that Elizabeth would help her. She tried hard to be diplomatic, reminding Elizabeth constantly that they were fellow queens, but now she distrusted her. Elizabeth had raised her hopes too many times, only to dash them again.

For her part, Elizabeth wrestled with the very real problem of what to do with Mary. She accepted that sending her back to Scotland was impractical and would only destabilise the situation there, and yet by holding her in England she was almost encouraging conspiracies against herself. There were always people ready to plot to depose her and replace her with Mary. There was the plan to marry Mary to the Duke of Norfolk and place them jointly on the throne of England, the Northern Rising of Roman Catholics, and then the Ridolfi Plot, which revived the idea of the Norfolk marriage and resulted in the execution of the Duke.[32] The worst of it was that foreign powers involved themselves in these plots. The Duke of Alva, Philip II's governor in the Netherlands, supported both the Northern Rebellion and the Ridolfi Plot while Pope Pius V, under the mistaken impression that the rising had been a success, issued a declaratory sentence against 'Elizabeth, Pretender Queen of England', deposing her and absolving her subjects from their oath of allegiance to her. Anyone who obeyed her orders would be excommunicated.[33]

This was extremely damaging, of course, and English Protestants were highly alarmed. Elizabeth decided to recognise James VI as King of Scots, something she had avoided doing before, because it meant that she was tacitly acknowledging Mary's abdication. A special committee of the Houses of Parliament was appointed to consider the problem of the Queen of Scots, and it advised Elizabeth bluntly to 'cut off her head and make no more ado about her'. She refused. Parliament then drafted another bill ruling out of the succession anyone who tried to claim the throne during Elizabeth's lifetime. Thanking the members for their concern, she turned this down too. Apart from her revulsion at the thought of signing the death warrant of another monarch, she had recently negotiated a new treaty with the French and she had no desire to jeopardise it by executing the King of France's former sister-in-law.[34]

The plots continued, Mary continued to long desperately for freedom, and in the 1580s it seemed for a time that a peaceful solution might be found to the dilemma. Elizabeth indicated interest in a new scheme to restore Mary to the Scottish throne, to rule jointly with her Protestant son, James VI. Ever since her forced abdication Mary had been strongly opposed to recognising him as King, but now she was willing to compromise. Elizabeth would obviously have to give her approval. However, the whole project foundered when it became evident in the spring of 1585 that, in spite of earlier assurances of support, James himself was against the idea. He had no desire to share his throne with his mother. Mary was bitterly disappointed by what was for her a dreadful betrayal by her only son. He then made his own agreement with Elizabeth, with no mention of his mother.[35]

Even so, it seemed that the threat to the English throne would never go away until Mary, Queen of Scots was dead. Cecil had by now reached the conclusion that Elizabeth would not execute Mary unless she were sufficiently frightened into doing so. Sir Francis Walsingham was running a highly efficient network of spies with the aim of rooting out conspiracies and he now set about initiating false plots against Elizabeth in the expectation that Mary would become irrevocably involved in them. In this he was correct. The Babington Plot of 1587 was by no means his first, but it was the most successful. Walsingham's spies had infiltrated Mary's household and he lured her into a secret correspondence with Sir Anthony Babington, who was plotting to assassinate Elizabeth. Correspondence between Babington and Mary was intercepted and, in case Mary's letters were not incriminating enough, Walsingham forged a postscript to one of them, giving the impression that Mary wanted details of the men who were to kill Elizabeth. Elizabeth was, not unnaturally, thrown into a panic when the plot was revealed to her, and she demanded a slow and lingering death for Babington and his fellow conspirators. Even then she drew back from the prospect of prosecuting Mary until Cecil convinced her that if she did nothing her life would be in constant danger.[36]

Mary was tried at Fotheringhay Castle in October 1587. 'I do not deny that I have earnestly wished for liberty,' she said when she was questioned, 'and done my utmost to procure it for myself. In this I have acted from a very natural wish, but can I be responsible for the criminal projects of a few desperate men, which they planned without my knowledge or participation?'[37] Her protests were in vain and she was found guilty. Until now, Elizabeth had shielded Mary by refusing to order her execution. Even at this time of crisis she could not bring herself to sign the death warrant until her exasperated advisers came up with a plan which would allow her to save face. On 1 February 1587 her secretary gave her a pile of papers for signature. She went through them, signing them with scarcely a glance, pretending that she did not know that the death warrant was among them.[38]

Afterwards, she claimed that she had signed the warrant by mistake, but of course she knew what she was doing and even at this late date she wrote to Mary's keeper, Sir Amyas Paulet, telling him she was very disappointed that he had found no private way of disposing of Mary. 'God forbid that I should make so foul a shipwreck of my conscience!' he replied. Mary was executed on 8 February 1587. The following year, Elizabeth's navy triumphantly defeated Philip II of Spain's avenging armada and she continued to rule successfully for a further sixteen years, dying on 24 March 1603. Her throne then passed to Mary's son James, Scotland and England were united, and on his orders Mary and Elizabeth now lie near each other in Westminster Abbey.[39]

Notes

1. Guy, *My Heart is my Own*, 203
2. Scarisbrick, *Henry VIII*, 135–355; Ives, *Anne Boleyn*, 47–234
3. Ridley, *Elizabeth I*, 22–3; Loades, *Mary Tudor*, 73–83
4. Scarisbrick, *Henry VIII*, 348–55; Loades, *Mary Tudor*, 95, 98, 99, 108, 114
5. Haynes, *Burghley State Papers*, 95–100; Hibbert, *The Virgin Queen*, 24, 29–35; Ridley, *Elizabeth I*, 38–41
6. Loades, *Mary Tudor*, 211–15, 283, 316, 322, 326; Ridley, *Elizabeth I*, 56–7, 94
7. Mumby, *Girlhood of Queen Elizabeth*, 234; Loades, *Mary Tudor*, 288–91; Ridley, *Elizabeth I*, 69–70
8. Loades, *Mary Tudor*, 274–314
9. Guy, *My Heart is my Own*, 96–7
10. Donaldson, *Scottish Historical Documents*, 121
11. Hay Fleming, *Mary, Queen of Scots*, 246n.
12. Guy, *My Heart is my Own*, 114; *Lettres*, ed. Labanoff, i, 62; vii, 288; Donaldson, *Mary, Queen of Scots*, 73
13. *Lettres*, ed. Labanoff, ii, 308; iii, 106–9; *cf. CSP Scot*, ii, 121
14. Melville, *Memoirs*, 38–9
15. *CSP Scot.*, i, 559
16. Turnbull, *Letters of Mary Stuart*, 144–5n., Poull, *La Maison ducale de Lorraine*, 204; *Foreign Correspondence*, 1548–57, 96–8, 146–7; Cloulas, *Diane de Poitiers*, 276; Chéruel, *Marie Stuart et Catherine de Médicis*, 35; *Lettres*, ed. Labanoff, i, 204, 209–13, 244–5, 248–9
17. *CSP Spanish*, i, 312–13; *CSP Scot.*, ii, 19; Melville, *Memoirs*, 35; Donaldson, *Mary, Queen of Scots*, 78; Guy, *My Heart is my Own*, 190–3; Fraser, *Mary, Queen of Scots*, 212–18

18. Melville, *Memoirs*, 45–7; Hay Fleming, *Mary, Queen of* Scots, 105–6; Fraser, *Mary, Queen of Scots*, 226–32; Ridley, *Elizabeth I*, 138–40
19. Guy, *My Heart is my Own*, 243 and 453n.
20. Melville, *Memoirs*, 45–7
21. Guy, *My Heart is my Own*, 276–80
22. *CSP Scot.*, ii, 529
23. Keith, *History*, ii, 702
24. *Lettres*, ed. Labanoff, ii, 59; Ridley, *Elizabeth I*, 150–1
25. *Lettres*, ed. Labanoff, vii, 139–41; ii, 97–9
26. *CSP Scot.*, ii, 428
27. Donaldson, *Mary, Queen of Scots*, 144, a point further developed in Guy, *My Heart is my Own, passim*
28. *Lettres*, ed. Labanoff, ii, 183–7
29. Donaldson, *First Trial, passim*
30. *Lettres*, ed. Labanoff, ii, 230
31. *CSP Scot.*, ii, 516
32. Williams, *A Tudor Tragedy*, 126–259; Fraser, *Mary, Queen of Scots*, 409–31
33. Ridley, *Elizabeth I*, 170–1
34. Fraser, *Mary, Queen of Scots*, 430–1; Guy, *My Heart is my Own*, 466
35. *Lettres*, ed. Labanoff, vi, 98–104, 107–9, 113–16, 122–6; Fraser, *Mary, Queen of Scots*, 455–74
36. *Lettres*, ed. Labanoff, vi, 275–90, 385–93, 440–1; Ridley, *Elizabeth I*, 255–7; Fraser, *Mary, Queen of Scots*, 475–500
37. Chantelauze, *Marie Stuart*, 490 *et seq.*; Fraser, *Mary, Queen of Scots*, 501–22
38. Nicolas, *Life of William Davidson*, 83; Fraser, *Mary, Queen of Scots*, 528
39. Fraser, *Mary, Queen of Scots*, 523–55; Guy, *My Heart is my Own*, 479–515

Conclusion

Mary, Queen of Scots, like so many other women, has been defined by the men in her life but, once identified, the female relatives, attendants, friends and enemies are no longer a ghostly band, glimpsed in the background. Some, like Catherine de Medici and Elizabeth I, are already very well-known, in the forefront of history. Others, such as the Dame de Parois, Guillemette de Sarrebruche and Margaret Erskine are largely unfamiliar, yet they emerge as strong personalities with interesting and dramatic lives of their own. What, then, may we conclude about Mary's relationships with them? Given the lack of their personal correspondence, it is difficult to find direct evidence, but Mary's own letters, the comments of male contemporaries, lists of gifts by the Queen and intended bequests allow us to glimpse something of her interaction with the women in her life.

Other female rulers might have seemed to be natural allies, but their dealings with each other were complicated by the fact that any personal impulses of friendship had to be subordinated to the demands of politics and foreign policy. Moreover, many of their transactions were carried out by male advisers with agendas of their own. Then again, during her long years of captivity Mary, Queen of Scots' power ebbed away and she was marginalised, easily ignored when alliances were discussed and treaties negotiated. Even the many plots to place her on the English throne were instigated not by Mary herself, but by ambitious courtiers. That said, there is no denying that many of her actions were in response to what was being done by those two powerful women, Catherine de Medici and Elizabeth I. The tragedy for Mary was that, while she looked instinctively to them for support in time of trouble, as one woman monarch to another, their hands were tied by diplomatic considerations and they could not act on any sympathy they may have felt.

As for Mary's courtiers and attendants, she had a close relationship with many of them, but it was never on equal terms. However affable and open she might be, she remained conscious of the fact that she was their monarch, the mother of her people, and even when she was scarcely out of her teens she required their presence, told them whom to marry, made them gifts of property and jewellery and garments, and acted as godmother to their daughters. Did she also employ them in political manoeuvering? It is hard to say. Only a few specific examples are known. As we have seen, she enlisted the Duchess of Arschot in her attempts to marry Don Carlos. Had Queen Elisabeth of Spain lived, Mary believed that they could make an arrangement whereby James VI would marry one of Elisabeth's daughters. During the 1570s, Lady Livingston apparently co-ordinated a group of Mary's supporters in Scotland. There may have been far more examples of women acting in this way but, by their very nature, these activities were hidden, secret, unrecorded.

Had her life been otherwise, Mary would very likely have relied on her women to be the means of ensuring their husbands' loyalty to the crown, encouraging them to stand by the Queen when their support inevitably wavered in the shifting sands of sixteenth-century politics. That certainly seems to have been so with Mary Fleming and her husband, William Maitland of Lethington, who oscillated in his support of the Queen but was finally in Edinburgh Castle when it was the last fortress to hold out in her name. Mary's forced abdication and captivity had changed everything, of course, shattering old friendships. It is no surprise that Agnes, Countess of Moray, once a favourite, changed her allegiance after her husband's assassination and looked to Elizabeth I for help. Yet the Earl of Huntly's wife, daughter and daughter-in-law and indeed Margaret, Countess of Lennox were apparently able to set aside the traumas of the past and renew their friendship with Mary in later years. Lady Lennox's motives may be suspect but, in less dramatic circumstances, there is no doubting the genuine devotion of people like Mary Seton, Renée de Rallay and Elizabeth Curle, who gave up everything to share their Queen's imprisonment.

Throughout her adult life Mary, Queen of Scots cherished the memory of her first husband, François II not so much, perhaps, because of his personal qualities but because he had brought her such a high position in life. During her captive years she seems to have given no thought to Lord Darnley, and within months of parting from Bothwell she was perfectly ready to divorce him if it meant improving her chances of freedom. Whatever passion she had felt for these men had faded, but her love for her own women relatives remained undiminished. She sent them affectionate messages whenever she could, and she never forgot the woman who had been most important of all to her, Mary of Guise, her mother. In the last year of her long captivity, she still had in her possession a portrait of 'the late Queen of Scotland, of the house of Guise, her mother' and a silver mirror decorated with little portraits, one of them a miniature of Mary of Guise. These treasured mementoes were listed in August 1586. In December of that year, Mary wrote to Elizabeth I from Fotheringhay Castle, where she was awaiting execution. After her death, she said, she would like her servants to be allowed to take her body to France for burial beside Mary of Guise. The request was not granted. However, in her stated view of her own role, her shrewd understanding of the people around her, her generosity, her concern for her retinue and ultimately in her dignity and courage on the scaffold, Mary, Queen of Scots was truly her mother's daughter.[1]

Notes

1. Labanoff, *Lettres*, vii, 216, 248; Fraser, *Mary, Queen of Scots*, 100n.

Bibliography

PRINTED BOOKS

APS The Acts of the Parliaments of Scotland eds. T. Thomson and C. Innes (Edinburgh 1814–75), ii

Accounts and Papers relating to Mary, Queen of Scots eds. Allan J. Crosby and John Bruce (Camden Society 1867)

Accounts of the Lord High Treasurer of Scotland ed. Sir James Balfour Paul and Charles T. McInnes (Edinburgh 1907–70), vii, xi, xii

Adams, S., 'The release of Lord Darnley and the failure of amity', in *Mary Stewart, Queen in Three Kingdoms* ed. Michael Lynch (Oxford 1988)

Adhémar, Jean and Moulin, Christine, *Les Portraits dessinés du XVIe siècle au Cabinet des Estampes*, in *Gazette des Beaux-Arts* (Paris September and December 1973)

Allen, J.W., *A History of Political Thought in the Sixteenth Century* (London 1928)

Amico, Léonard N., *Bernard Palissy: In Search of Earthly Paradise* (Paris and New York 1996)

Anderson, James, *Collections relating to the history of Mary, Queen of Scotland* (Edinburgh 1727)

Anselme, de la Vierge Marie [Pierre de Guibours], *Histoire Généalogique et Chronologique de la Maison Royale de France … continuée par M. du Fourny* (Paris 1726–33), i–ix

The Art of Jewellery in Scotland eds. Rosalind K. Marshall and George Dalgleish (National Galleries of Scotland 1991)

Aubespine, Sebastien de l', Bishop of Limoges, *Négociations, lettres et pièces diverses relatives au règne de François II* (Paris 1841)

Baillargeat, René and Regnault, P., *Histoire du Mausolée d'Anne de Montmorency* (Mémoires de la Société historique et archéologique de Pontoise, du Val-d'Oise et du Vexin Paris 1970), ii

Bardon, Françoise, *Diane de Poitiers et le Mythe de Diane* (Paris 1963)

Baumgartner, Frederic J., *Henry II, King of France, 1547–59* (Durham, N.C. 1988)

Beaugé, Jean de, *Histoire de la guerre d'Ecosse* (Maitland Club 1830)

Bell, Susan Groag, *The Lost Tapestries of the City of Ladies* (California 2004)

Benger, Elizabeth Ogilvie, *Memoirs of the Life of Mary, Queen of Scots, with anecdotes of the Court of Henry II* (London 1823), i, ii

Bentley-Cranch, Dana, 'The Château of Beauregard and the Robertet Family', in *Bibliothèque d'Humanisme et Renaissance*, xlix (Geneva 1987)

Bentley-Cranch, Dana, 'Clément Marot's *Etrennes aux Dames de la Court*', in *Renaissance Reflections: Essays in memory of C.A. Mayer* eds. Pauline M. Smith and Trevor Peach (Paris 2002)

Bentley-Cranch, Dana, 'L'iconographie de Marguerite de Savoie (1523–1574)', in *Culture et pouvoir au temps de l'Humanisme et de la Renaissance* (Geneva 1978)

Bentley-Cranch, Dana and Marshall, Rosalind K., 'John Stewart, Duke of Albany, Lord Governor of Scotland, and his political role in 16th century France: a reassessment in the light of new information', in *Proceedings of the Society of Antiquaries of Scotland*, cxxxiii (Edinburgh 2003)

Bertière, Simone, *Les Reines de France au temps des Valois*, ii *Les années sanglantes* (Paris 1994)

Bingham, Caroline, *Darnley: A Life of Henry Stuart, Lord Darnley* (London 1995)

Bouillé, René de, *Histoire des Ducs de Guise* (Paris 1849)

Brantôme, Pierre de Bourdeille, Seigneur de, *Memoires contenant les vies des dames illustres de France de son temps* (London 1739)

Brantôme, Pierre de Bourdeille, Seigneur de, *Mémoires de messire Pierre de Bourdeille, seigneur de Brantôme, contenant les vies des hommes illustres et grands capitaines françois de son temps* (Leyden 1699), i–iv

Brantôme, Pierre de Bourdeille, Seigneur de, *The Lives of Gallant Ladies* transl. Alec Brown (London 1961)

Bibliography

Bresc-Bautier, Geneviève, 'Le Tombeau de Claude de Lorraine, Duc de Guise, et d'Antoinette de Bourbon-Vendôme 1550–1552', in *Primatice, Maître de Fontainebleau* ed. Dominique Cordellier (Paris 2004)

Broglie, Raoul de, *Les Clouet de Chantilly: catalogue illustré (Extrait de la Gazette des Beaux-Arts)* (Paris, May–June 1971)

Brosse, Jules de la, *Histoire d'un Capitaine Bourbonnais au XVIe siècle, Jacques de la Brosse, 1485–1562* (Paris 1929)

Buchanan, Patricia H., *Margaret Tudor, Queen of Scots* (Edinburgh and London 1985)

CSP Foreign: Calendar of State Papers Foreign ed. Joseph Stevenson *et al.* (London 1861–1950), Edward VI, Mary I and Elizabeth I

CSP Scot.: Calendar of State Papers relating to Scotland and Mary, Queen of Scots, 1547–1603 ed. Joseph Bain *et al.* (Edinburgh 1898–1952), i–xi

CSP Spanish: Calendar of State Papers Spanish, Henry VIII, Elizabeth I ed. Martin Hume (London 1892–9), i–iv

CSP Venetian: Calendar of State Papers relating to Venice eds. Rawdon Brown and G.C. Bentinck (London 1890), vii

Carleton Williams, Ethel, *Anne of Denmark* (London 1970)

Carpenter, Sarah, 'Performing Diplomacies: The 1560s Court Entertainments of Mary, Queen of Scots', in *Scottish Historical Review*, lxxxii, 2, no. 214 (Edinburgh, October 2003), 194–225

Carroll, Stuart, *Noble Power during the French Wars of Religion: The Guise Affinity and the Catholic Cause in Normandy* (Cambridge 1998)

Castelnau, Jacques, *Catherine de Médicis* (Paris 1954)

Castelot, André, *Diane, Henri, Catherine, le triangle royal* (Paris 1997)

Chantelauze, R., *Marie Stuart, son procès et son exécution, d'après le journal inédit de Bourgoing* (Paris 1876)

Chappuys, Claud, *Poésies Intimes* ed. Aline Mary Best (Geneva 1967)

Cheetham, Keith, *Mary, Queen of Scots: The Captive Years* (Sheffield 1982)

Chéruel, Pierre Adolphe, *Marie Stuart et Catherine de Médicis: étude historique sur les relations de la France et de l'Ecosse dans la seconde moitié du 16e siècle* (Paris 1975)

Chevalier, Bernard, 'Marie d'Anjou, une reine sans gloire', in *Autour de Marguerite d'Ecosse: Reines, princesses et dames du XVe siècle* eds. Geneviève et Philippe Contamire (Paris 1999)

Clan Campbell Letters, 1559-1583 ed. Jane E.A. Dawson (Scottish History Society 1997)

Clément Marot, Les Epigrammes ed. C.A. Mayer (London 1970)

Clément Marot, Oeuvres Diverses ed. C.A. Mayer (London 1966)

Clément Marot, Oeuvres Lyriques ed. C.A. Mayer (London 1964)

Clément Marot, Oeuvres Satiriques ed. C.A. Mayer (London 1962)

Cloulas, Ivan, Catherine de Médicis: la passion du pouvoir (Paris 1999)

Cloulas, Ivan, Diane de Poitiers (Paris 1997)

A collection of Inventories and other records of the Royal Wardrobe and Jewelhouse ed. Thomas Thomson (Edinburgh 1815)

A Collection of State papers . . . left by William Cecil, Lord Burghley ed. Samuel Haynes (London 1740)

Collinson, Patrick, The English Captivity of Mary, Queen of Scots (Sheffield 1987)

'Compte des dépenses de Catherine de Médicis', in Archives Curieuses de l'Histoire de France depuis Louis XI jusqu'à Louis XVIII ed. M.L. Cimber (Paris 1836), ix

Cosandey, Fanny, La reine de France: Symbole et pouvoir XVᵉ - XVIIIᵉ siècle (Paris 2002)

Coste, Hilarion de, Les Eloges et les Vies des Reynes (Paris 1647), ii

Crossley, E.W., 'A Temple Newsam inventory, 1565', in Yorkshire Archaeological Journal, xxv (Leeds 1918-20)

Dawson, Jane E.A., The Politics of Religion in the Age of Mary, Queen of Scots (Cambridge 2002)

Dictionnaire de Biographie Française eds. M. Prevost, R. D'Amat et al., v (Paris 1951), ix (Paris 1961)

Discours particulier d'Ecosse (Bannatyne Club 1824)

A Diurnal of Remarkable Occurrents (Bannatyne and Maitland Clubs 1833)

Donaldson, Gordon, All the Queen's Men (London 1983)

Donaldson, Gordon, The First Trial of Mary, Queen of Scots (London 1969)

Donaldson, Gordon, Mary, Queen of Scots (London 1974)

Donaldson, Gordon, Scottish Historical Documents (Edinburgh and London 1970)

Dumont, Georges-Henri, Marguerite de Parme, bâtarde de Charles Quint (1522-1586) (Brussels 1999)

Duncan, Thomas, 'The Queen's Maries', in *Scottish Historical Review*, ii (Edinburgh 1905)

Durant, David N., *Arbella Stuart, a Rival to the Queen* (London 1978)

Durant, David N., *Bess of Hardwick* (London 1977)

Durkan, John, 'The Library of Mary, Queen of Scots', in *Mary Stewart, Queen in Three Kingdoms* ed. Michael Lynch (Oxford 1988)

Elder, John, *Copie of a Letter sent in to Scotlande* (London 1555)

Erlanger, Philippe, *Diane de Poitiers* (Paris 1955)

Fleming, John Arnold, *The Four Maries* (Glasgow 1951)

Fontette, Micheline de, *Les Religieuses à l'âge classique du Droit Canon* (Paris 1967)

Foreign Correspondence with Marie de Lorraine, 1537–48, 1548–57 ed. Marguerite Wood (Scottish History Society 1923, 1925)

Forneron, H., *Les Ducs de Guise et Leur Epoque* (Paris 1887)

Francisque-Michel, *Les Français en Ecosse: les Ecossais en France* (London 1862)

Fraser, Antonia, *Mary, Queen of Scots* (London 1969)

Fraser, William, *The Douglas Book* (Edinburgh 1885), ii

Fraser, William, *The Lennox*, (Edinburgh 1874), i and ii

Fraser, William, *The Sutherland Book*, i (Edinburgh 1892)

Frieda, Leonie, *Catherine de Medici* (London 2003)

Garrisson, Janine, *Catherine de Médicis, L'impossible harmonie* (Paris 2002)

A Genealogical Deduction of the Family of Rose of Kilravock (Spalding Club 1848)

George Buchanan: The Political Poetry eds. Paul J. McGinnis and Arthur H. Williamson (Scottish History Society 1995)

Gore-Browne, Robert, *Lord Bothwell* (London 1937)

Greengrass, M., 'Mary, Dowager Queen of France', in *Mary Stewart, Queen in Three Kingdoms* ed. Michael Lynch (Oxford 1988)

Guiffrey, Georges, *Dianne de Poytiers: Lettres Inédites* (Geneva 1982 reprint of Paris 1866 edn)

Guy, John, *My Heart is my Own: The Life of Mary, Queen of Scots* (London 2004)

Hackenbroth, Yvonne, *Renaissance Jewellery* (London 1979)

Hamilton Papers ed. Joseph Bain (Edinburgh 1890), ii

Hay Fleming, David, *Mary, Queen of Scots from her birth to her Flight into England* (London 1898)

Haynes, see *A Collection of State Papers . . . left by William Cecil, Lord Burghley*

Herries, Lord, *Historical Memoirs of the reign of Mary, Queen of Scots* (Abbotsford Club 1836)

Hibbert, Christopher, *The Virgin Queen: The Personal History of Elizabeth I* (London 1990)

The Historie and Cronicles of Scotland . . . by Robert Lindesay of Pitscottie ed. A.J.G. Mackay (Scottish Text Society 1899–1911), ii

Holinshed, Raphael, *Holinshed's Chronicles of England, Scotland and Ireland* (London 1807–8)

Hollingsworth, Mary, *The Cardinal's Hat: Money, Ambition and Housekeeping in a Renaissance Court* (London 2004)

Inventaires de la royne descosse douairière de France: catalogues of the jewels, dresses, furniture, books and paintings of Mary, Queen of Scots, 1556–1569 ed. Joseph Robertson (Bannatyne Club 1863)

Ives, Eric, *Anne Boleyn* (Oxford 1986)

James, Susan E., 'Lady Margaret Douglas and Sir Thomas Seymour by Holbein: Two miniatures re-identified', in *Apollo* (London, May 1998)

Jamieson, John, *A Dictionary of the Scottish Language* (Edinburgh 1827)

Jollet, Etienne, *Jean et François Clouet* (Paris 1997)

The Journal of King Edward's Reign, written in his own hand (Clarendon Historical Society 1884)

Keith, R., *History of the Affairs of Church and State in Scotland down to 1567* ed. J.P. Lawson (Spottiswoode Society 1844)

King, Catherine, *Renaissance Women Patrons: Wives and Widows in Italy, c.1300–1550* (Manchester 1998)

Knecht, R.J., *Catherine de' Medici* (New York 1998)

Knecht, R.J., *Francis I* (Cambridge 1982)

Knecht, R.J., *Renaissance Warrior and Patron: the Reign of Francis I* (Cambridge 1994)

Knecht, R.J., *The Valois: kings of France, 1328–1589* (London 2004)

Knox, John, *History of the Reformation in Scotland* ed. William Croft Dickinson (London 1949)

LPFD: Letters and Papers, Foreign and Domestic, Henry VIII (Vaduz, Kraus Reprint 1965)

Laing, David, 'Notes on the Moray Tomb', in *Proceedings of the Society of Antiquaries of Scotland*, i (Edinburgh 1855)

Lang, Andrew, 'The Household of Mary, Queen of Scots in 1573', in *Scottish Historical Review*, ii (Edinburgh 1905)

Larcade, Veronique, 'Le Duc d'Epernon et les Guises', in *Le Mécénat et l'influence des Guises* ed. Yvonne Bellenger (Paris 1997)

Lee, Maurice, *James Stewart, Earl of Moray* (New York 1953)

Lees, J. Cameron, *St Giles', Edinburgh: Church, College and Cathedral* (Edinburgh and London 1889)

Lesley, John, *The History of Scotland from the Death of King James I in the year 1436 to the year 1561* (Bannatyne Club 1830)

Letters to the Argyll Family ed. Alexander MacDonald (Maitland Club 1839)

Lettres du Cardinal Charles de Lorraine ed. Daniel Cuisiat (Geneva 1998)

Lettres de Catherine de Médicis ed. Hector de la Ferrière (Paris 1880), i–x

Lettres, Instructions et Mémoires de Marie Stuart, Reine d'Ecosse ed. Prince Alexandre Labanoff (London 1844), i–vii

Letters of Mary Stuart, Queen of Scotland ed. William Turnbull (London 1845)

Levey, Santina, *An Elizabethan Inheritance: The Hardwick Hall Textiles* (London 1998)

Loades, David, *Mary Tudor: A Life* (Oxford 1989)

Lomas, Richard, *A Power in the Land: The Percys* (East Linton 1999)

Louda, Jiri and MacLagan, Michael, *Lines of Succession* (London 1981)

Lovell, Mary S., *Bess of Hardwick: First Lady of Chatsworth, 1527–1608* (London 2005)

Lynch, Michael, 'Queen Mary's Triumph: the Baptismal Celebrations at Stirling in December 1566', in *Scottish Historical Review*, lxix, 1, no. 187 (April 1990), 1–21

Macdougall, Norman, *James IV* (East Linton 1997)

Madden, Frederick, *Privy Purse Expenses of the Princess Mary, daughter of King Henry the Eighth, afterwards Queen Mary* (London 1831)

Mahoney, Irene, *Madame Catherine* (London 1976)

Maidment, J., *Analecta Scotica* (Edinburgh 1834)

Marshall, Rosalind K., *Elizabeth I* (London 1991)

Marshall, Rosalind K., *John Knox* (Edinburgh 2000)

Marshall, Rosalind K., *Mary I* (London 1993)

Marshall, Rosalind K., *Mary of Guise* (London 1977)

Marshall, Rosalind K., *Mary of Guise, Queen of Scots* (Edinburgh 2001)

Marshall, Rosalind K., 'Mary, Queen of Scots: a Flemish Connection', in *The Flemish-Scottish Connections* ed. Annette Hardie-Stoffelen (Brussels 1996)

Marshall, Rosalind K., '"This lady and princess is a notable woman": the public persona and private personality of Mary, Queen of Scots', in *Enfers et délices à la Renaissance* eds. François Laroque and Franck Lessay (Paris 2003)

Marshall, Rosalind K., *Queen of Scots* (Edinburgh 1986)

Marshall, Rosalind K., *Scottish Queens* (East Linton 2003)

Marshall, Rosalind K., *Virgins and Viragos: A History of Women in Scotland 1080–1980* (London 1983)

Martienssen, Anthony, *Queen Katherine Parr* (London 1973)

Mayer, C.A. and Bentley-Cranch, D, *Florimond Robertet (?–1527), Homme d'Etat Français* (Paris 1994)

Mayer, C.A. and Bentley-Cranch, Dana, 'François Robertet: French sixteenth-century civil servant, poet and artist', in *Renaissance Studies*, ii, no. 3 (Oxford 1997)

McCrie, Thomas, *The Life of John Knox* (Edinburgh 1960)

McGowan, Margaret M., *L'entrée de Henri II à Rouen 1550* (Amsterdam 1977)

McGowan, Margaret M., *Ideal Forms in the Age of Ronsard* (California 1985)

McGowan, Margaret M., *The Vision of Rome in Late Renaissance France* (Yale 2000)

Le Mécénat et l'influence des Guises ed. Yvonne Bellenger (Paris 1997)

Melville, Sir James, of Halhill, *Memoirs of his Own Life* ed. Gordon Donaldson (London 1969)

Merigot, C., *La Vie Serenissime Philippe de Gueldres* (Paris 1627)

Meulemans, André, 'Op zoek naar de woning van Barbara Moubray en Elisabeth Curle', in *Antwerpsche Tydinghen*, 4 (Antwerp 1991)

Millar, Oliver, *The Tudor, Stuart and early Georgian Pictures in the Collection of Her Majesty The Queen* (London 1963)

Montelos, Jean-Marie Pérouse de, *Fontainebleau* (London 1998)

Mumby, F.A., *The Girlhood of Queen Elizabeth* (London 1909)

Nau, Claude, *The History of Mary Stuart* ed. Joseph Stevenson (Edinburgh 1883)

Nicolas, Nicholas H., *Life of William Davidson, secretary of state and privy councillor to Queen Elizabeth* (London 1823)

'Observations on a picture representing the cenotaph of the Lord Darnley', in D. Jacques, *A Visit to Goodwood* (Chichester 1822)

Original Letters illustrative of English History ed. Henry Ellis (London 1825), 1st series, i

Oxford Dictionary of National Biography (Oxford 2004), articles cited in full in footnotes

Paul, James Balfour, *The Scots Peerage*, (Edinburgh 1904), i–viii

Perry, Maria, *Sisters to the King* (London 1998)

Phillip, J., *A Commemoration of the right noble and vertuous Lady Margrit Douglasis, Countis of Lennox* (London 1578)

Pierre de Ronsard, Oeuvres Complètes ed. Gustave Cohen (Paris 1950), ii

Pierre de Ronsard, Poésies Choisies ed. Françoise Joukovsky (Paris 1969)

Pimodan, Gabriel de, *La Mère des Guises: Antoinette de Bourbon, 1494–1583* (Paris 1925)

Poull, Georges, *La Maison ducale de Lorraine devenue La Maison impériale et royale d'Autriche, de Hongrie et de Bohême* (Nancy 1991)

Queens, Dynasts and Potentates ed. Theresa M. Vann (Cambridge 1993)

RMS: Register of the Great Seal of Scotland ed. J. Maitland Thomson (Edinburgh 1866, reprint 1984), iv

RPC: Register of the Privy Council of Scotland ed. P. Hume Brown (Edinburgh 1904), v

RSS: Register of the Privy Seal of Scotland ed. James Beveridge and Gordon Donaldson (Edinburgh 1908–), iv, v, vi

Records of the Scots Colleges at Douai, Rome, Madrid, Valladolid and Ratisbon, i (New Spalding Club 1906)

Registrum Honoris de Morton ed. Thomas Thomson and Cosmo Innes (Bannatyne Club 1853), i

The Reign of Elizabeth I, ed. Christopher Haigh (London 1984)

Ridley, Jasper, *Elizabeth I* (London 1987)

Ridley, Jasper, *John Knox* (Oxford 1968)

Ruble, Alphonse de, *La première jeunesse de Marie Stuart (1542–61)* (Paris 1891)

Russell, Joycelyne G. *Peacemaking in the Renaissance* (London 1986)

Sanderson, Margaret H.B., *A Kindly Place? Living in Sixteenth-Century Scotland* (East Linton 2002)

Sanderson, Margaret H.B., *Mary Stewart's People* (Edinburgh 1987)

Scarisbrick, Diana, *Jewellery in Britain, 1066–1837* (Norwich 1994)

Scarisbrick, Diana, *Tudor and Jacobean Jewellery* (London 1995)

Scarisbrick, J.J., *Henry VIII* (London 1969)

Schutte, Kim, *A Biography of Margaret Douglas, Countess of Lennox, 1515–1578: niece of Henry VIII and mother-in-law of Mary, Queen of Scots* (New York 2002)

Scottish Ballad Poetry ed. G. Eyre-Todd (Glasgow 1893)

Seton, George, *A History of the Family of Seton during eight centuries*, i (Edinburgh 1896)

Solnon, Jean-François, *La Cour de France* (Paris 1987)

Somerset, Anne, *Ladies-in-Waiting from the Tudors to the present day* (London 2002)

The State Papers and Letters of Sir Ralph Sadler ed. Arthur Clifford (Edinburgh 1809), 87

Stevenson, David, *Scotland's Last Royal Wedding: The Marriage of James VI and Anne of Denmark* (Edinburgh 1997)

Stevenson, Jane, *Women Latin Poets: language, gender and authority, from antiquity to the eighteenth century* (Oxford 2005)

Stoddart, J.T., *The Girlhood of Mary, Queen of Scots* (London 1908)

Strickland, Agnes, *Lives of the Queens of Scotland* (Edinburgh 1851–96), vi

Stuart, John, *A Lost Chapter in the history of Mary, Queen of Scots* (Edinburgh 1874)

Sutherland, N.M., *The French Secretaries of State in the age of Catherine de Medici* (London 1962)

Swain, Margaret, *The Needlework of Mary, Queen of Scots* (New York and London 1973)

Tait, Hugh, 'Historiated Tudor Jewellery', in *The Antiquaries Journal*, xlii (Oxford 1962)

Teulet, A., *Papiers d'Etat, pièces et documents inédits* (Bannatyne Club 1860)

Teulet, A., *Relations Politiques de la France avec l'Ecosse au XVIe siècle* (Paris 1862)

Thierry, Adrien, *Diane de Poitiers* (Geneva and Paris 1955)

Treasurer Accounts, see *Accounts of the Lord High Treasurer of Scotland*

Trombert, Florence, 'Une Reine de Quatre Ans à la Cour de France: Marguerite d'Autriche, 1484–1485', in *Autour de Marguerite d'Ecosse: Reines, princesses et dames du XV*ᵉ *siècle*, eds. Geneviève et Philippe Contamire (Paris 1999)

Turnbull, William, *Letters of Mary Stuart* (London 1845)

Two Missions of Jacques de la Brosse ed. Gladys Dickinson (Scottish History Society 1942)

Vertue, George, 'Observations on a Picture representing the Cenotaph of the Lord Darnley', in D. Jacques, *A Visit to Goodwood* (London 1822)

Viard, Georges, 'La religion d'Antoinette de Bourbon, duchesse de Guise', in *Les Cahiers Haut-Marnais: Joinville et les Guises* (Chaumont 1990)

Visschers, P., *Aenteekening nopens het Eergraf van Barbara Moubray en Elizabeth Curle, staetdamen van de Koningen Maria Stuart in St Andries kerk te Antwerpen* (Antwerp 1857)

Whiteley, Jon, *Catalogue of the Collection of Drawings in the Ashmolean Museum, Oxford,* vi (Oxford 1996)

Wilkinson, Alexander S., *Mary Queen of Scots and French Public Opinion, 1542–1600* (Basingstoke 2004)

Williams, Neville, *A Tudor Tragedy: Thomas Howard, Fourth Duke of Norfolk* (London 1964)

Williams, H. Noel, *The Brood of False Lorraine* (London 1918)

Williams, H. Noel, *Henri II: His Court and Times* (London 1910)

Yates, Frances A., *The French Academies of the Sixteenth Century* (London 1988 edn)

MANUSCRIPTS

NAS   National Archives of Scotland (formerly Scottish Record Office)

NLS   National Library of Scotland

Moray Muniments, listed in National Register of Archives Scotland Survey 0217: Correspondence and other papers of Lady Agnes Keith, Countess of Moray

NAS E33/6/2 *Despences de la maison royale*, Household book of Mary, Queen of Scots, 1562

NAS E34/23 Household papers and accounts, Lists of household of Mary of Guise, *c.* 1543, n.d.

NAS E34/27 Household papers and accounts, List of household of Mary, Queen of Scots, 1555-6

NAS, Mar and Kellie Muniments, GD124/15/5 Note on jewel sent by Mary, Queen of Scots to the Countess of Atholl; GD124/15/6 Letter of the Countess of Lennox, 1571

NAS, Ogilvy of Inverquharity Muniments, GD205/19/lxiv (3) Incomplete testament, probably of David Beaton of Melgund, 1593

NAS, Register of Acts and Decreets, C57/186 f.252r Case concerning payment in connection with the marriage of Lucrece Bethune's daughter Christian, 1599

NAS, Register of Acts and Decreets, CS7/10 f.415v Letters purchased at the instance of Janet and Margaret Carwood against John Fleming, 1554.

NAS, Register of Deeds, viii, 9, 232 Marriage contract of Lady Jane Gordon and the Earl of Bothwell

NAS, Register of Testaments, Edinburgh Commissary Court, CC8/8/35 Testament of Lucrece Bethune, 1601

NLS Adv. MS.541.1.4 Letter from Mary, Queen of Scots to Henri d'Angoulême, son of Lady Fleming, 1564

NLS, Balcarres Papers, Adv. MSS, 29.2.1.82-3 Letters of Catherine de Medici

NLS, Balcarres Papers, Adv. MSS, 29.2.5 Accounts of expenditure of Mary of Guise

NLS MS.3647 Letters of Sir Amyas Paulet and others, relating to the captivity of Mary, Queen of Scots, 1585–7

NLS, Sutherland Muniments, 313/910, 1592, 1593, 1597, 3323 Papers relating to Jane Gordon, Countess of Bothwell, later Countess of Sutherland

Index

Monarchs are indexed by first name; peers and ecclesiastics by title; married women by maiden name; single women by surname. The abbreviation *s.j.* means 'in her own right'.

Aberdeen 127

Aberdeenshire 126, 160

Adamson, John, merchant 157

Ainslie Bond 131

Alba, Ferdinand of Toledo, Duke of 206

Albon, Catherine d', Demoiselle de Saint-André 80

Alègre, Yves d' 82

Alluye, Françoise d', attendant of Antoinette de Bourbon, Duchess of Guise 168

Amboise 41, 63, 79, 181

Amboise, Marie d', wife of Robert de Sarrebruche, Count of Roucy and Brenne 68

Amiens 11

Anet 31, 41

Angoulême, Jeanne d', illegitimate sister of François I of France 76

Angus 126

Angus, Archibald Douglas, 6th Earl of 107–8, 112

Angus, earldom of 112

Anne Boleyn, second Queen Consort of Henry VIII of England 108, 111, 193–4

Anne of Brittany, Queen Consort of Charles VIII and then Louis XII of France 57

Anne of Denmark, Queen Consort of James VI of Scotland 185

Annency, Church of Notre Dame d' 66

Antwerp 189

Antwerp, Siege of 82

Antwerp, St Andrew's Church 189

Aquila, Alvarez de Quadra, Bishop of, Spanish ambassador to England 113

Argyll and Moray, Lady Agnes Keith, Countess of *see* Keith, Lady Agnes

Argyll, Archibald Campbell, 4th Earl of 91, 102

Argyll, Archibald Campbell, 5th Earl of 91–5, 102

Argyll, Archibald Campbell, 7th Earl of 102

Argyll, Colin Campbell, 6th Earl
of 94, 102–3
Argyll, Countess of *see*
Cunningham, Lady Jean;
Keith, Lady Agnes;
Stewart, Lady Jean
Argyllshire 93
Arnault, Monsieur *see*
Colomniers, Arnault de
Arnault, Monsieur, daughter of,
chamberwoman to Mary,
Queen of Scots 170
Arran, James Hamilton 2nd Earl
of *see* Châtelherault,
Duke of
Arran, James Hamilton, 3rd Earl
of Arran 30, 69
Arschot, Anne de Lorraine,
Duchess of *see* Lorraine
Arthur, Prince of Wales, brother of
Henry VIII of England 193
Arthur, Thomas, royal tailor
90–1
Arundel Castle 184
Arundel, Countess of *see* Dacre
Asquin, Mademoiselle d' *see*
Erskine, Marie
Asteane, Margaret, midwife to
Mary, Queen of Scots 171
Astel, Madame *see* Fleming,
Margaret
Atholl, Forest of 167
Atholl, John Stewart, 4th Earl of
193, 166–7
Aubigny 114
Aumale, Claude de Lorraine,
Marquis of Mayenne then
Duke of 30, 66
Atholl, Countess of *see*
Fleming, Margaret

Aumale, Duchess of *see* Brézé,
Louise de
Aumale, François, Duke of
Aumale *see* Guise,
François, 2nd Duke of
Aumont, Jean, Marshal of 78
Avantigny, Renée d',
Mademoiselle de la
Touche, governess to the
maids of honour of Mary
of Guise 159

Babington, Sir Anthony 208
Babington Plot 152, 208
Babou, Françoise, Demoiselle de
la Bourdaisière, wife of
Antoine d'Estrées, Marquis
of Coeuvres and maid of
honour to Mary, Queen of
Scots 82, 86
Babou, Marie, Demoiselle de la
Bourdaisière, wife of
Claude de Beauvilliers,
Count of Saint-Aignan
and maid of honour to
Mary, Queen of Scots 82,
86
Banffshire 126, 129
Bar-le-Duc 19
Barbancoys, Anne de, wife of
Monsieur de Fonterpuys
and lady-in-waiting to
Mary of Guise, 81
Bastian *see* Pages, Sebastian
Batarnay, Anne de, friend of
Mary of Guise 80
Baudreuil, Anne de, wife of
Lyonnet de Breüil,
Seigneur de Palua 48
Baxter, Christian, nurse to Lady

Jean Stewart, Countess of
Argyll 90
Beaton family 143
Beaton, Andrew, master of the
household to Mary, Queen
of Scots 150–1, 160, 162
Beaton, Cardinal David *see* St
Andrews, Archbishop of
Beaton of Melgund, David 161
Beaton, David, son of David
Beaton of Melgund 161
Beaton, Elizabeth, mistress of
James V, King of Scots 90,
143
Beaton, James *see* Glasgow,
Archbishop of
Beaton of Creich *see* Rainville,
Jeanne de la
Beaton of Creich, Sir John 90
Beaton, John, master of the
household to Mary, Queen
of Scots 150
Beaton, Lucrece, wife of (1)
David Beaton of Melgund
and (2) Andrew Wishart of
Mylneden, maid of honour
to Mary, Queen of Scots,
160–1, 169, 183
Beaton, Margaret, wife of Arthur
Forbes of Rires ('Lady
Rires') 167
Beaton, Mary, wife of Alexander
Ogilvy of Boyne, lady-in-
waiting to Mary, Queen of
Scots, one of the Four
Maries 130, 141–7, 157–8,
160, 172
Beaton of Creich, Robert 143,
158
Beaton (Beton), Silla de,

chamberwoman to Mary,
Queen of Scots 143
Beaucaire, Gilbert de, gentleman
carver to Mary, Queen of
Scots 48–9
Beaucaire, Marie de Beaucaire,
Demoiselle de Péguillon,
wife of Sebastian de
Luxembourg, 4th Viscount
of Martigues and maid of
honour to Mary, Queen of
Scots 50–1
Beaulieu 108
Beaune, Claude de, wife of (1)
Louis Burgensis (2) Claude
Gouffier, Duke of
Rouannais, and lady-in-
waiting to Catherine de
Medici 51
Beauregard *see* Rallay, Renée
Bellenden, John of Auchnoul
Berlandière, Dame de *see*
Marconnay, Hilaire de
Bertrand, Jean, first President of
the Paris Parlement,
Keeper of the Seals of
France 79
Bertrand, Marguerite, wife of
Germain-Gaston de Foix,
Marquis of Trans and lady-
in-waiting to Mary, Queen
of Scots 79
Bettoncourt 169
Bettoncourt, Madame de *see*
Piédefer, Jeanne
Bettoncourt, Pierre de Joisel,
Seigneur de, master of the
household to Mary, Queen
of Scots 161, 168–9
Biencourt, Jeanne de,

Demoiselle de Poutrincourt, attendant of Mary, Queen of Scots 53

Biggar 170

Bingueton, Catherine, chamberwoman to the maids of honour of Mary, Queen of Scots 170

Blois, Castle of 32, 41, 49, 77, 181

Boc, Hélenè *see* Bog, Helen

Bog, Helen (Boc, Hélène), chamberwoman to Mary, Queen of Scots 170-1, 183-4

Bolton 185

Borgia, Lucretia, grandmother of Anne d'Este, Duchess of Guise 61

Bothwell, Countess of *see* Gordon, Lady Jane; Gordon, Margaret; Stewart, Lady Isabel

Bothwell, James Hepburn, 4th Earl of, third husband of Mary, Queen of Scots 2, 23, 33, 35, 117-9, 126-35, 146-9, 165, 182, 202-3, 213

Bothwell, Patrick Hepburn, 1st Earl of Bothwell 129

Bothwell, Patrick Hepburn, 3rd Earl of Bothwell 131

Bouillon, Mademoiselle de *see* Marck, Antoinette de la

Bouillon, Duchess of *see* Brézé, Françoise; Sarrebruche, Guillemette de

Bouillon, Robert de la Marck, Duke of, Marshal of France 68

Bouillon, Robert de la Marck, Duke of 68, 69, 85

Boullères, siege of 77

Boulis, Bonaventure de Beaucaire, Sieur de, cupbearer to Mary, Queen of Scots 48

Bourbon, Antoinette de, wife of Claude, 1st Duke of Guise, grandmother and lady-in-waiting to Mary, Queen of Scots 4-5, 10, 18, 19-36, 39, 40, 42-3, 45, 47, 61-2, 66-7, 76, 83, 85, 130, 166, 168, 182

Bourbon, Louis de Bourbon, Cardinal of, brother of Antoinette de Bourbon 20

Bourbon, Louise de, Abbess of Fontevrault, sister of Antoinette de Bourbon, great-aunt of Mary, Queen of Scots 20

Bourbon, Marie de *see* Poissy, Prioress of the Priory of St Louis

Bourbon, Renée de, wife of Antoine de Lorraine, Duke of Lorraine, great-aunt of Mary, Queen of Scots 23

Bourbon-Montpensier, Suzanne de, wife of Claude, Sieur de Rieux, Count of Harcourt 66

Bourdaisière, Françoise, Dame de la *see* Robertet, Françoise

Bourdaisière, Demoiselle de la *see* Babou, Françoise; Babou, Marie

Bourdaisière, Jean Babou, Sieur de la, master of the wardrobe to Henri II of France 78

Bours, Jean de Montmorency, Chevalier de 82

Brantôme, Pierre de Bourdeille, Abbé de 44, 63, 65, 76, 78

Braye, Catherine, maiden to the gentlewomen of Mary, Queen of Scots 187

Brenne, Abbey of Saint-Yved of 70

Brenne, Countess of *see* Sarrebruche, Guillemette de

Brenne, Countess of Roucy and Brenne *see* Amboise, Marie d'

Brenne, Robert de Sarrebruche, Count of Roucy and 68

Breüil, Guyonne du, wife of Jean de Beaucaire, Sieur de Péguillon and lady of the bedchamber to Mary, Queen of Scots 47–50, 80, 85, 156, 163, 166

Brézé, Artus de Maillé, Monsieur de 43

Brézé, Françoise de, wife of Robert de la Marck, Duke of Bouillon and lady-in-waiting to Mary, Queen of Scots 68–70, 85–6

Brézé, Louis de *see* Maulevrier, Count of

Brézé, Louise de, wife of Claude de Lorraine, Marquis of Mayenne, later Duke of Aumale, aunt by marriage

and lady-in-waiting to Mary, Queen of Scots 30, 66

Briante, Madame de *see* Pierres, Marie

Briante, Pierre de Clovis, Seigneur de 157

Bridlington Bay 112

Brion, Demoiselle de *see* Chabot, Anne

Brittany 9, 21

Brosse, Jacques de la, French ambassador to Scotland 157

Brussels 69

Brydges, Winifred, wife of Sir Richard Sackville 113

Buchan, Countess of *see* Stewart, Christina

Buchan, earldom of 97

Buchanan, George, neo-classical poet and tutor of James VI of Scotland 146

Buggenout and Maignelay, Antoine de Hallwin, Seigneur de, Grand Wolf-Hunter of France 75, 77

Burgensis, Agathe, chamber-woman to Mary, Queen of Scots 52

Burgensis, Jacqueline, chamber-woman in the household of the children of Henri II of France 52

Burgensis, Louis, French royal doctor 51–2

Burgensis, Simon, French royal doctor 52

Burghley, Lady *see* Cooke, Mildred

Burghley, William Cecil, 1st Lord 116, 118–21, 148, 177–8, 181–2, 199–201, 203–4, 206–8

Burntisland 185

Butler, Elizabeth, laundress to Mary, Queen of Scots 187

Buxton 177

Cabrianne, Anne, (Anna Cabriana), Demoiselle de la Guyonnière, wife of Philibert de Lignerolles and maid of honour to Mary, Queen of Scots 83, 86

Caen, Abbey of La Trinité 70

Cagnioli, Timothy, steward and purse-bearer to Mary, Queen of Scots 187

Caithness 111

Calais 64

Calder, Lady *see* Keith, Lady Mary

Callendar House 182

Camp, Isabelle, Demoiselle de Cobron, lady-in-waiting to Mary, Queen of Scots 80, 84, 163, 166

Campbell, Lady Agnes, daughter of Colin Campbell, 6th Earl of Argyll 102

Campbell, Colin, son of Colin Campbell, 6th Earl of Argyll 102

Carberry Hill 2, 118, 135–6, 146, 149, 203

Carlisle 149

Carlos, Don, son of Philip II of Spain 33, 200, 212

Carmichael, Mary, fictitious character in the ballad, 'Marie Hamilton' 141–2

Carnavalet (Kernevenog), Dame de *see* Hurault

Carnavalet (Kernevenog), François, Sieur de 80

Carre, Marie (Kerr, Mary), washerwoman to Mary, Queen of Scots 171, 186

Carrières, House of 40

Carwood House 170

Carwood, Janet, sister of Margaret Carwood 170

Carwood, Margaret, (Marguerite) chamberwoman to Mary, Queen of Scots 169–70, 172

Carwood, William of that Ilk 170

Casket Letters 146, 205

Cassillis, Gilbert Kennedy, 3rd Earl of 10, 184

Castellane, Philippe, Baron de 45

Castelnau-Mauvissière, Michel de, French ambassador to England 22, 180–1

Castro, Duchess of *see* Diane de France

Castro, Horace Farnese, Duke of 75

Cateau-Cambrésis, Treaty of 31

Catherine of Aragon, first Queen Consort of Henry VIII of England 193–5

Catherine de Medici, Queen Consort of Henri II of France, first mother-in-law of Mary, Queen of Scots

10, 12, 15, 18, 21, 24–36, 39,
41, 43–4, 47, 51, 59–63, 65–7,
69–70, 74–83, 85–7, 161, 163,
187, 200, 205, 211
Caumont, Geoffrey, Baron de
80
Caumont, Baronne de *see*
Lustrac, Marguerite
Cavendish, Charles, son of Bess
of Hardwick 180
Cavendish, Elizabeth, wife of
Charles, 5th Earl of Lennox
121–2
Cavendish, Frances, wife of
Pierrepont, Sir Henry 179
Cavendish, William, son of Bess
of Hardwick 180
Cecil, Mildred *see* Cooke,
Mildred
Cecil, William *see* Burghley
Cerisay, Antoinette de, wife of
François Olivier,
Chancellor of France 79,
82–3, 84–6
Chabot, Anne, Demoiselle de
Brion, wife of Charles
Hallwin, Duke of Hallwin
and lady-in-waiting to
Mary, Queen of Scots 76–7
Chabot, Charles, husband of
Louise de Hallwin 76
Chabot, Dame de *see* Longwy,
Françoise de
Chabot, Philippe de, Admiral of
France and governor of
Burgundy 77
Chambre, Estienette de la, lady-
in-waiting to Mary, Queen
of Scots 79
Chambre family, de la 79

Champigny 77
Chantilly 41, 69, 74
Charles V, Holy Roman Emperor
24–6, 75, 84, 193–5
Charles VI of France 50
Charles VIII of France 57, 78
Charles IX of France (Charles-
Maximilien) 10, 32–4, 41,
49, 205, 207
Chartley 123, 163, 187
Chaseabout Raid 98, 117
Chasteigner, Marguerite de, wife
of Jean de Gaignon,
Seigneur de Saint-Bohaire
51
Châteaudun 5
Châtelard, Pierre de, poet 144
Châtelherault, dukedom of 76
Châtelherault, James Hamilton,
2nd Earl of Arran and
Duke of, Lord Governor of
Scotland 6–8, 10–11, 15,
30, 50, 69, 76, 109–10, 114,
128, 157
Chatsworth 121
Cheverny, Countess of *see*
Thou, Anne de
Cheverny, Philippe Hurault,
Count of 161
Chisholm, William *see*
Dunblane, Bishop of
Claude, first Queen Consort of
François I of France 25, 39,
57
Claude de France, Princess,
sister-in-law to Mary,
Queen of Scots 41, 45, 196
Clerk, Alexander, tailor 100
Clouet, François, portrait painter
18, 59, 69

Cobron, Bonaventure de, Demoiselle de Saint-Léger, wife of Pierre Totigoti and maid of honour to Catherine de Medici 80, 156

Cobron, Demoiselle de see Camp, Isabelle

Coeuvres, Antoine d'Estrées, Marquis of 82

Coeuvres, Marquise of see Babou, Françoise

Colomniers, Arnault de, (Monsieur Arnault), doctor to Mary, Queen of Scots 170–1

Colquhoun, Jane, fool to Mary, Queen of Scots 171

Comenges, Demoiselle de, see Langest, Anne de

Condé, Louis de Condé, Prince of 63

Constant, Suzanne, Demoiselle de Fonterpuy, maid of honour to Mary, Queen of Scots 81–2, 86, 156, 166, 172

Contay, Françoise de, wife of Jean, Monsieur de Humières and lady governess to the daughters of Henri II 41

Contine, La see Mirandola, Livia della

Cooke, Mildred, wife of William Cecil, 1st Lord Burghley 117

Corrichie, Battle of 127, 166

Courcelles, Claude de, French ambassador to Scotland 152

Courcelles, Marie, maid of honour to Mary, Queen of Scots 151, 164, 169, 171, 183

Courdion, Barde, chamberwoman to Mary, Queen of Scots 52

Coutras, Battle of 77

Craig, John, doctor of medicine 103

Craigmillar Castle 202

Crawford, Bessie, serving maid to Lady Jane Gordon, Countess of Bothwell 132–3

Crichton Castle 130, 134

Cricq (Creich) see Rainville, Jeanne de la

Critoflat, Jacqueline, governess to Nicole la Jardinière 163–4, 169, 184

Cromar 160

Cromwell, Thomas, chief minister to Henry VIII of England 109

Cunningham, Lady Jean, wife of Archibald Campbell, 5th Earl of Argyll 94

Curel, Charles de la Haye, Sieur de 43

Curel, Dame de see Essartz, Mahanet des

Curle, Barbara see Mowbray, Barbara

Curle, Elizabeth, chamberwoman to Mary, Queen of Scots 188–9, 213

Curle, Gilbert, secretary to Mary, Queen of Scots 162, 187–9

Curle, Hieronymous, Rector of

the Scots College, Douai
189
Curle, James, elder, Edinburgh
burgess 187
Curle, James, younger, brother
of Gilbert Curle 187
Curle, Janet, wife of Timothy
Cagnioli, purse-bearer to
Mary, Queen of Scots
187
Cypière, Dame de see Hallwin,
Louise de
Cypière, Philibert de Marsilly,
Seigneur de 77

Dacre, Anne, wife of Philip
Howard, 1st Earl of
Arundel 184
Dacre, Elizabeth, wife of Lord
William Howard 117
Daillon, Anne de, lady-in-
waiting to Mary, Queen of
Scots 79–80
Dalkeith Castle 182
Damville, Henri de
Montmorency, Seigneur de
13, 69, 78
Dandolo, Matteo, Venetian
ambassador to France 26
Dannemarie (Dammarie),
Demoiselle de see Maye,
Le
Darnaway Castle 102–3
Darnley, Henry Stewart, Lord
(born and died 1545) 110
Darnley, Henry Stewart, Lord,
second husband of Mary,
Queen of Scots 2, 23, 33,
64, 90, 95, 98–9, 107, 110–21,
126, 131, 141, 146–7, 149, 157,

166, 170, 179, 182, 185, 192,
201–4, 213
Davidson, William, secretary to
Elizabeth I of England
208
Derbyshire 178
Diane de France, wife of (1)
Horace Farnese, Duke of
Castro (2) François de
Montmorency, later 2nd
Duke of Montmorency,
half-sister-in-law and lady-
in-waiting to Mary, Queen
of Scots 13, 70, 74–6, 78
Dickson, Thomas, apothecary
103
Dieppe 11, 112
Dombasle, d'Ormes and Parroye,
Gérard-Sicard
d'Haraucourt of, Steward
of Lorraine and Grand
Baillie of Nancy 45
Dominican confessor of Mary,
Queen of Scots see
Mamerot, Roche
Dornoch Cathedral 136
Douai, Scots College 189
Douglas, Lady Agnes, wife of
Alexander Livingston, 5th
Lord Livingston 143
Douglas, David, nephew of
Archibald Douglas, 6th
Earl of Angus 112
Douglas, Sir George, brother of
Archibald Douglas, 6th
Earl of Angus 110, 112
Douglas, George, brother of Sir
William Douglas of
Lochleven 138
Douglas of Lochleven, Lady see

Erskine, Margaret; Leslie, Agnes

Douglas, Lady Margaret, wife of Matthew Stewart, 4th Earl of Lennox, aunt and second mother-in-law to Mary, Queen of Scots 107–23, 126, 178–9, 201, 212–13

Douglas of Lochleven, Sir Robert 96, 137

Douglas, Robert, son of Sir Robert Douglas of Lochleven 98

Douglas of Lochleven, Sir William, later Earl of Morton 137–8

Douglas, Willie, nephew of Sir William Douglas of Lochleven 138

Dreux, Battle of 80

Drummond of Riccarton, Henry 147

Drury, Andrew *see* Galloway, Bishop of

Drury, Sir William, English ambassador to Scotland 138

Duci, Filippa, mistress of Henri II of France 74

Duff, Alexander, minister of Golspie 136

Duffus, parson of 101

Dumbarton 9, 42, 168

Dunbar Castle 131

Dunblane, William Chisholm, Bishop of 133

Duncan, Thomas, historian 142

Duncan, William, in Dundee 101

Dundee 101

Dunkeld 157

Dunoon 102

Dunottar Castle 100, 102

Dunrobin Castle 134–6

Ecosse, Hippolyte d', Demoiselle de Richebourg, maid of honour to Mary, Queen of Scots 82, 86

Edinburgh 3, 9, 33, 71, 81, 93, 96–7, 99, 102–3, 114, 127–8, 131, 133–4, 146
  Commissary Court (Roman Catholic) 133 (Protestant) 93, 132
  Holyrood Abbey 94
  Kirk o' Field 2, 99, 117, 123, 182, 185, 202
  Palace of Holyroodhouse 80, 98, 114, 116, 129, 131, 149, 160, 170, 181, 185, 201
  St Giles' Church (later Cathedral) 97, 100, 103–4, 133
  Tolbooth 185

Edinburgh Castle 15, 94–5, 97, 144, 148–9, 212

Edinburgh, Treaty of 196, 202

Edouard-Alexandre de France *see* Henri III of France

Edward III of England 57

Edward VI of England 8, 109–11, 194–5

Elboeuf, Marquise of *see* Rieux, Louise de

Elboeuf, René de Lorraine, Marquis of 66

Elder, John, tutor to Henry, Lord Darnley 111–12

Eleanor of Austria, second
Queen Consort of François
I of France   58, 61, 66,
69–70, 81, 85

Elgin Cathedral   128

Elisabeth de France, third Queen
Consort of Philip II of
Spain, sister-in-law of
Mary, Queen of Scots
23–4, 31, 33, 39, 41, 45, 205,
212

Elizabeth I of England   1–2, 15,
34–5, 44, 58–9, 79, 93–4,
97–102, 111–23, 134, 149, 167,
176–80, 186, 189–90, 192,
194–213

Elizabeth of York, Queen
Consort of Henry VII and
mother of Henry VIII of
England   194

Enfant, Anne l', chamberwoman
to Mary, Queen of Scots
170–1, 183

Enfant, Michel l', secretary to
Mary, Queen of Scots   171

England   6, 8, 34–6, 57–8, 79,
98–9, 107–10, 112–13, 117,
119–20, 122, 135, 152, 157,
159, 167, 176, 178–83, 186,
192–3, 195–7, 199, 201–6,
209

Erskine of Blackgrange, Arthur,
equerry to Mary, Queen of
Scots   138, 160

Erskine, John Erskine, 5th Lord
9, 13, 28, 137

Erskine, John Erskine, 6th Lord
see Mar, 1st Earl of

Erskine, John,   see Mar, 2nd Earl
of

Erskine of Dun, John   97

Erskine, Margaret, wife of Sir
Robert Douglas of
Lochleven and mistress of
James V, King of Scots
96–8, 100–1, 137–9, 165, 211

Erskine, Marie (Mademoiselle
d'Asquin), lady-in-waiting
to Mary, Queen of Scots
168

Erskine, Mary, daughter of John
Erskine, 6th Lord Erskine
95–6

Essartz, Mahanet des, wife of
Charles de la Haye, Sieur
de Curel, and lady of the
bedchamber to Mary,
Queen of Scots   42–3, 45,
47, 166, 183

Estamville, Françoise d', Dame
de Parois, lady governess
to Mary, Queen of Scots
29, 45–7, 67, 211

Este, Anne d', wife of (1)
François de Lorraine, 2nd
Duke of Guise (2) Jacques
de Savoie, Duke of
Nemours, aunt by
marriage and lady-in-
waiting to Mary, Queen of
Scots   61–6, 75, 83–5, 186

Este, Cardinal Ippolito d', 62, 75

Eworth, Hans, portrait painter
98, 111

Falkirk   182

Falkland Palace   6

Fame, Margaret, chamberwoman
to Mary, Queen of Scots
171

Faremoutiers, Antoinette de Lorraine, Abbess of, daughter of Claude, 1st Duke of Guise, aunt to Mary, Queen of Scots 20

Faucher, Captain de 168

Ferrara Cathedral 62

Ferrara, Duchess of *see* Renée de France

Ferrara, Ercole d'Este, Duke of 61

Fife 94, 143

Flanders 68

Fleming, Anne (Agnes), wife of William Livingston, 6th Lord Livingston, cousin and maid of honour to Mary, Queen of Scots 42, 50, 150, 177, 182, 212

Fleming, James Fleming, 4th Lord 42, 50

Fleming, John, illegitimate son of Malcolm Fleming, 3rd Lord Fleming 170

Fleming, Lady *see* Hamilton, Lady Barbara; Stewart, Lady Jane

Fleming, Malcolm Fleming, 3rd Lord 42, 170

Fleming, Margaret, wife of John Stewart, 4th Earl of Atholl, cousin and lady-in-waiting to Mary, Queen of Scots 162, 166–7, 172

Fleming, Mary, wife of (1) William Maitland of Lethington (2) George Meldrum of Fyvie, cousin and lady-in waiting to Mary, Queen of Scots and one of the Four Maries 42,

142, 144, 147–9, 152, 158, 170, 172, 212

Flodden, Battle of 107

Florence 23–5

Fontainebleau 41, 82, 181

Fonterpuys, Demoiselle de *see* Constant, Suzanne

Fontpertuys, Madame de *see* Barbancoys, Anne de

Fontpertuys, Monsieur de, servant to Mary of Guise 81

Forbes of Rires, Arthur 167

Forster, Alice, laundress to Mary, Queen of Scots 187

Forth, River 185

Fotheringhay Castle 2, 163, 181, 184, 186–8, 208, 213

Four Maries, the *see* Beaton, Mary; Fleming, Mary; Livingston, Mary; Seton, Mary; 49–50, 54, 80–1, 86, 130, 141–53, 156, 158, 160, 166, 168, 170, 172

France 1, 6–7, 9, 10, 14–15, 18–20, 22, 25, 31, 39, 44, 48–9, 52, 57, 69, 71, 74, 77, 80–1, 83, 91, 97, 99, 108–10, 112–3, 141, 143–4, 147, 151, 156–60, 162–4, 166, 169, 172, 176, 182–3, 186, 192, 195–6, 200, 203, 207, 213

François I of France 4, 19–20, 24–8, 57, 66, 70, 76, 78, 87

François II of France, first husband of Mary, Queen of Scots 1, 8, 13–16, 21–3, 27–8, 30–3, 39, 41, 44, 51, 53, 57, 60, 62–3, 76, 78–9, 87, 112–13, 171, 199, 213

François, Dauphin, son of François I 26–7

Françoise, maid of honour to Mary, Queen of Scots 164

Gaignon, Marie de, Demoiselle de Saint-Bohaire ('Mademoiselle Sunboire'), later wife of Claude Gouffier, Duke of Rouannais, and maid of honour to Mary, Queen of Scots 50–1, 80

Galloway, Andrew Drury, Bishop of 11

Galloway, Alexander Gordon, Bishop of 130

Germany 19

Glasgow 176, 182

Glasgow, James Beaton, Archbishop of, and Mary, Queen of Scots' ambassador to France 96, 122, 150–1, 158, 160, 183, 185–6

Glencairn, Alexander Cunningham, 4th Earl of 94

Gobelin, Claude, nurse to François II 171

Gobelin, Marie, chamberwoman to Mary, Queen of Scots 170–1, 183

Golspie 136

Gondy, Peronnelle de, attendant in the households of the children of Henri II and of Mary, Queen of Scots 52

Goodman, Gabriel *see* Westminster, Dean of

Gordon, Adam, son of George

Gordon, 4th Earl of Huntly 128

Gordon, Alexander *see* Bishop of Galloway

Gordon, Lord George *see* Huntly, George Gordon, 5th Earl of

Gordon, Sir John, son of George Gordon, 4th Earl of Huntly 127–8

Gordon, Lady Jane, wife of (1) James Hepburn, 4th Earl of Bothwell (2) Alexander Gordon, 12th Earl of Sutherland (3) Alexander Ogilvy of Boyne 126–36, 146–7, 165, 212

Gordon, Lady Margaret, fiancée of Archibald Campbell, 5th Earl of Argyll 91

Gordon, Margaret, great-aunt of Lady Jane Gordon 129

Gordon, Robert, son of Alexander Sutherland, 12th Earl of Sutherland 136

Granvelle, Antoine de Perrenot, Cardinal 200

Gray, James, goldsmith 103

Greenwich Palace 108

Greenwich, Treaties of 8

Grenoble 62

Grey, Lady Jane 68

Grisel (Goisel, Joisel) maid of honour to Mary, Queen of Scots 161, 169

Gueldres, Philippa of, wife of René de Lorraine, Duke of Lorraine, great-grandmother of Mary, Queen of Scots 4, 20

Guise family 157–8
Guise, Claude de Lorraine, 1st
Duke of 4, 10, 19, 23, 53,
62, 77
Guise, Duchess of, *see*
Bourbon, Antoinette de;
Este, Anne d'
Guise, François de Lorraine, Duke
of Aumale then 2nd Duke
of, 11–12, 18, 21–2, 31–3, 40,
44, 61–5, 75, 80, 84–5
Guise, Henri de Lorraine, 3rd
Duke of 35
Guise, Louis de Lorraine,
Cardinal , son of Claude
de Lorraine, 1st Duke of
Guise 20
Guyonnière, Demoiselle de *see*
Cabrianne, Anne

Hackney 122
Haddington 148
Haddington, Treaty of 9
Hallwin, Charles Hallwin, Duke
of 77
Hallwin, Charles, eldest son of
Charles Hallwin, Duke of
Hallwin 77
Hallwin, Charles, fifth son of
Charles Hallwin, Duke of
Hallwin 77
Hallwin, Duchess of *see*
Chabot, Anne
Hallwin, Florimond de, son of
Charles Hallwin, Duke of
Hallwin 77
Hallwin, Jeanne de, Dame de
Piennes, wife of
Florimond Robertet the
younger 75, 87

Hallwin, Leonor de, son of
Charles Hallwin, Duke of
Hallwin 77
Hallwin, Louise de, wife of
Charles Chabot 76
Hallwin, Louise de, wife of
Philibert de Marsilly,
Seigneur de Cypière and
lady-in-waiting to Mary,
Queen of Scots 77–8
Hallwin, Louise de, wife of
François, Seigneur de
Mesvilliers 77
Hallwin, Robert de, son of
Charles Hallwin, Duke of
Hallwin 77
Hambal, chamberwoman to
Mary, Queen of Scots 163
Hamilton 135, 176
Hamilton, Lady Anne, wife of
George Gordon, 5th Earl of
Huntly 128–9, 212
Hamilton, Lady Barbara, wife of
James Fleming, 4th Lord
Fleming and maid of
honour to Mary, Queen of
Scots 50
Hamilton family 114
Hamilton, Gavin *see*
Kilwinning, Abbot of
Hamilton of Bothwellhaugh,
James, assassin 100
Hamilton, John *see* Glasgow,
Archbishop of
Hamilton, Mary, fictitious char-
acter in the ballad, 'Marie
Hamilton' 141–2
Hanet, Marie, chamberwoman
to Mary, Queen of Scots
184–5

Haraucourt, Monsieur, son of the Dame de Parois 45

Haraucourt *see Dombasle*

Harbottle Castle 107–8

Harcourt, Claude, Sieur de Rieux, Count of 66

Harcourt, Countess of *see* Bourbon-Montpensier, Suzanne de

Hardwick 178

Hardwick, Elizabeth ('Bess of Hardwick'), wife of George Talbot, 6th Earl of Shrewsbury 121–2, 150, 177, 181, 187

Hardwick, John, father of Bess of Hardwick 178

Hatfield Palace 194

Hay, Captain 171

Hay, Mrs, chamberwoman to Mary, Queen of Scots 171

Henri II of France 1, 8–12, 14, 18, 22–8, 30–2, 39–40, 42–5, 50, 52–3, 57–8, 60, 67, 74–6, 78, 80, 85, 87, 95, 112, 196–7

Henri III of France (Edouard-Alexandre) 34–5, 41, 79

Henry VII of England 192, 198, 201

Henry VIII of England 6–8, 107–10, 192–5, 197, 200

Herries, John Maxwell, 4th Lord 176

Hesdin, siege of 69, 75

Hog, Christine, wife of Bastien Pages 184–7, 189

Holbein, Hans, portrait painter 108

Home, Alexander Home, Master of, later 5th Lord Home 95

Howard, Charles, brother of Queen Katherine Howard 109

Howard, Lady William *see* Dacre, Elizabeth

Howard, Lord Thomas, uncle of Queen Anne Boleyn 108

Huick, Dr, physician to Elizabeth I of England 117

Humières, Dame d' *see* Contay, Françoise

Humières, Jean de, Governor of the household of the children of Henri II of France 39

Huntly, Countess of *see* Hamilton, Anne; Keith, Elizabeth

Huntly, George Gordon, 4th Earl of 10, 91, 126–8, 166

Huntly, George Gordon, 5th Earl of 128–9, 132, 135

Hurault, Anne, wife of François de Carnavalet and lady-in-waiting to Mary, Queen of Scots 80

Inchmahome, Island of 8

Ireland 196

Issoire 82

Italy 27, 31, 63, 74, 78

Jacqueline *see* Critoflat

James II, King of Scots 109

James IV, King of Scots 42, 58, 107, 126

James V, King of Scots 1, 3–7, 44, 48, 90–1, 96, 98, 107, 137–8, 143, 187, 198

James VI, King of Scots 2, 64,

93, 95–6, 99, 101, 117–20,
122, 135, 145–6, 148–9, 152,
158, 165–7, 171, 180, 185,
202, 205, 207, 209, 212
James, Prince of Scotland, half-
brother of Mary, Queen of
Scots 5, 39, 49
Jamieson, John, lexicographer
141
Jane Seymour, third Queen
Consort of Henry VIII of
England 194
Jannequin, Clément, composer
20
Jardinier, dwarf in the retinue of
Mary of Guise 163
Jardinière, Catherine La, dwarf
in the retinue of Catherine
de Medici 163
Jardinière, Nicole La, dwarf in
the retinue of Mary, Queen
of Scots 163–4, 169, 171–2
Jeanne d'Albret, Queen of
Navarre 65
Jeanne de France, Princess, twin
daughter of Henri II of
France 28
Joinville 19–21, 23, 42, 62, 168
Joinville, Church of St Laurent
23

Katherine Howard, fifth Queen
Consort of Henry VIII of
England 108–9
Katherine Parr, sixth Queen
Consort of Henry VIII of
England 194–5
Keith, Lady Agnes, wife of (1)
James Stewart, 1st Earl of
Moray (2) Colin Campbell,

6th Earl of Argyll, half-
sister-in-law to Mary,
Queen of Scots 90,
96–104, 134, 137, 165, 212
Keith, Lady Elizabeth, wife of
George Gordon, 4th Earl of
Huntly 126–9, 165, 212
Keith, James 101
Keith, Margaret, wife of William
Keith, 4th Earl Marischal
96
Keith, Lady Mary, wife of John
Campbell of Calder 165
Kelso 101
Kennedy of Cassillis family 184
Kennedy, Jane (Jehanne de
Kierie), wife of Andrew
Melville and chamber-
woman to Mary, Queen of
Scots 184–5, 188–9
Kennedy, Lady Jean, wife of
Robert Stewart, 1st Earl of
Orkney, half-sister-in-law
to Mary, Queen of Scots
184
Kernevenog *see* Carnavalet
Kerr, Mary *see* Carre, Marie
Killigrew, Sir Henry 48
Kilwinning, Gavin Hamilton,
Abbot of 13
Kirk o' Field *see* Edinburgh
Kirkcaldy, Dame Margaret *see*
Learmonth
Kirkcaldy of Grange, Sir William
148–9, 152
Knollys, Sir Francis 149, 177,
204, 206
Knox, John, reformer and
minister of St Giles'
Church (now Cathedral),

Edinburgh 7, 15–16, 92, 95,
    97–8, 100, 130, 138, 142,
    144–5, 155

La Ferté-Milnon 75
La Rochelle, Siege of 66
Langest, Anne de, Demoiselle de
    Comenges, lady-in-waiting
    to Mary, Queen of Scots
    80
Langside, Battle of 2, 84, 119,
    135, 146, 148–9, 176, 182,
    187, 203
Lascaris, Anne, s.j. Countess of
    Tende, wife of René,
    Bastard of Savoy, Count of
    Villars 70
Learmonth, Margaret, wife of Sir
    William Kirkcaldy of
    Grange, later Abbess of
    Saint Pierre-les-Dames,
    Rheims 152
Leeds 110
Leicester, Robert Dudley, Earl of,
    favourite of Elizabeth I of
    England 115, 178, 201
Leith 11, 15, 81, 148, 185
Leith, siege of 51
Lennox, Charles Stewart, 5th
    Earl of 112, 114, 118,
    121–2, 179–80
Lennox, Countess of see
    Cavendish, Elizabeth;
    Douglas, Lady Margaret
Lennox, Matthew Stewart, 4th
    Earl of, Regent of Scotland
    96, 101, 109–20, 146, 201
Lennox Jewel, The 115
Lennoxlove see Lethington
    Tower

Lesley, John see Ross, Bishop of
Leslie, Lady Agnes, wife of Sir
    William Douglas, later 5th
    Earl of Morton 138–9
Leslie of Parkhill, John, assassin
    138
Leslie, Norman, assassin 138
Lethington Tower (now
    Lennoxlove) 148
Lignerolles, Dame de see
    Guyonnière
Lignerolles, Philibert de 83
Limousin, Leonard, enamellist
    18
Lindsay of the Mount, Sir David,
    poet and herald 137
Lindsay of the Byres, Patrick,
    Lord 129
Linlithgow 100, 139, 181
Linlithgow Palace 7
Livingston, Alexander
    Livingston, 5th Lord 9,
    143, 168
Livingston, Lady see Douglas,
    Lady Agnes; Fleming, Lady
    Anne (Agnes); Piédefer,
    Jeanne
Livingston, Magdalen, wife of (1)
    Arthur Erskine of
    Blackgrange (2) Sir James
    Scrymgeour of Dudhope
    and maid of honour to
    Mary, Queen of Scots 138
    151, 160–1, 169, 172
Livingston, Mary, wife of John
    Sempill, lady-in waiting
    of Mary, Queen of Scots
    and one of the Four
    Maries 142–6, 151, 160,
    168, 172

Livingston, William Livingston, 6th Lord 50, 145, 182
Lochleven Castle 2, 33, 92–3, 99, 136–9, 146, 148–9, 164, 170, 176, 182, 203
Lochleven, Newhouse of 137
London 98, 108–10, 113–4, 120, 180, 188, 199, 201
  Coldharbour Palace 118
  Palace of Westminster 110, 206
  St James's Palace 109
  Tower of London 108, 113, 116–17, 122–3, 195
  Westminster Abbey 122, 209
  Whitehall Palace 116
Longueville, François d'Orléans, Duke of, half-brother of Mary, Queen of Scots 4–5, 9, 11, 21, 48, 52, 62
Longueville, Louis d'Orléans, Duke of Longueville, first husband of Mary of Guise 4,5
Longueville, Louis d'Orléans, half-brother of Mary, Queen of Scots 4
Longwy, Françoise de, wife of Philibert de Chabot, Admiral of France 77
Longwy, Jacqueline (Jacquette), wife of Louis de Bourbon, Duke of Montpensier and lady-in-waiting to Mary, Queen of Scots 67, 76–7, 159
Lorne, Lord of see Argyll, Colin Campbell, 6th Earl of
Lorraine 20, 23, 45, 68, 77, 80, 158, 169, 185

Lorraine, Anne de, wife of Philippe de Croy, 1st Duke of Arschot, cousin of Mary of Guise 200, 212
Lorraine, Antoine de Lorraine, Duke of 4, 19, 23, 200
Lorraine, Catherine Marie de, cousin of Mary, Queen of Scots 63
Lorraine, Charles de Lorraine, Cardinal of 11–12, 16, 18, 20–2, 31–3, 40–2, 45, 47–8, 52, 61, 63, 65–7, 69, 80, 84–5, 158–9, 171, 176
Lorraine, Charles de, cousin of Mary, Queen of Scots 66
Lorraine, Duchess of see Bourbon, Renée de; Gueldres, Philippa of
Lorraine, François de, Grand Prior General of the Galleys 45
Lorraine, Jean de see Metz, Bishop of
Lorraine, Marie de see Mary of Guise
Lorraine, Marie de, cousin and god-daughter of Mary, Queen of Scots 66
Lorraine, René de Lorraine, Duke of, King of Sicily 19
Lorraine, Renée de see Saint Pierre-les-Dames, Abbess of
Louis IX of France (St Louis) 19
Louis XII of France 19, 57, 61–2, 78
Louise of Savoy see Savoy, Louise of
Louis de France, Prince, second

son of Henri II of France 27, 41

Lude, Guy de Daillon, Count of, attendant to the sons of Henri II of France 80

Lustrac, Marguerite de, wife of (1) Jacques d'Albon, Marshal of Saint-André (2) Geoffrey, Baron de Caumont and lady-in-waiting to Mary, Queen of Scots 80, 84

Luxembourg, Guillemette de, wife of Amé de Sarrebruche, Count of Roucy 68

Luxembourg, Marie de, wife of François de Bourbon, Count of Vendôme 19

Lyons 62

Madeleine de France, Princess, first Queen Consort of James V, King of Scots 58, 137, 187

Maitland, James, son of William Maitland of Lethington 148, 152

Maitland, Margaret, daughter of William Maitland of Lethington 148

Maitland, Marion, daughter of William Maitland of Lethington 147

Maitland of Lethington, William, secretary of state to Mary, Queen of Scots 97, 127, 147–8, 152, 197, 200–1, 212

Mamerot, Roche, Dominican

confessor to Mary, Queen of Scots 35

Mar family 168

Mar, Countess of *see* Murray, Annabella

Mar, James Stewart, Earl of *see* Moray, James Stewart, 1st Earl of

Mar, John Erskine, 6th Lord Erskine then 1st Earl of, Regent of Scotland 95–6, 120, 160

Mar, John Erskine, 2nd Earl of 96

Marconnay, de, family 79

Marconnay, Hilaire de, wife of the Sieur de Berlandière and lady-in-waiting to Mary, Queen of Scots 79

Marconnay, Jean de, royal cup-bearer 79

Marck, Antoinette de la, Mademoiselle de Bouillon, maid of honour to Mary, Queen of Scots 30, 68–70, 83

Margaret Tudor, Queen Consort of James IV, King of Scots, grandmother of Mary, Queen of Scots 58, 107–8

Marguerite de France, Princess, Duchess of Savoy 24, 76–7

Marguerite (Margot) de France, Princess, daughter of Henri II of France, sister-in-law of Mary, Queen of Scots 29, 39

Marguerite *see* Carwood, Margaret

Maricourt, Françoise, attendant

of Mary, Queen of Scots
53
Maricourt, Jean de Maricourt,
Seigneur de 53
Marignano, Battle of 19
Marischal, Countess *see*
Margaret Keith
Marischal, William Keith, 3rd
Earl 126
Marischal, William Keith, 4th
Earl 96–7
Marischal, William, Lord Keith,
Master of, son of William,
4th Earl Marischal 103
Marna, chamberwoman to Mary,
Queen of Scots 164
Marne, River 19
Marot, Clément, poet 69
Marseilles 25
Martigues, Marie de, god-
daughter of Mary, Queen
of Scots 51,80
Martigues, Marie de Beaucaire,
Demoiselle de Péguillon
then Viscountess of, maid
of honour to Mary, Queen
of Scots 50–1
Martigues, Sebastian de
Luxembourg, 4th Viscount
of 51
Martigues, Viscountess of *see*
Beaucaire, Marie de
Mary, Queen of Scots:
Life:
childhood in Scotland 3–4,
6–9, 39, 49
childhood in France 1, 9–14,
20–22, 28–9, 39–54, 62–3,
87, 143
as Queen Consort of France

1, 15–16, 31–2, 48, 57–89,
159, 163–4
personal rule 2, 90–104,
107–19, 126–34, 137–9,
141–9, 155–72, 176, 182
imprisonment in England 2,
34–6, 119–23, 146–51, 157–8,
162–3, 167, 172, 176–90,
192–209
*Female attendants: (see also indi-
vidual names, e.g Pages,
Marie, chamberwoman to
Mary, Queen of Scots):*
accommodation 164
age 61, 83, 86, 158, 172
analyses of female members
of household 53–4, 57, 81,
83–7, 158–9, 166, 169, 172,
187
duties 42, 46–7, 58–9, 156–7,
162–3, 165, 182
education 50, 58–9, 165
food 164–5
marital status 84, 86, 158
morality 87, 155
occupations of male relatives
84–5
religion 85–6
salaries 47, 49, 50, 68, 171, 186
*Female attendants of comparative
royal households of:*
Anne of Brittany, Queen of
France 57
Catherine de Medici , Queen
of France 51, 60–2, 65–6, 70,
75, 79, 81–3, 85–7, 161, 163
Claude, Queen of France 57
Eleanor of Austria, Queen of
France 58, 61, 66, 70, 81,
85

Elizabeth I, Queen of England 58–9

Madeleine, Queen of Scots 58

Margaret Tudor, Queen of Scots 58

Mary I, Queen of England 58

Mary of Guise, Queen of Scots 39, 42–3, 48, 58, 81, 85, 91, 143, 157–9, 163, 168, 172

Philippa of Hainault, Queen of England 57

and Louise of Savoy, not a queen, but mother of François I of France 57

Mary I of England 58, 108–12, 123, 194–7

Mary of Guise, wife of (1) Louis d'Orléans, Duke of Longueville and (2) second Queen consort of James V, King of Scots, mother of Mary, Queen of Scots 1–16, 21–2, 27–30, 39–48, 52–3, 58–9, 62–3, 67–8, 80–1, 85–6, 90–1, 95, 97, 109, 131, 137, 143, 145, 150, 157–9, 162–3, 168–9, 172, 196, 199, 213

Massacre of St Bartholomew's Day 18, 182

Maulevrier, Louis de Brézé, Count of, husband of Diane de Poitiers, Duchess of Valentinois 26, 31

Maye, Anne le, Demoiselle de Dannemarie (Dammarie), lady-in-waiting to Mary, Queen of Scots 79

Mayenne, Louise, Marquise of *see* Brézé, Louise de

Mayenne, Marquis of *see* Aumale, Claude de Lorraine, 1st Duke of

McLeod, Marie, chamberwoman to Mary, Queen of Scots 171

Medici, Clarissa de, wife of Philip Strozzi 24–5

Medici, Lorenzo de *see* Urbino, Lorenzo de Medici, Duke of

Medici, Lorenzo de, 'Lorenzo the Magnificent' 24

Meldrum of Fyvie, George 149

Melville, Andrew, steward to Mary, Queen of Scots 185

Melvill of Halhill, Sir James, Scottish ambassador to England 115-6, 131, 201

Menteith, Lake of 8

Mesnil, Demoiselle du *see* Pons, Claude du

Mesvilliers, Dame de *see* Hallwin, Louise de

Mesvilliers, François Mesvilliers, Seigneur de 77

Metz 77, 80

Metz, François de Beaucaire, Bishop of, super-intendent of the French finances of Mary, Queen of Scots 48

Metz, Jean de Lorraine, Bishop of 20

Metz, siege of 66

Meudon 12, 63

Millot, Claude, schoolmaster of Mary, Queen of Scots 41

Mirandola, Fulvia della, attendant to the children of
Henri II of France 52

Mirandola, Livia Pica della, 'La
Contine', attendant to the
children of Henri II of
France and to Mary, Queen
of Scots 52–3

Mirandola, Lodovico Pico, Count
della 52

Mirandola, Silvia della, attendant to the children of
Henri II of France 52

Montagne, Jean de Balsac,
Seigneur de 83

Montcrabeau, siege of 79

Montmorency, Anne de
Montmorency, Duke of,
Constable of France 13,
27, 41, 67, 69–71, 74–5, 78, 84

Montmorency, Anne de, Abbess
of La Trinité, Caen 70

Montmorency, Church of St
Martin de 71

Montmorency, Duchess of see
Savoie, Madeleine de

Montmorency, François de, later
2nd Duke of
Montmorency 75

Montmorency, Hippolyte de,
wife of Pierre, Marquis of
Richebourg 82

Montmorency, Louise de, nun
70

Montmorency, Madeleine de,
Abbess of La Trinité, Caen
70

Montpensier, Duchess of see
Longwy, Jacqueline
(Jacquette)

Montpensier, Louis de Bourbon,
Duke of 76

Montreuil, Madame de, lady
governess to Princess
Madeleine of France 58

Moray, Countess of see Keith,
Lady Agnes; Stewart,
Elizabeth

Moray, James Stewart, 1st Earl
of, for a time Earl of Mar,
Regent of Scotland 23, 34,
93, 96–103, 116–7, 119–20,
127, 132, 137–8, 146, 148,
164, 167, 204–6

Moray, James Stewart, 2nd Earl
of 102

Morel, Camille, poet 59

Morton, Countess of see
Leslie, Agnes

Morton, James Douglas, 4th Earl
of, Regent of Scotland 94,
102, 122, 146, 149, 182, 205

Morton, William Douglas, 5th
Earl of see Douglas of
Lochleven, Sir William

Mowbray, Barbara, wife of
Gilbert Curle and gentle-
woman to Mary, Queen of
Scots, 187–9

Mowbray, Gilles, gentlewoman
to Mary, Queen of Scots,
later wife of Sir John
Smith of Barnton 188

Mowbray, John, Laird of
Barnbougle 187

Murray, Annabella, wife of John,
6th Lord Erskine, later 1st
Earl of Mar 90, 95–6, 104

Murray of Tullibardine, William
95

Nancy 4, 23, 45
Nau, Claude, secretary to Mary,
    Queen of Scots 179
Nemours, Jacques de Savoie,
    Duke of 64–6
Nesle, Marquise of *see* Olivier,
    Madeleine
Nesle, Louis de Sainte-Maure,
    Marquis of 83
Nether Hailes 131
Netherlands 75, 206
Norfolk 109
Norfolk, Thomas Howard, 4th
    Duke of 148, 182, 206
North Sea 185
Northamptonshire 2
Northern Rebellion 150, 207
Northumberland 107
Norton, Christopher, suitor of
    Mary Seton 150
Norton of Norton Towers, Sir
    Richard 150

Ogilvy, Alexander, Laird of
    Boyne 129–30, 136, 146
Oisel, Henri Cleutin, Sieur d',
    master of the household
    to Mary, Queen of Scots 42
Olivier, Dame d' *see* Cerisay,
    Antoinette de
Olivier, François, Chancellor of
    France 79, 82–3, 86
Olivier, Jeanne, Demoiselle, later
    wife of Antoine de
    Monchy, Seigneur de
    Senarpont and Voisines,
    possible maid of honour
    to Mary, Queen of Scots
    82–3, 86
Olivier, Madeleine, Demoiselle,

wife of (1) Louis de Sainte-
    Maure, Marquis of Nesle
    (2) Jean de Balsac,
    Seigneur de Montagne 83
Orkney, Countess of *see*
    Kennedy, Lady Jean
Orkney, Robert Stewart, 1st Earl
    of, half-brother of Mary,
    Queen of Scots 184
Orléans 23, 32
Orléans, siege of 64
Orléans, Charles, Duke of,
    brother of Henri II of
    France 26
Orsini, Alfonsina, grandmother
    of Catherine de Medici 24
Oxfordshire 195

Pages, Christine *see* Hog
Pages, Marie, chamberwoman to
    Mary, Queen of Scots
    185–6, 189
Pages, Sebastian (Bastian)
    185–6
Palua, Dame de *see* Baudreuil,
    Anne de
Palua, Lyonnet de Breüil,
    Seigneur de 48
Paris 28, 41, 47, 66, 76, 143, 151,
    158, 187, 196
    Cathedral of Notre Dame 14
    Château des Tournelles 31
    Church of St Paul 19
    Hôtel d'Angoulême 76
    The Louvre 31, 68
    Sorbonne 151
Parois (Parroye, Parroys), Dame
    de *see* Estamville,
    Françoise d'
Parois, Sieurs de 45

Paulet, Sir Amyas, custodian of Mary, Queen of Scots 187–8, 209

Pavia, Battle of 24–5

Péguillon, Dame de *see* Breüil, Guyonne du

Péguillon, Demoiselle de *see* Beaucaire, Marie de

Péguillon, Jean de Beaucaire, Sieur de, master of the household to Mary, Queen of Scots 45, 48–9

Perron, Antoine de, Seigneur de 79

Perron, Dame de *see* Pierrevive, Marie-Catherine

Peter the Great, Tsar of Russia 142

Peterborough
  Bishop's Palace 189
  Cathedral 188–9

Philip II of Spain 31, 33, 96, 111, 189, 195–7, 200, 205–6, 209

Philippa of Hainault, Queen Consort of Edward III of England 57

Pica, Livia *see* Mirandola, Livia Pica della

Piédefer family 168

Piédefer, Guillaume, clerk in the Chambre des Comptes 168

Piédefer, Jeanne de, wife of (1) Alexander Livingston, 5th Lord Livingston (2) Pierre de Joisel, Seigneur de Saint Rémy-en-Bouzemont and de Bettoncourt 168–9, 183

Piédefer, Robert, counsellor in the Paris Parlement 168

Piennes, Dame de *see* Hallwin, Jeanne de

Pierres, Marie, wife of (1) George Seton, 4th Lord Seton (2) Pierre de Clovis, Seigneur de Briante, and lady-in-waiting to Mary, Queen of Scots 80, 143, 150, 157–8, 163, 166, 172, 183

Pierrepont, Elizabeth (Bess), god-child of Mary, Queen of Scots 179

Pierrepont, Sir Henry 179

Pierrepont, Lady *see* Cavendish, Frances

Pierrevive, Marie-Catherine de, wife of Antoine, Seigneur de Perron and lady-in-waiting to Mary, Queen of Scots 52, 79, 83

Pinkie, Battle of 8, 42, 137

Pizan, Christine de, writer 50

Pochomnères, chamberwoman to Mary, Queen of Scots 170–1, 183

Pochomnères, Louis de Forestz, called, usher of the chamber to Mary, Queen of Scots 171

Poissy, Françoise de Vieuxpont, Prioress of the Priory of St Louis of 50

Poissy, Marie de Bourbon, Prioress of the Priory of St Louis of 50

Poissy, Priory of St Louis of 50, 143

Poitiers, Diane de, s.j. Duchess of

Valentinois, wife of Louis de Brézé, Count of Maulevrier 26–31, 41, 43–4, 60, 65–9, 74, 80
Poitou, County of 33
Pons, Demoiselle de Mesnil, Claude de, governess of the maids of honour to Mary, Queen of Scots 52, 60, 81, 86, 159
Pont à Mousson, Convent of the Poor Clares 4
Pope Clement VII 6, 20, 25, 193
Pope Julius II 193
Pope Paul III 75, 137
Pope Pius V 207
Poutrincourt, Demoiselle de *see* Biencourt, Jeanne de
Poutrincourt, Florimond de Biencourt, Sieur de, master of the household to Catherine de Medici 53
Preston, Elizabeth, maid of honour to Mary, Queen of Scots 169
Primrose, Gilbert, surgeon 103

Quadra, Alvarez de *see* Aquila, Bishop of
Quelay, maid of honour to Mary, Queen of Scots 169

Rainville 158
Rainville, Jeanne de la, (Madame Cricq/Creich) wife of Robert Beaton of Creich and lady-in-waiting to Mary, Queen of Scots 143, 158, 160, 163, 166, 172
Rallay, chamberwoman to Mary, Queen of Scots 52, 160–2, 169, 183
Rallay, Renée, alias Beauregard, chamberwoman to Mary, Queen of Scots 162–3, 187, 213
Randolph, Thomas, English ambassador to Scotland 81, 97, 99, 145, 192
Renée de France, wife of Ercole d'Este, Duke of Ferrara 61
Rheims 23, 151
  Abbey of Saint Pierre-les-Dames 23, 151–3
Riccio, David, secretary to Mary, Queen of Scots 2, 64, 92, 99, 117, 129, 147, 158, 160
Richebourg, Demoiselle de *see* Ecosse, Hippolyte d'
Richebourg, Marquise of *see* Montmorency, Hipployte de
Richebourg, Pierre, Marquis of 82
Ridolfi Plot 34, 206–7
Rieux, Louise de, wife of René, Marquis of Elboeuf, aunt by marriage and lady-in-waiting to Mary, Queen of Scots 66
Rires, Lady *see* Beaton, Margaret
Robert of Scotland, Prince, half-brother of Mary, Queen of Scots 5
Robertet, Florimond, the Elder, Treasurer of France 75, 78
Robertet, Florimond, the Younger 75, 78
Robertet, Françoise, wife of (1)

Jean Babou, Sieur de la
Bourdaisière (2) Jean,
Marshal d'Aumont, and
maid of honour to Mary,
Queen of Scots 78–9, 82
Rohan, Françoise de, maid of
honour to Catherine de
Medici 65, 87
Rome 6, 24–5, 75, 193
Ronsard, Pierre de, poet 22, 184
Roscoff 9
Ros(s), maid of honour to Mary,
Queen of Scots 164
Ross, John Lesley, Bishop of
169
Rothes, Andrew Leslie, 5th Earl
of 138
Rothes, George Leslie, 4th Earl
of 138
Rouannais, Claude Gouffier,
Marquis of Boisy and
Duke of 51
Rouannais, Duchess of see
Beaune, Claude de;
Gaignon, Marie; Tour-
Landry, Antoinette de la
Rouen 4, 11, 48
Cathedral 26
Russia 142
Ruthven, Patrick Ruthven, 3rd
Lord 92
Ryotell, John, mason 100

Sackville, Lady see Brydges,
Winifred
Sackville, Sir Richard 113
Sadler, Sir Ralph, English
ambassador to Scotland,
later custodian of Mary,
Queen of Scots 7–8

Saint-Aignan, Claude de
Beauvilliers, Count of 82
Saint-Aignan, Countess of see
Babou, Marie
Saint-André, Dame de see
Lustrac, Marguerite de
Saint-André, Demoiselle de see
Albon, d', Catherine
Saint-André, Jacques d'Albon,
Marshal of 80
Saint-Bohaire, Dame de see
Chasteigner, Marguerite de
Saint-Bohaire, Demoiselle de
see Gaignon, Marie de
Saint-Bohaire, Jean de Gaignon,
Seigneur de 51
Saint-Leger, Demoiselle see
Cobron, Bonaventure de
Saint Pierre-les-Dames, Renée
de Lorraine, Abbess of,
daughter of Claude, 1st
Duke of Guise and aunt of
Mary, Queen of Scots 23,
151, 188
Saint-Remy-en-Bouzemont,
Seigneur de see
Bettencourt
Saint-Vallier, Jean de Poitiers,
Sieur de 26
Sarrebruche (Saarbrücken) 68
Sarrebruche, Guillemette de, s.j.
Countess of Brenne, wife
of Robert de la Marck,
Duke of Bouillon and
lady-in-waiting to Mary,
Queen of Scots 67–70, 83,
211
Saubole, Roger Comminges,
Sieur de, Governor of Metz
80

Index

Saubonne, Michelle de, Baronne de Soubise 61
Sauvaige, Adrian, butler of kitchen vessels to Mary, Queen of Scots 161
Sauvaige, La, maid of honour to Mary, Queen of Scots 161, 169
Savoie, Madeleine de, wife of Anne de Montmorency, Duke of Montmorency, lady-in-waiting to Mary, Queen of Scots 65, 67, 70–1, 74, 79, 159
Savoy, Emmanuel Philibert, Duke of 22, 77, 195
Savoy, Louise of, mother of François I of France 19, 57
Scotland passim
Scott, Sir Walter, writer 142
Scrymgeour of Dudhope, Sir James 160
Sempill, James, son of John Sempill 145–6
Sempill, John, husband of Mary Livingston 145–6
Sempill, Mary see Livingston, Mary
Sempill, Robert Sempill, 3rd Lord 145–6
Senarport and Voisines, Antoine de Monchy, Seigneur de 83
Senarport and Voisines, Dame de see Olivier, Jeanne
Senlis, Battle of 77
Seton Palace 129, 149
Seton, George Seton, 4th Lord Seton 52, 143, 157

Seton, George Seton, 5th Lord 151
Seton, Mary, lady-in-waiting to Mary, Queen of Scots, one of the Four Maries 86, 141–6, 149–53, 157–8, 160, 162–4, 172, 177, 182, 213
Seton, Mary Jane, chamber-woman to Mary, Queen of Scots 52
Seton, Lady see Pierres, Mary
Seton, James, son of George Seton, 4th Lord Seton 157
Seton, Robert, son of George Seton, 4th Lord Seton 157
Settrington House 112, 121
Seymour, Thomas, second husband of Queen Katherine Parr 194–5, 198
Sharpe, Alice, laundress to Mary, Queen of Scots 187
Sharpe, Charles Kirkpatrick, antiquarian 142
Sheen 113, 117
Sheffield 177
Shrewsbury, Countess of see Hardwick, Elizabeth
Shrewsbury, George Talbot, 6th Earl of 150, 177, 180–1, 184, 187
Sigismund, King of Poland 61
Silva, Don Diego Guzman da, Spanish ambassador to England 116
Sinclair, Jean, nurse to Mary, Queen of Scots 39, 49, 54
Smith of Barnton, Sir John 188
Solway Firth 119, 176
Solway Moss, Battle of 6

Somerset, Edward Seymour,
Duke of, Lord Protector of
England 8, 195
Sondrelan *see* Sunderland,
Barbara
Soubise, Baronne de *see*
Saubonne, Michelle de
Souche, Mademoiselle de la,
governess to the maids of
honour of Mary, Queen of
Scots 159, 163, 169, 183
Spain 31, 34, 119, 193, 195, 205
St Andrews 5, 99, 137
St Andrews University 97
St Andrews, Cardinal David
Beaton, Archbishop of
138, 161
St Andrews, John Hamilton,
Archbishop of 133, 135
St Denis, Battle of 71
St Germain-en-Laye 9, 21, 40–1,
44, 50, 53, 62, 143
St Mars, Dame de *see* Tour-
Landry, Antoinette de la
St Quentin, Siege of 22
St Rémy-en-Bouzemont 169
Stewart, Alexander, chamberlain
at Darnaway 103
Stewart, Alexander, in Kelso 101
Stewart, Lady Annabel, daughter
of James, 1st Earl of Moray,
niece of Mary, Queen of
Scots 99
Stewart, Christina, s.j. Countess
of Buchan, 97–8
Stewart, Elizabeth, s.j. Countess
of Moray, niece of Mary,
Queen of Scots 99, 101–3,
165
Stewart, Isabel (or Agnes), wife

of Adam, 3rd Earl of
Bothwell and mistress of
James IV, King of Scots
42
Stewart, Lord James *see* Moray,
James Stewart, 1st Earl of
Stewart, Sir James,
Commendator of
Inchcolm 102
Stewart, Lady Jane, wife of
Malcolm Fleming, 3rd Lord
Fleming and lady
governess to Mary, Queen
of Scots 9, 42–6, 54, 87,
142, 166
Stewart, Lady Jean, half-sister of
Mary, Queen of Scots and
wife of Alexander
Campbell, 5th Earl of
Argyll 90–5, 104, 138, 143
Stewart, John, husband of
Margaret Carwood 170
Stewart, Lady Margaret,
daughter of James, 1st Earl
of Moray, niece of Mary,
Queen of Scots 100, 102–3
Stewart, Margaret, possible ille-
gitimate daughter of
James V, King of Scots 95
Stirling 5, 91, 102, 120, 144, 148
Stirling Castle 3, 8, 120, 131
Stirling Castle Chapel Royal
120
Stirlingshire 182
Strathbogie Castle 126, 134–5
Strozzi, Philip 24
Stuart, Lady Arabella, niece of
Mary, Queen of Scots 122,
178–9
Stuart, John, historian 134

Sunboire, Mademoiselle de *see*
    Gaignon, Marie de
Sunderland (Sondrelan), Barbara,
    maid of honour to Mary,
    Queen of Scots 169
Suriano, Michele, Venetian
    ambassador to France 16,
    32
Sutherland 136
Sutherland, Alexander Gordon,
    12th Earl of 135–6, 147
Sutherland, Countess of *see*
    Gordon, Lady Jane
Sutherland, John Gordon, 13th
    Earl of 136
Sutherland, John Gordon, 14th
    Earl of 136
Syon House 109

Temple Newsam 110, 112, 116
Tende, Countess of *see* Lascaris,
    Anne
Thire, Mademoiselle *see* Thore
Thore (Thire, Torrie),
    Mademoiselle, maid of
    honour to Mary, Queen of
    Scots 161, 169
Thou, Anne de, wife of Philippe
    Hurault, Count of
    Cheverny 161
Thou, Christophe de, First
    President of the
    Parlement of Paris 161
Thou, Mademoiselle, maid of
    honour to Mary, Queen of
    Scots 161, 169
Throckmorton, Sir Nicholas,
    English ambassador to
    France, and then Scotland
    118, 134, 196, 203

Torrie, Mademoiselle *see* Thire
Totigoti, Bonaventure *see*
    Cobron, Bonaventure de
Touche, Françoise de la, maid of
    honour to Mary of Guise
    159
Touche, Mademoiselle de la,
    see Avantigny, Renée d'
Touche, Monsieur de la 159
Touche, Urbain de la, carver to
    Mary of Guise 159
Tour-Auvergne, Madeleine de
    la, wife of Lorenzo de
    Medici, Duke of Urbino
    24–5
Tour-Landry, Antoinette de,
    Dame de St Mars, wife of
    Claude Gouffier, Duke of
    Rouannais and attendant
    of Mary, Queen of Scots
    53
Tours 21
Trans, Germain-Gaston de Foix,
    Marquis of 79
Trans, Marquise of *see*
    Bertrand, Marguerite
Turenne, duchy of 33
Tutbury Castle 162, 177, 206
Tweedie, Margaret, nurse to
    Mary, Queen of Scots 171

Urbino, Lorenzo de Medici, Duke
    of, father of Catherine de
    Medici 24
Urbino, Duchess of *see* Tour
    d'Auvergne, Madeleine de
    la
Valentinois, Duchess of *see*
    Poitiers, Diane de
Vallery 80

Valois, Henry (Harry) de, illegitimate son of Lady Fleming and Henri II of France 44–5
Vaudemont, Nicolas de Lorraine, Count of 46
Vendôme, Countess of see Luxembourg, Marie de
Vendôme, François de Bourbon, Count of 19
Verger, Gilles du Verger, Seigneur du, member of the Council of the jointure lands of Mary, Queen of Scots in France 183
Verger, Mademoiselle du, wife of Gilles du Verger, Seigneur du Verger and lady-in-waiting to Mary, Queen of Scots 183
Victoire de France, Princess, twin daughter of Henri II of France 28
Villars, Countess of see Lascaris, Anne
Villars, René, Bastard of Savoy, Count of 70
Villegaignon, Nicolas Durant, Sieur de, Captain of the Royal Galleys 42
Vieuxpont, Françoise de see Poissy, Prioress of
Vogeleer, Lieven de, artist 118

Walker, Murdoch, mason 100
Walsingham, Sir Francis 208
Wardlaw, maid of honour to Mary, Queen of Scots 164
Westminster, Gabriel Goodman, Dean of 117
White, Nicholas, correspondent of William Cecil 182
Winchester Cathedral 111
Wishart of Mylneden, Andrew 161
Wishart, George, reformer 96
Woodstock 195
Wyatt, Sir Thomas 195

York 148, 177, 205
Yorkshire 109, 118, 121